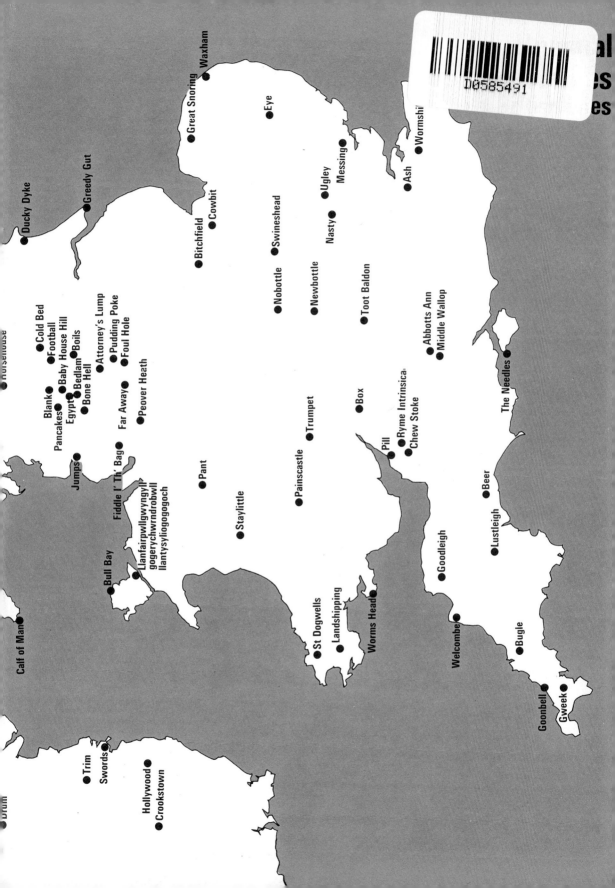

The Guinness
Book of Names

The Guinness
Book of Names

Leslie Dunkling

Guinness Superlatives Limited
2 Cecil Court, London Road, Enfield, Middlesex

CREDITS

For permission to print short extracts of copyright material the author and publisher are grateful to the following:

Methuen & Co. Ltd. (*Why Piccadilly?* by E. Stewart Fay) p. 166; A. D. Peters & Co. (*A Name to Conjure with*, by G. B. Stern) p. 120; Punch Publications Ltd. p. 232; The Bodley Head (*British Warship Names*, by T. D. Manning and C. F. Walker) p. 217; Wolfe Publishing Ltd. (*How Dare you Call me that*, by Roger Price and Leonard Stern) p. 77.

ILLUSTRATIONS reproduced by kind permission of:

Associated Newspapers Group p. 91; Associated Press Ltd. p. 95; B.B.C. p. 75; The Blazonym Enterprise p. 232; Brewers' Society p. 179; Campbell Connelly & Co. Ltd. (Louise) p. 79; Central Press Photos Ltd. pp. 45, 76 (left), 110; E. Delderfield (Drunken Duck) cover; The Economist Diary pp. 40, 160, 169; English Country Cheese Council (cheeses) cover; B. Feldman & Co. Ltd. (Tip toe through the Tulips with me) p. 79; Janet "Rusty" Field (tattooed lady) cover; Francis Day & Hunter Ltd. (Daisy Bell) p. 79; Globe Management p. 108 (right); Guildhall Museum pp. 84, 179 (top), 206; Arthur Guinness Son & Co. Ltd. (Guinness tanker) cover; ITC Incorporated TV Co. Ltd. p. 72 (right); Keystone Press Agency Ltd. (Miss England) cover; London Weekend TV p. 108 (left); Mary Evans Picture Library pp. 13, 20, 21 (top), 31, 76 (right), 90, 98, 119, 123, 124, 149, 151, 201, 211, 218, 223, 224, 225, 227; National Geographic Society (Hawaii) cover; National Portrait Gallery p. 35; Northern Songs Ltd. © 1965 (Michelle) p. 79; Radio Times Hulton Picture Library pp. 19, 21, 105, 127, 131, 135, 147, 154, 173, 202, 215; B. A. Reeves (Flying Scotsman) cover; Mrs. P. M. du Sautoy p. 58; United Artists Corporation Ltd. p. 72 (left); Universal Pictorial Press pp. 44, 46, 73; Harry Wheatcroft Gardening Ltd. (Peace rose) cover; Zoological Society of London (panda) p. 215.

Index compiled by Gordon Robinson.

© 1974 Guinness Superlatives Ltd

Published in Great Britain by
Guinness Superlatives Ltd, 2 Cecil Court,
London Road, Enfield, Middlesex

SBN 0 900424 21 4

Set in Monophoto Baskerville Series 169
Printed and bound in Great Britain by
Jarrold and Sons Ltd, Norwich

Designed by Francis Morgan

Contents

Acknowledgements

This book could not have been written without the helpful advice, comments and friendly assistance of a great many people. It is unfortunately not possible to mention by name the three thousand or more correspondents who have written to me in the last few years about names of one kind or another. Many of them are members of The Names Society; some are authors of books listed in the Bibliography; many others are members of the public who responded to newspaper appeals for information. I am most grateful to all of them.

A special word of thanks must go to C. V. Appleton, who made available to me the results of his very extensive first name researches. These are referred to in the text as being based on the 'Somerset House records.' In fact, the Registrar General's Indexes of Births, Marriages and Deaths for England and Wales have recently moved to St. Catherine's House, but their association with Somerset House will long be remembered. A further point about Mr. Appleton's surveys is that it takes a considerable time for the indexes to be prepared and made available to the public, and still more time for a count based on a very large sample to be made. The figures for 1971 were therefore the latest available while this book was being written. Other figures, such as those drawn from newspaper surveys, have been given for the same year to allow comparisons to be made.

Of the newspaper surveys, the best known was that conducted by my late friend, John Leaver, based on the birth announcements in *The Times*. It was a sad blow to his relations and many friends when John died while this book was at the printer's. I hope the discussion of his researches in the chapters on first names will serve as a memorial to him. I know that Mrs. Jodi Campbell, who has kindly allowed me to reproduce her figures for Australian first name frequencies, was another of John's admirers.

Very specific help with the book has also been given by Adrian Room, Beatrice Frei, Richard Luty, Anne Kirkman, Alec Jeakins, Joe Hambrook, Gordon Wright, Rev. Peter Sutton, John Field, Dr. Kelsie Harder, Elsdon C. Smith, Gillian Skirrow, Kathleen Sinclair, Cecily Dynes, J. Bryan III, Muriel Smith, A. A. Willis, Darryl Francis, Philip Riley, Pauline Quemby, George F. Hubbard and Sue Beaty.

My wife, Nicole, has in her own way made it possible for the book to come into being. The poet was right: *a gode womman is mannys blys*.

Preface

'A preface,' wrote Isaac Disraeli, 'being the entrance to a book, should invite by its beauty. An elegant porch announces the splendour of the interior.'

It's a fine thought, but 'splendour' is not really what I want to offer in this book. Instead I have tried to bring together a mixture of information, entertainment, ideas and enthusiasm. The last of these I can at least guarantee to be present. Few authors can so have enjoyed immersing themselves in a subject, and I hope this will be clear on every page.

As for information, I asked myself at the outset what my potential reader would want to know about names. I thought he would certainly be interested in first names and surnames, in where those names came from and what they originally meant. In chapters on those subjects, therefore, I briefly summarise the historical and linguistic facts, and give the origins of as many names as possible. But I must say that, though I understand the interest in name origins, I think they are almost irrelevant in modern life. Far more to the point, it seems to me, is the consideration of why certain first names come into fashion or go out of fashion; why parents choose one name rather than any other at a given point in time; what associations are aroused in people's minds by certain names. There are a host of similar topics that concern the psychological and sociological aspects of names. I discuss such matters, having first presented firmly based tables of name frequencies that make a sensible discussion possible.

In these areas I try to offer a fresh approach, not merely to collate what is already in print. The usual books on first names are in any case very disappointing. I find no trace in any of them of an objective attempt to establish which names are currently being used. As a result they contain long articles about names such as **Griselda** and **Letitia**, while vital names such as **Tracey**, **Joanne** and **Sharon** are virtually ignored.

To complete the survey of personal names I deal with nicknames in a separate chapter. Nicknames have an inbuilt liveliness which makes them of special interest. The names are entertaining in themselves, whatever one says of them.

I thought my potential reader would next be interested in place names, and accordingly I turn in that direction. The interpretation of early English place names is a matter for the specialist, the scholar who has devoted a great deal of time to the study of certain languages and cultures.

I received a preliminary training in philology, and my main hope is that this will have enabled me to interpret the findings of the experts without too much distortion. The place names of the New World have also been well studied by historians and linguists, and once again I summarise their work.

Personal and place names are the concern of a major part of this book, but the interest of names really does not end there. The rest of the book is concerned with street names and pub names, house names and trade names, boat names, locomotive names, animal names, and still more names. *All* names are fascinating, and I try to explain why. In this latter section of the book the scales are slightly loaded in favour of entertainment rather than information, especially in the chapter on 'Name Games'.

In an earlier section of the book, however, I bring together some ideas and theories about names. It is by no means as easy as it might seem to define 'name', for instance. I also discuss categories of names in an attempt to impose some order on what otherwise might seem to be chaos. There are countless thousands of names in use, but they do fall naturally into certain groups which are worth describing. In this theoretical section I provide readers with an opportunity to take part in a naming experiment.

Finally, I include at the end of the book details of where to obtain further information about particular name topics. There is a Bibliography which mentions books such as the one from which I borrowed my opening quotation, Isaac Disraeli's *Curiosities of Literature*. It is there because among dozens of other interesting essays it contains those on the 'Influence of a Name', the 'Orthography of Proper Names', 'Names of Our Streets' and 'Political Nicknames'. Disraeli was clearly a names enthusiast: I hope there are many more like him.

St. Genevieve's Day, 1974   Leslie Dunkling

Glossary of Name Terms

The words used in name studies are mainly based on *name* itself (Old English *nama* and common to the Germanic languages), Greek *onoma*, 'name' and Latin *nomen*, 'name'. Several of the terms given below are well established among name students; others are used in this book for the first time or with a special meaning.

Acronym an initial name that forms a word, e.g. ERNIE (Electronic Random Number Indicating Equipment)

Activity name a descriptive name that refers to an activity associated with the named entity. See page 34.

Ananym a name that is a word or name spelt backwards.

Appellation occasionally used as a synonym for *name*.

Blended name a name formed by blending or putting together parts of other names or words. See page 38.

Byname a non-hereditary personal nickname, forerunner of a surname. See page 84.

Code name a name that consists of letters and numbers in a random order, e.g. **XG112**. See page 37.

Common name a noun, such as 'table', not really a name within the context of this book. See page 28.

Converted name a name formed by converting a non-descriptive word or phrase to name status. See page 35.

Descriptive name a name that in some way describes what is being named. Many sub-categories, for which see page 34.

Eponym one who gives his name to an entity, e.g. **Cecil Rhodes—Rhodesia**.

First name used in this book to describe the first Christian name, as opposed to other Christian names or surnames which may be used as *middle names*.

Generic name the name of a class of entities rather than an individual entity. See page 28.

Incident name a name that arises because of an incident that occurs at or near the time of naming, e.g. **Sirena**, for a girl born during an air raid.

Initial name a name consisting of initial letters, but not forming a word.

Invented name a name formed of letters or numbers to form a combination not previously in existence as a word or name. See page 37.

Link name a name based on all or part of an existing name or names. See page 38.

Locative name a kind of descriptive name that locates what is named in time or space. See page 35.

Nomenclature a system of names, e.g. house names, boat names.

Number name a number used to identify an entity rather than to quantify a group of entities. See page 39.

Onomastics used in this book to describe the simultaneous study of a range of naming systems with a view to defining their common characteristics and features.

Onomatology the historical study of personal and place names.

Patronymic a name derived from the father's name, e.g. **Johnson**.

Personal name the single name that identified a person before the first name/surname system evolved. Also a general term for a name that applies to a person.

Personal name modifier a social or professional 'title'. See page 25.

Personal name substitute a term to replace a personal name; the traditional *vocative*. See page 24.

Proper name the name of an individual entity. For a full discussion see Chapter 2.

Provenance name a name which indicates where the named entity comes from.

Sequential name a kind of *locative* name. See page 35.

Sobriquet/Soubriquet a personal nickname, meant to be insulting. See page 115.

Theonym the name of a god.

Title a synonym of *name* in some contexts, e.g. the 'title' of a book.

To-name a nickname that is used in a community where a large number of people have the same surname. See page 115.

Toponym a place name.

Transferred name a name transferred from one entity to another.

Chapter 1
What's in a Name?

In *Romeo and Juliet* Shakespeare gives Juliet the lines:

> What's in a name? that which we call a rose
> By any other name would smell as sweet.

Juliet's beautiful speech, which in context is a passionate plea for what is known to be a lost cause, is often misinterpreted. Juliet does not believe what she says even as she says it, and Shakespeare certainly did not believe it. He gives quite a different answer to his own question many times in his plays and poems. With his usual genius, however, he makes Juliet ask herself a timeless question which has an infinity of answers. The innumerable sub-editors who have echoed the question at the head of a thousand columns simply acknowledge the fact. We must also acknowledge it, and attempt to find some answers.

A name's meaning

A name has different kinds of meaning. In one sense, for instance, **Romeo** means the character in Shakespeare's play. The name is also so generally associated with the idea of a romantic young lover that it can be used humorously to describe any such person. The original meaning of Romeo, which probably indicated that the bearer came from Rome, is quite another matter.

Names have general meanings and private meanings. **Lamorna Valley**, for example, is a place in Cornwall. This simple fact about the name is a general meaning that is given in any gazetteer. To somebody who was born in Lamorna, or who lives there, the name obviously means

far more. It conjures up immediately memories and associations. The name has an extended, particular meaning as well for those who have been to Lamorna on holiday or for their honeymoon and have subsequently transferred the name to their house.

When such a transfer has taken place, a further extension of meaning is possible. A young couple who hope to own their own house one day see a house which is called **Lamorna**. For them that house is everything they dream about. Perhaps they fall in love with the name itself, with its form and sound. When they call their own house Lamorna years later they may still be unaware of the name's general meaning. It has a private meaning for them, and that is what counts.

John Stuart Mill was certainly not correct in saying that 'proper names have strictly no meaning: they are mere marks for individual objects'. He was no doubt thinking that the original meaning of a name may not be the same as its modern meaning. A man whose surname is **Swift** is not necessarily a fast runner, even though his ancestor might well have been.

A name's origin

Just as many kinds of meaning are possible, so different kinds of name origins may be described. Primary origin refers to the way in which the name first becomes a name. For instance, if in the middle of a dark wood there is a clearing where the sun streams down, that spot might well be described by those who know it as 'the bright clearing'. A thousand years ago those words would have looked more like 'the sheer lea'. Such a description was applied to a place in Surrey, and the general description gradually became a particular name. 'The sheer lea' is still so called today, though it has a slightly different pronunciation and is written **Shirley**.

But once such a name has come into being it can be transferred constantly from one entity to another. We spoke of Lamorna becoming a house name. By a similar process of transfer, Shirley became a surname. Then, as frequently happens with surnames, it began to be used as a boy's first name. In 1849 Charlotte Brontë wrote a novel in which the *heroine* was called Shirley, because:

> 'her parents, who had wished to have a son, finding that . . . Providence had granted them only a daughter, bestowed on her the same masculine family cognomen they would have bestowed on a boy, if with a boy they had been blessed.'

The novel was popular and must have gone a long way in establishing Shirley in many people's minds as a girl's name. As it happened, in 1880, the Reverend W. Wilks cultivated in the garden of Shirley Vicarage at Croydon a poppy to which he transferred the name Shirley. A few years later it became fashionable to give girls flower names. Shirley was one of many candidates to be considered, and it had the advantage of being partly established in that role already by Charlotte Brontë's novel. The final step was for Shirley Temple to come along in the 1930s and associate the name with an ideal little girl and international stardom. Shirley quickly became one of the most popular names for a girl. It enjoyed a brief spell in the limelight before retiring to a more modest position, but it is certainly established permanently now as a girl's name. For many people it must be that first and foremost, and some may be quite unaware of its place name, surname, boy's name and flower name connections.

With **Shirley**, then, we see how the principle of secondary origin applies. Names are passed from one naming system to another, just as words are passed from one language to another. It would be well to consider how many naming systems, or nomenclatures, surround us.

Name density

On a normal day—which can itself be identified by many different names—most of us meet a number of people who are known to us by name. We may know, and use, their first names, surnames or nicknames which are drawn from different, but overlapping, systems. We will also meet people whose names we do not know, and here we may have to make use of a complicated personal name substitution system.

One way of 'naming the day'. **Shrove Tuesday**—or **Pancake Day**.

In our newspaper (named) we will read of many more people who are known to us by name, but whom we have never met. We will read, too, of places all over the world, most of whose names are familiar to us though we have not been to them. When we leave our houses, which usually have number names but may have other names, we walk through named streets. In a town we will pass shops which have names and which are crammed with named products. In the country we will be passing named fields and natural features.

If we live near the sea, or near a river (named), we may be exposed to ship or boat names. In some parts of the English-speaking world we will almost certainly see the traditionally well illustrated names of public houses.

Our job or profession will bring us into contact with still more names. They may be the names of other companies, or the names of products. If these products are simply components, not usually seen by the public, they may well have code names consisting of letters and numbers. The form will have changed, but these are still names.

Every occupation has its accompanying nomenclatures. The professional gardener must cope with vast numbers of plant names. A builder uses not just bricks but particular kinds of bricks that have names. A librarian becomes familiar with an ever-increasing number of names, though in his case they masquerade as book 'titles'.

Eight Ball

Harry Fat

BEE/KNEE/

Olympiad

Some examples of named type faces.

All this only hints at the true name density which surrounds us. To stay with books for a moment, you are reading now a page that is identified by a number name, which has words printed by a named type-face (**Baskerville**, after its inventor) on named paper (**Nimrod**). The ink that has been used also has a name (**Fishburn**) black and warm red.

A similar situation exists everywhere. Almost any generic term, even a word like 'table' or 'chair', conceals a naming system. A named chair may sound strange, but a company that manufactures chairs presumably makes several different models. A salesman from such a company might refer to the chair you are sitting on as an **Elizabethan**, say, or a **K52**. The simple word 'chair' would be meaningless on his order-forms.

So it is with specialists of all kinds. A man who works in a wholesale fruit market is probably surrounded by apples, but it is unlikely that he uses that word. He deals in boxes of **Coxes**, say, or **Granny Smiths**.

Such names differ from those that identify people, places, houses, boats and the like. They do not individualise, but serve to distinguish members of one group from those of another. There is obviously an important difference between generic names, such as **King Edward** for a potato, and what we may continue to call proper names, such as **Edward King** when it identifies an individual.

Proper names are more important than generic names from one point of view, since man has always tended to bestow an individual name on something that he considers to have a personality. In the past a fighting man was quite likely to name his sword, because he looked upon it as a friend who helped him in times of trouble. Soldiers in the Second World War named their tanks in a similar way. In many parts of the country individual trees have proper names, not just common names such as 'oak' or 'cedar'. Local folk-tales become attached to them and lead to names like **The Kissing Tree**.

But generic names have a vital part to play in our language system, and are certainly not less important in communication terms. There is great confusion, incidentally, as to the exact definition of generic names. No one is quite sure when they cease to be names and become words. We will look into this problem in a later chapter.

The 'name-print' theory

Linguists know that no two speakers of a language use the language in quite the same way. Because of where and when they were born they use one dialect or another; because of their educational, professional and social backgrounds they know and use different words, or use the same words in different ways. Every speaker of a language has a personal dialect, an idiolect, which is like his linguistic finger-print. Similarly, one can safely say that no two people know and use the same body of names. We have all what might be called an onomastic finger-print, a 'name-print'.

This fact is sometimes exploited in general-knowledge tests. Candidates are shown a list of personal names, for example, and are asked to say whether the people concerned are engineers or writers, musicians, scientists or whatever. Properly applied, such a test can reveal very efficiently in which areas a candidate is well read, and how specialised his knowledge is.

An individual's 'name-print'—to use this playful term for a moment as shorthand for a highly complicated concept—is constantly changing. We hear a new song on the radio, see a new film, read a new book, and we add to our store of names or change the private meanings of old ones. We have no means of counting how many names a person knows at any one time, any more than we can count how many words he knows, but one's subjective impression is that whereas our store of words increases very slowly after the age of eighteen or so, we continue to add to our store of names at a steady rate all our lives. As we get older we are able to use our general vocabulary to talk of more and more specific entities—named entities. One wonders whether we reach a point where we know more names as such than words.

Previous name studies

At first sight there appears to be general recognition of the importance of names because so much has been written about them. Elsdon C. Smith, in his excellent bibliography of works on personal names, listed nearly 3,500 books and articles. That was in 1952, and he extends the list with newly published works and new 'discoveries' every year.

Geographical names have also received an enormous amount of attention, but there the matter virtually ends. It is possible to find the occasional books that deal with street names, house names, pub names, field names, ship names, pet names, nicknames, plant names, locomotive names and the like, but they are relatively few and far between. I give details of as many as possible in the Bibliography at the end of this book.

What is serious about the situation is that statements about names, by writers on language and similar topics, invariably refer to personal and place names only or pay the merest lip-service to the existence of other nomenclatures. The position is thus very similar to the one that pertained 400 years ago in language studies, when it was only considered necessary to study seriously a handful of the world's languages. It was assumed that all other languages followed the same pattern as those few, and the then minor languages such as English were forced into a mould which was itself based on a misunderstanding.

Names—naming

As it happens, we cannot even claim that personal and place names have been thoroughly studied, in spite of the number of books about them. It is not just that a high proportion of those books are merely imitative, and often inaccurately so. Those studies which are sound and which make a real contribution to our knowledge are almost exclusively concerned with name origins. There appears to be no major study of naming processes from a psychological or sociological point of view. The psychology of naming has been made the subject of many short articles, but psychologists have on the whole left the field clear to the philologists.

The result of this has been to give—in my own opinion—a totally wrong emphasis to name studies. The interpretation of philological data is obviously valuable for historians and the philologists themselves, but the interpretation of what the choice of names, for example, tells us about human thought processes would be equally valuable to scholars in many other fields.

To study the naming process one must have access to the namers as well as the names. The philologists have dominated name studies for so long that a myth seems to have grown up that only historically based name studies are academically respectable. We need to know about names *and* naming, just as when we study a language we need to know its vocabulary and its grammar. The one is virtually useless without the other.

The above remarks are obviously not meant to lay any blame at the feet of the philologists. It is perfectly natural that they should have pursued their own interests, and the best of them have done it remarkably well. I criticise the psychologists, sociologists and linguists who do not seem to have given names and naming the attention they deserve.

The world of names

Because of the situation described above, our opening question: 'What's in a name?', can only be partly answered in this book. Just as an early cartographer, who wished to draw a map of the world, had very unevenly distributed information at his disposal, so a writer on the world of names is faced with an unbalanced situation. If a naming system is thought of as a country, then a few have been thoroughly explored and mapped—though in a specialist way. Others are almost virgin territories where one may wander for the first time. What follows must therefore be only a sketch-map at times—a first report. I hope that my traveller's tales will encourage others to visit these lands and fill in the details.

Chapter 2
What is a Name?

We have already talked of generic names and proper names. Let us now look at these terms more closely and try to define them. We can begin with the traditional definition of 'proper name'. Most of us were taught at school that a proper name is a word that identifies a particular person, place or thing.

It is unlikely that we questioned our teachers very closely about this definition when we heard it. It was just as well. They were simply passing on yet another piece of traditional grammar which was authoritative only because it was there in print before them. And after all, **John** is a name, and it does identify a particular person; **London** is a name, and it does identify a particular place; **Concorde** is a name, and it does identify a particular thing.

The problem is that there are hundreds of boys called John, so it can hardly be said that John identifies a particular person. Similarly, **New York** is two words, so is it still a name? And if it is a name, why do we call it 'proper'?

Duplication and transfer

Two important onomastic processes account for the names that apply to more than one particular object. These are *natural duplication* and *transfer*. Natural duplication means that different namers, faced with the problem of naming whatever is to be named, independently arrive at the same solution. Transfer was discussed in Chapter 1 in connection with **Shirley**. It means that a name that is already known to exist is borrowed and applied to a new entity, either within the same nomenclature or outside it.

Centuries ago natural duplication was no doubt a common phenomenon. The fact that there are many English places called **Burton**, or **Acton**, means that different groups of people in the past instinctively commented on the nearness of a fortified manor-house or on the profusion of oak trees when they named their locality. People with common English surnames do not all descend from the same ancestors. Once again the names reflect ideas that occurred spontaneously to different groups of namers. Some names that *appear* to be the same actually started from different sources, but there is ample evidence that natural duplication occurs. When settlers in a new country, however, consciously name a town after their home-town, as with **Richmond**, **Boston** and countless others, transfer is taking place.

So it is in the case of the multiple **John**s. Where our first names are concerned, it is normal to transfer names rather than invent them. It is a convention of that particular naming system. In spite of the situation that inevitably arises, where there are a great many bearers of the same name, first names still manage on the whole to identify individuals. There is usually only one person with each name in a family group. Outside the family, in larger social groups, this is often still the case. If it isn't, surnames, nicknames and personal name substitutes can be used instead or additionally in order to achieve the desired result. Presumably something similar happens in those families where family tradition leads to the son being named after his father.

Proper words

As to the second point about **New York**, a name can consist of any number of words which need have little or no logical or grammatical connecting links. A record catalogue on my desk refers to **Three Dog Night**, **The Who** and **Frigid Pink**, for example. These are legitimate names. They are even recognisably the names of pop groups because of their slightly startling word juxtapositions. (A possible orgin of Three Dog Night, incidentally, is the old Australian saying: 'When it's cold at night, a dog keeps you warm; when it's colder, you need two dogs; a really frigid night is a three dog night.')

Finally, there is a use of *propre* in French which gives the clue to what the early grammarians had in mind when they used 'proper names'. At one time in English it was possible to speak of one's 'proper possessions', meaning one's own, particular possessions. By 'proper name', then, the grammarians meant something like 'special to the object being referred to'.

A lot more questions could be asked about the definition of 'name'. For instance **Paris** identifies a particular place and is clearly a name but 'the capital of France' identifies the same place equally well. Why isn't that phrase a name? Again a **sandwich** is so called because of the person who is said to have 'invented' it—the fourth Earl of Sandwich. Should we write 'sandwich' with a capital 'S' to signify that it is a name?

The phrase 'the capital of France' does not, of course, constitute a name, although it certainly contains nominal potential. Paris is a convenient piece of shorthand not only for 'capital of France', but for any of a hundred other descriptive phrases that could be applied to the same city. A great many names begin life as descriptions of one kind or another. Only when a formal or unspoken agreement is reached that a particular description will consistently be applied to what is being named does a 'name' come into being. 'The muddy place of the Parisii tribe—the ship people' was the descriptive phrase that eventually became shortened to Paris, long before the city *was* the capital of France.

Some descriptive phrases of places are used so often, perhaps deliberately for advertising purposes, that they also achieve name status. **The**

Emerald Isle, **Venice of the North**, **Garden of England**, for instance, identify **Ireland**, **Stockholm** and **Kent** almost as readily as the place names themselves. The phrases have thus become accepted nicknames.

Conventional usage

We should return to our traditional definition of 'proper name', therefore, to amend it to 'a name is a word or words which by conventional usage or agreement identify a particular person, place or thing'. While changing it one might also replace the rather clumsy 'person, place or thing' part of it with the word 'entity', which will serve just as well.

One becomes particularly aware of this need for conventional usage to establish itself when something new appears on the social scene that needs to be named. There is often a period of fluidity in which many potential names are bandied about before agreement is reached. Before cinemas became 'cinemas' they were variously described as picture palaces, picture theatres, picture dromes, picture houses, picture pavilions, electric theatres, electric palaceums, electric empires, cinematograph halls, talkie theatres, kinemas, kinematic theatres and pictoriums. Although 'launderette' is now the generally accepted generic term in Britain for a self-service laundry, one may still see a wide variety of

A fore-runner of today's 'cinemas'.

descriptions appearing over the launderettes themselves. They are laundermats, laundraterias, washaterias, wash-o-mats, laundrometers, laundricoins, laundertoriums and even coin laundries, where presumably one can clean up one's filthy lucre. A firm listed in a Manchester directory that I came across was **Lorna Drette**—enough to make R. D. Blackmore turn in his grave.

Just as it takes time for new words to settle down, so a newcomer to a social group may at first be referred to by a number of names until a particular nickname is agreed on. In the case of nicknames, certain features will lead almost inevitably to standard names. The boy who is fatter than normal or who has bright red hair will automatically become **Porky** or **Carrot Tops**. Less conventionalised nicknames, such as **Balloon** for someone who keeps saying: 'Don't let me down', may take a very long time to develop, though as incident names they may also come into being on the spur of the moment.

Names into words

With the 'sandwich' example we go immediately to the other end of the scale. Here we have an undisputed name that is renouncing its name status and becoming an ordinary, generic term. Some would consider it an honour for their name to pass into the language in this way, but it can have its drawbacks. If a name becomes known to everyone while remaining a name, that is national recognition and true fame. If the name takes on a general meaning which swamps the original, particular meaning or associations that the name had, it will be the name that suffers. The point is of vital importance to trade names, which we will be looking at later. Meanwhile, on pages 22 and 23 I give examples of other 'sandwich'-type words that derive from names.

Words or names?
(*opposite*) The **Ferris Wheel** at Chicago, built by George **Ferris**; Mrs. **Bloomer** wearing the garment that took her name; the **Norfolk** jacket, originally worn in Norfolk; Captain **Boycott**, who earned a strange kind of fame when his name entered several languages as a verb. (*this page*) Sandwich-board men, linked in a metaphorical way to the **Earl of Sandwich**.

A Selection of Names Turned Words

academy from the name of a grove near Athens where Plato taught. The grove was named in honour of the hero **Akademos**.

amp the usual form of *ampère*, from the name of André **Ampère**, 1775–1836, a French scientist.

aphrodisiac from the name of the goddess of love, **Aphrodite**, 'foam born'.

badminton the game was first played at **Great Badminton** in Gloucestershire, the Duke of Beaufort's seat.

bayonet first made at the French city of **Bayonne** in the seventeenth century.

bedlam from **Bethlehem**. The hospital of St. Mary of Bethlehem was converted into a lunatic asylum in 1547. London pronunciation turned Bethlehem into bedlam in the previous centuries.

bourbon first made in **Bourbon County** (Kentucky), which in turn derived its name from Bourbon in France. The French place name is thought to be Celtic or pre-Celtic and refers to hot springs.

bowdlerize from the name of Dr. Thomas **Bowdler**, 1754–1825, who edited Shakespeare so that the poet could 'with propriety be read aloud in a family'.

boycott The Irish Land League treated Charles **Boycott** in this way in 1880.

bungalow a building characteristic of **Bengal** (Hindu *bangla*, 'habitation of the Bangs').

bunkum or *buncombe*, from the name of **Buncombe County** in North Carolina. The Member of Congress insisted, in 1820, on showing his constituents that he was active on their behalf by making a wearisome speech 'for Buncombe'.

caesarian Julius **Caesar** is usually said to have been born by means of what we now call a 'caesarian operation', his name deriving from a word meaning 'to cut'.

canter pilgrims on their way to **Canterbury** to visit the shrine of *St. Thomas à Becket* would go at a 'Canterbury pace', later shortened to 'canter'.

cardigan from the name of James Thomas Brudenell, 1797–1868, the seventh Earl of **Cardigan** ('land of Ceredig').

cashmere from **Kashmir** ('sea of Kasyapa') in India and the goats bred there.

champagne from **Champagne**, province in eastern France, a 'level ground' originally.

china the clay for making it came from **China**. The name dates back to *c.* 1650.

colt a pistol patented by Samuel **Colt** in 1835.

copper originally the metal of **Cyprus**.

currant a corruption of the name **Corinth** as pronounced in the French equivalent of 'grapes of Corinth'.

damson from an earlier 'damascene', 'of **Damascus**'.

duffle/*duffel* a fabric first made in **Duffel**, near Antwerp.

epicure **Epicurus** was a Greek philosopher who taught that the highest good was pleasure.

erotic from **Eros**, the god of sexual love.

gallery held to be from **Galilee** ('district of the Gentiles'). A galilee was a porch at the entrance of a church.

gauze from **Gaza** ('strong') in Palestine.

gipsy once thought to come from **Egypt**.

guillotine invented by Joseph **Guillotin**, 1738–1814, a French doctor. His surname derives ultimately from **Guillaume** ('**William**').

guinea originally gold from **Guinea** ('black') was used for the coins.

guy from **Guy** Fawkes, whose first name appears in several European languages and may derive from 'wood, forest'.

hackneyed a hackney carriage was hired out, so hackneyed came to mean 'much used, unoriginal'. From **Hackney** in London, originally 'Haca's island'.

hamburger formerly a **Hamburg** steak. The 'ham' in the place name means either 'inlet' or 'wood', while 'burg' is 'fortress'. By folk-etymology the word has been analysed as 'ham' + 'burg' = sandwich.

jacket from French *jaquette*, 'peasant's coat'. Peasants were often addressed as **Jacques**, the popular form of **Jacob**, regardless of their true names.

jeans the cloth was first made in **Genoa** (*Gênes* in French).

jersey was once '**Jersey** cloth'. The Channel Island name is commonly said to derive from 'Caesar's island'.

jockey from **Jock**, Northern form of **Jack**.

jovial based on the name of the god **Jove**.

juggernaut from **Jagannath**, the Hindi name of Krishna, whose idol was dragged in a huge cart in the annual procession through the streets of Puri. Jagannath is 'world lord'.

limerick from **Limerick** ('bare earth') in Ireland, but possibly influenced by *learic*, from Edward **Lear**.

limousine the inhabitants of the French province **Limousin** ('muddy') wore hoods. Early closed motor-cars resembled these hoods.

lynch either from **Lynch**'s law, after Charles Lynch, 1736–96, who presided over unofficial courts in Virginia, or from **Lynch's Creek** in South Carolina where groups of unofficial law-enforcers gathered.

mackintosh patented in 1823 by Charles **Mackintosh** ('son of the chieftain').

madeira from **Madeira** ('timber'). The cake called 'Madeira' was presumably flavoured originally by madeira wine.

magnet and *magnesium* from **Magnesia** in Thessaly. Originally 'stone of Magnesia'.

magpie the 'mag-' is ultimately **Margaret** and was added to the name of the bird.

marionette a little Marian or puppet, ultimately from **Maria**.

maverick Samuel **Maverick** neglected to brand his cattle. A maverick became 'a rover or stray', applied metaphorically to people as well as cattle.

mayonnaise formerly *mahonnaise*, from **Port-Mahon**, capital of Minorca.

meander from a particular river in Turkey that was winding, the **Menderes**.

mesmerize Franz Anton **Mesmer**, 1734–1815, an Austrian physician, who believed in a theory of animal magnetism.

nicotine Jacques **Nicot** took some tobacco plants back to France with him from Portugal, 1561. Nicot ultimately derives from **Nicholas**.

ohm for Georg Simon **Ohm**, 1787–1854, a German physicist.

panic thought to be caused by the god **Pan**.

pasteurize a method of sterilising milk discovered by Louis **Pasteur**, 1822–95, ('shepherd').

peach its French form *pêche* leads back to **Persia**.

platonic from the name of the Greek philosopher, **Plato**.

romantic a *romance* was formerly a novel, and before that a story written in the everyday speech of **Rome** as opposed to Classical Latin.

rugby from the school at **Rugby** in Warwickshire where the game is popularly thought to have had its origins in 1823.

sardine found off the coast of **Sardinia**.

saxophone invented by a Belgian named **Sax**, *c.* 1840.

sherry earlier *sherris*, *Xeres* from the Spanish place name **Jerez**.

silhouette originally a portrait rapidly traced on a wall, following a person's shadow, a comment on Etienne de **Silhouette**, died in 1767, an unpopular French politician.

slave it was the **Slavs** who were once reduced to slavery.

suède from gloves originally made in **Sweden**.

teddy bear alluding to **Theodore (Teddy) Roosevelt**, 1859–1919, a great bear-hunter in his spare time.

tobacco the natives of **Tobago** smoked pipes (Haitian *tambaku*), which led to the place name and word.

trilby ultimately from the name of George du Maurier's fictional heroine **Trilby** in the novel of that name, nineteenth century.

turkey the American bird gets its name because guinea-fowl, imported from Africa through **Turkey**, came to be called turkey-cocks. The name was then transferred to the other bird.

tuxedo from a fashionable club and park at **Tuxedo** in New York, 1886.

vandal the **Vandals** were a Germanic tribe who sacked Rome, AD 455.

vaudeville originally songs composed in the *Vau* ('valley') *de Vire* (Normandy). *Vire* became *Ville* ('town') when the songs reached Paris.

volt from the Italian physicist Count Alessandro **Volta**, 1745–1827.

wellingtons named in 1817 after the Duke of **Wellington**.

Yankee if used originally of Dutch inhabitants of New York, probably from **Jan (John) Kes**.

Words can become names, then, and names can become words: the same lexical item can be both word and name at the same time. But the traditional definition of 'proper name', as it stands, does not acknowledge the fact. We should really add another qualifying phrase. A name is now 'a word or words which in a given context and by conventional usage, etc.' How else can we distinguish in speech between a word like 'peace' when used to refer to a desirable human state and the name **Peace** when used to refer to a particular variety of rose?

The English orthographic convention, shared by some other languages, whereby a name is given an initial capital letter, is in many ways misleading. It makes it seem easy to say when one is dealing with a name rather than a word. Obviously it is no real help, even in writing, and by far the greater proportion of our linguistic activity is, in any case, spoken. If a linguist were asked to devise a series of tests that would enable a name to be diagnosed in any linguistic context, he would certainly not mention capital letters.

Linguistic diagnosis is far too specialised a subject for our present purpose. We can speculate instead about another significance of a name's initial capital. Are we acknowledging instinctively that human communication revolves round these central points, named entities?

Personal name substitutes

More questions about the definition of 'name' arise when we come across a passage like this, in Congreve's *The Way of the World*:

> Mrs. Millamant: And d'ye hear, I won't be called names after I'm marry'd; positively I won't be called names.
>
> Mirabell: Names!
>
> Mrs. Millamant: Ay, as *wife, spouse, my dear, joy, jewel, love, sweetheart*, and the rest of that nauseous cant, in which men and their wives are so fulsomely familiar. . . .

What Mistress Millamant refers to as 'names' are more accurately *personal name substitutes*. They are subject to many restrictions in use and are certainly not interchangeable with personal names in all circumstances. A husband who habitually calls his wife *sweetheart*, for example, would presumably not say to a friend: 'Sweetheart has just bought a new hat.'

This particular restriction does not apply to all personal name substitutes. By an accepted convention children hardly ever address their parents by their first names. *Mum* and *Dad* or other versions of these words are used as permanent substitutes, and the fact that most writers instinctively award the terms initial capital letters shows that they are felt to be names. But while it is possible to say something like: 'Dad has just painted the kitchen', treating 'Dad' like a name, other restrictions still apply. Only his children (and possibly his wife) can properly refer to him in that way. Social restrictions as to who may use a name can certainly apply to nicknames and first names, but such restrictions are rarely as narrow as that.

Personal name modifiers

Personal name substitutes are normally used vocatively, that is, when the person concerned is being directly addressed by the speaker. They are closely linked to *personal name modifiers*, and can be back-formations from these. A modifier can be a polite social or professional title, such as *Mister* or *Professor*, or a general term of friendliness or unfriendliness. It is possible to be both polite and friendly at the same time by saying something like: 'My dear Mrs. Brown.'

Both modifiers and substitutes allow a speaker to show his attitude towards the person he is addressing. The use of the first name itself does this to some extent, but *David, darling* is that much more definitely friendly than the use of David on its own. For friendly purposes name modifiers often come in to expand the name. For unfriendly and insulting purposes substitution is more normal, so that David might become *you stupid fool*.

Substitution is also normal, for obvious reasons, when a person whose name is unknown has to be addressed. Sometimes generic terms are raised temporarily to name status, and the taxi-driver becomes *driver*, the girl on the switchboard *operator*. In Britain far less use is made of *sir* and *madam* in such situations than the equivalent terms in other countries. We tend to reserve the terms for special environments such as shops, or for well-defined hierarchies such as the armed forces.

We seem to have launched into rather a detailed discussion of Mrs. Millamant's 'names', and it is worth continuing with it briefly. It is especially necessary to show that substitutes and modifiers, which often seem to have the characteristics of names, are not true names. They differ from them in several points of usage. The use of personal names is straightforward on the whole, with first names being used by mutual consent immediately or surnames and polite social titles such as *Mr.* and *Mrs.* continuing. Special situations arise occasionally when one person expects to be addressed by surname and title but addresses the other by first name, but this is one of the very few complications. The use of the substitutes and modifiers, on the other hand, is quite complex.

Use of substitutes and modifiers

Sexual restrictions apply to some name substitutes. A woman can address a man or a woman by such terms as *love* or *my dear*, and a man can address a woman by the same terms. Most people would find it strange, however, to hear a man using them to address another man. Then there are expressions such as *you silly*, which one would normally expect to be used only by a woman. *Bastard* is technically applicable to both men and women, but someone being addressed in this way would almost certainly be a man.

There are also age restrictions. *Old man* was a common name substitute at one time, but it could not be used by a young man to an old man. This would have had the effect of converting 'old' as a term of affection back to its more usual meaning, making the expression a very tactless one. 'Young' has always retained its true sense, and *young man* remains an irritatingly patronising term.

Certain professions sometimes impose sub-rules on the system. In England it would be incorrect to address a surgeon, although he holds a doctorate, as *doctor*. It would be wrong, at least, for his professional colleagues to call him that. They would know that he prefers to be called *mister*. A research scientist, however, attached to the same hospital, would insist on the *doctor* if he had the right to the title.

Mr. David Jones can be addressed by many different *personal name substitutes* and *modifiers*.

Mention of 'titles', which is an everyday synonym for name modifiers that then become name substitutes, reminds one that many of us are at something of a loss on those rare occasions when we have to address a bishop, peer, ambassador or the like. It is not for nothing that books like *Debrett's Correct Form*, by Patrick Montague-Smith, are there on the library shelves. We are by no means 'safe', even when we are native speakers, in this question of always being able to select the right name substitute.

Perhaps the chief trap for an outsider who is trying to use the more ordinary substitutes lies in the fact that so many of them are only used by a person of a certain social and professional class. *Mate* and *old boy* can both be used to a man in a friendly way, but they would convey different information about the person addressing him. In many cases, too, these terms are like slang in that they date quickly.

Love names

Personal name substitutes and modifiers, then, are not 'names' in the way that we have attempted to define them. They can be conventional in form and be applied consistently to the same person, but the various restrictions on their use, described above, must make us treat them differently. Sometimes they come very close indeed to being nicknames. A member of The Names Society, for example, once revealed in **Viz.**, the Society's newsletter, the 'love names' used by her fiancé to address her. They included *chunkie, porky, slurpy, floppy, big softie, hot chops, cuddly duddly, tatty head, rumble tum, kipper feet, twizzle, lucky legs* and *lucky lips*. To become nicknames these would have to be used by several speakers, and in the third person as well as vocatively. As it was they were described as being 'a small selection' of *ad hoc* inventions, part of a game in which the fiancé proved his linguistic virility. One shudders to think how Mrs. Millamant would have reacted to them.

Hate names

Name substitutes, as we have mentioned, are frequently used to convey a negative attitude as well as a positive one. Once again the border-line between name substitute and nickname is often difficult to define. When we retorted in the school playground:

> Sticks and stones may break my bones
> But names will never hurt me,

we were defending ourselves against both substitutes and nicknames.

We tend to use more words when we want to insult someone than when we want to be affectionate. One or two words are common in friendly name substitutes, but we usually need at least three to express our disgust. We begin with *you*, add a *dirty*, *filthy*, *little*, *stupid*, *bloody* or equally aggressive word, then round off with a scathing noun. If emotion does not choke us we are quite likely to follow the example of Lucky Jim when he is annoyed with Bertrand, and be very wordy indeed. One of the many insulting name substitutes that Jim levels at him is *you bloody old towser-faced boot-faced totem-pole on a crap reservation.*

Names as name substitutes

By a strange twist of linguistic fate, names can actually operate as name substitutes. The point is made by Josef Reinius in his Uppsala dissertation *On Transferred Appellations of Human Beings*: 'any name of note and of allusion obvious to some group of persons may acquire appellative use'. In other words, it is possible for any man, regardless of his real name, to be addressed as **Lord Fauntleroy**, **Sherlock**, **Dr. Watson**, **Samson**, **Rip Van Winkle** or any of a hundred others in certain circumstances. Most nurses have probably been addressed as **Florence** at some time in their careers. Apart from literary and historical names, though, there are well-known national names such as **Jock**, **Mac**, **Paddy**, **Pat** and **Taffy** that are loosely applied. Occasionally these become transferred names used as nicknames, but they are frequently name substitutes.

One's good name

'Name' has more than one meaning, then, to the layman. As we have seen, we cannot bring personal name substitutes and modifiers under the same umbrella as 'proper names'. Yet another meaning of 'name' is illustrated by a Shakespearean quotation, this time from *Othello*. The words are given to that appalling hypocrite Iago to utter, but that does not change their truth or beauty:

> Good name in man and woman, dear my lord,
> Is the immediate jewel of their souls:
> Who steals my purse steals trash; 'tis something, nothing;
> 'Twas mine, 'tis his, and has been slave to thousands;
> But he that filches from me my good name
> Robs me of that which not enriches him,
> And makes me poor indeed.

Here 'name' has come to mean 'reputation', and the fact that it has done so is full acknowledgement of a name's private meaning. We all know what is meant by 'one's good name', and apart from ordinary social considerations it can have great commercial value. By contrast the old proverb has long recognised that if you give a dog a bad name, you might as well hang him.

This use of 'name' takes us a long way from the definition we are trying to establish for 'proper name'. Perhaps it is time to set this down, bearing in mind the various points that have arisen. For practical purposes—which means that it is still very over-simplified—we may say that a proper name is a word or group of words which in a given context and by conventional usage is habitually intended to identify a particular entity and only that entity. A 'generic name', which is a term I use for a sub-division of the traditional 'proper name', would be defined by changing 'entity' to read 'class of entities'.

It would be pleasant to be able to end the chapter at that point as if the problem were solved, but we have not yet mentioned another confusing use of 'name' when something other than a proper name is meant. This is what the traditional grammarians called 'the common name'. By this any noun is a name, because it is a word which identifies in some way what it refers to. If somebody is showing me his garden and says: 'I've got some potatoes and turnips, or dahlias and roses', he is 'naming' the vegetables and flowers in the sense we are now discussing. But it is only when he tells me that the roses on the right are of the variety **Show Lady** while those on the left are **Chrysler Imperial** that he begins to use what I call generic names.

A further example might be of someone being questioned about the vehicle he owns. What kind of vehicle? A car. What kind of car? A **Vauxhall**. What kind of Vauxhall? A **Victor**. And possibly he calls his very own Vauxhall Victor—**Daisy**. Here we have generic terms, or common names—vehicle, car; generic names—**Vauxhall**, **Victor**; a proper name—**Daisy**.

We especially think of generic terms as 'names' when we contrast different classes of objects. We metaphorically name our categories, but stay within the ordinary lexical system. If we link our categories to established names, however, we arrive at generic names.

The question of when a generic name becomes a generic term, or vice versa, could easily occupy us for the rest of this book if we allowed it to do so. As Ernest Weekley has said, in his *Words and Names*, 'the literature on the subject is immense'. The fact is that there are degrees of nameness, and nouns in particular are far more name-like in some contexts than in others. There also appears to be a tendency to call a generic term that describes living things a 'name' more easily than a term which applies to something like furniture.

The concept of the common name is well established, and usefully recognises that some words, such as 'oak', 'bulldog' and 'driver', are inherently more name-like than words such as 'useful', 'blue', etc. In the title of this book and throughout it 'name' primarily refers to a proper or generic name, but we would not want to deny common names their right to be called names. When Juliet says that a rose by any other name would smell as sweet, she uses 'name' in the traditional common name sense, which is really a metaphorical naming. A similar use of words will allow us, in the next chapter, to name names.

Chapter 3
Naming Names

The vast numbers of names that surround us seem to have little in common with one another. It is possible to impose some kind of order on the chaos, however, by grouping them into various categories. Naturally we then 'name' those categories.

There are at least four ways in which names can be classified:

- by their linguistic status,
- by their formal characteristics,
- by type of origin,
- by the nomenclature to which they belong.

The last of these is the most familiar to the non-specialist. We all know what is meant by 'surname', 'house name', 'boat name', 'street name', etc. This is the simplest classification of all to make, and it is essential to mention it when discussing any name in detail. Many naming systems have their own conventions and some, such as racehorse names, have formal sets of rules which restrict the choice of names.

Linguistic status

Classifying names by their linguistic status is certainly not as simple, but neither is it as useful. As we have already seen, we cannot say that our vocabulary consists of words on the one hand and names on the other. We can say that there are words like 'yellow' which almost always function as words, and names like **Laurence** which usually remain names, but we must allow for either of them to change roles.

The average native speaker of English, however, has an inbuilt store of knowledge about how often he has heard an item used as a word and how often as a name. He also knows that certain lexical items belong to the word-hoard, even though frequency of usage makes them appear to be names in modern English. (**Smith** is an example.) Such knowledge enables him to say, usually, that in one instance a name is functioning as a word, while in another a word has assumed name status.

Putting the problem of common names to one side for a moment, let us assume that our vocabulary does consist of words and names, and that the former have verbal characteristics, while the latter have nominal characteristics. We could then go on to say that when an item functioning as a name consists of one nominal element, such as **Eleanor**, **Godfrey**, **Canberra**, **Chicago** and the like, it is a *single name*. When the name consists of two or more nominal elements, as with **Robert Edward Lee**, **George Bernard Shaw**, it is a *block name*. A name that consists of one primarily verbal element, such as **Lucky**, **Spot**, **Ginger**, would be a *single verbal name*. Names consisting of two or more *words*, such as **War and Peace**, **Castle Street**, would be *block verbal names*. Finally, names that combine nominal and verbal elements, such as **Little John**, **Downing Street**, could be called *complex names*.

They could be called anything we like and it would not advance us very far. We would simply be drawing attention once again to the constant interchange between words and names, and setting ourselves logistic problems that few of us have the time to solve. Is **Baker Street**, for example, a complex name or a block verbal name? It would need a linguistic Sherlock Holmes to solve that one. As it happens, the famous London street with which he was connected was named after Sir Edward **Baker** in 1794, but there are probably many other streets in the country which bear a similar name where 'baker' was originally the generic term.

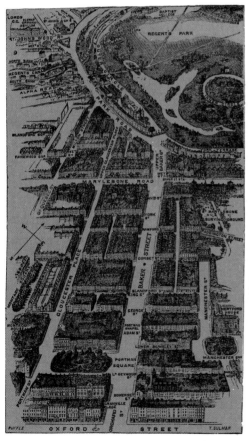

Sherlock Holmes and Baker Street, where he is supposed to have lived.

Formal characteristics

A name can be expressed in figures, as in the trade name **4711**, in initial letters, as in **BBC**, and in letters and numbers, as in the names of motorways such as the **M1**. These we may call *number names*, *initial names* and *code names* respectively. Initial names become *acronyms* when the letters form what is then treated as a single word. **UNESCO** is a well-established example of what has become a fashionable trend in recent years. An indication of this is the *Acronyms and Initialisms Dictionary* (Gale Research Co.) which has swelled to over 100,000 entries in its fourth edition. This is essential reading, incidentally, for the kind of person who notices a **DKW** car, say, and then walks under a bus because he is trying to work out what it means. (It originally spelt out as *Dampf Kraftwagen*, 'Steam power vehicle', but was subsequently interpreted as *Das Kleine Wunder*, 'The Little Wonder'.)

The order of letters in a name may be deliberately changed to create what is formally a new name. *Anagrams* or *ananyms* are the result. Ananyms, or back-spellings, are surprisingly popular and occasionally have some kind of logic about them. A husband who had quarrelled with his wife, **Linda**, for example, reportedly named his daughter **Adnil**, saying that he wanted her to be as unlike his wife as possible. I know of one couple who returned from Canada and therefore named their bungalow **Adanac**.

Another kind of formal change involves either a deliberate or accidental change in spelling. The deliberate misspeller (if he happens to be a heavy drinker as well) calls his house **Shay When** in order to blend **Chez Nous** and **Say When**. Accidental misspelling can arise through ignorance or a genuine mistake. An interesting example of the latter occurred in Mitcham, where a street name was intended to honour a local family of some note. The family's name was **Milholland**, but the council official to whom the documents came assumed that this was a mistake for **Mulholland**. Having 'corrected' the name, the road was duly signposted. By the time the family concerned came to point out the mistake, residents in the street had ordered printed stationery and become used to Mulholland. In any case, they rightly pointed out, if the street were to become Milholland all their friends would react as the council official had done and think that a mistake had been made. One wonders whether anyone had the nerve to ask the Milholland family to change their name.

Transmission of a name through the centuries frequently alters its form, so does transfer from one language to another. The kind of difficulty an explorer may have when asking a native informant what a place is called is well illustrated by an anecdote in *1001 British Columbia Place Names*, by G. P. V. and Helen Akrigg: 'The Indian gave two sneezes and a hiccough, then whistled for a while, choked and said: "Have you got that down?"' It is not surprising, in such circumstances, that the explorer writes down **Klemtu** when the Indian was in fact trying to say **Klemdoo Oolk**, 'the impassable place'.

A name can be visually represented in a kind of hieroglyphic form, or as I would prefer to say, in *allographic* form. I once visited a shop in Leicester which displayed its name as **&**. This symbol should be verbalised as

Ampersand, but I am sure that many customers referred to the shop as **And**. Allographic names are rare, to say the least, and it is perhaps fitting that the newsletter of The Names Society, **Viz.**, is such a name. If one came across 'viz.' in a text one would normally *say* 'namely', just as if one came across '+' one would *say* 'plus'. 'Viz.' represents the Latin *videlicet*, which translates as 'that is to say', or 'in other words', 'namely'. At one time it was no more than a conventional symbol, an abbreviation that one not only expanded but immediately translated. Nowadays I am sure that many speakers actually pronounce it as it is spelt, which is what readers of *Viz.* do, I might add.

Type of origin

By far the most useful kind of classification system for names considers how they come into existence. There are three major classes of primary origin, one which hovers between primary and secondary origin and one class that accounts for secondary origin pure and simple. Naturally there are a great many subdivisions which must be made within these great classes, but these really are like dialects within languages and rightfully spoken of as subdivisions, not separate classes.

Name the island, then see what kind of name you choose.

This point is best illustrated by a little experiment. Look at the illustration of the desert island. Imagine that you are a castaway on that island. You have ample supplies of everything you need, but you are to be alone there for a while. All you have to do now is give the island a name. Once you have your name you can see whether it fits into one of the categories I shall then be describing.

Primary origin

If you have now chosen your island name we can look at the three classes of primary origin.

> *Descriptive*. There are names which describe in some way all or part of the entity being used, literally or metaphorically.
> *Converted*. These are names which consist of a word or phrase which does not describe what is being named and does not link it with another named entity.
> *Invented*. These are neologisms, or groups of letters, or combinations of letters and numbers, which are not part of the vocabulary of any known language.

Descriptive names

These are directly inspired by some aspect of what is named. The most obvious sub-category is that of *generic description*. This would lead to a name like **The Island**, **The Isle** or **The Desert Island** for the island, **The Bungalow** as a name for a bungalow, and so on. When there is only one island off the mainland, or one bungalow in a street, such a name is perfectly justified.

Generic descriptions are sometimes made more exotic by translating them into other languages—a usual trick with commonplace names of all kinds. But **L'Île**, or the equivalent expression in any other language, remains a simple generic description while adding a little further information, perhaps, about the namer. Slightly more subtle is the use of rarer words within the native language. **The Ait** might serve as an example in the case of the island. 'Ait' is usually, but not necessarily, applied to an island in the middle of a river. It would be a relatively *learned* generic description to apply. One can also allow for *dialectal* generic descriptions, but it is clear that foreign, learned and dialectal factors can be present in any type of name, not just in generic descriptions where they are nevertheless frequent.

Direct description

The immediate appearance of what is being named frequently leads to a *direct description*. The island is roughly triangular, so it becomes **Triangle Island**, or **Three-cornered Island**. A person is tall, so he becomes **Lofty**, or because *antonyms* are popular, he is **Shorty**. This tendency towards opposite description presumably links with the fondness for back-spellings which we have already noticed. One thinks, too, of back-slang.

Even more common is *metonymical description*. This is where a distinctive feature of the entity being named is seized upon and used to identify the whole. It would lead to names like **Palm Island** or **Sandy Isle** for the island, and to caricature-type nicknames for people. In a perverse kind of way, *negative description* belongs here, for this produces names which draw attention to something that is missing. Since one distinctive feature that is absent when it is about to be named is the name itself, **Noname** becomes a name quite often, just as **Nonumber** or **Nono** is a common house-name joke.

Many descriptive names focus attention on something strongly associated with, but not actually part of, what is named. *Environmental descriptions* would be of the **Sunny Isle** or **Windy Isle** type, while *activity descriptions* would comment on a strongly associated activity. This would be my own way of describing what are normally called *occupational* surnames, such as **Taylor** and **Miller**, and I would include **The Vicarage** type of house name.

When an entity is large enough for the namer to be within it, the name he gives may be a kind of *outward description*. He might comment on what can be seen, using a name like **Seaview Island**, or he will refer to other sensual experiences with names like **Surfsong Island**, **Seatang Isle**. Next comes a general description of the regular inhabitants or owners of what is being named. If a name or part of a name is mentioned in this connection we have a transferred or link name, but a general description such as **My Island**, or **Seagull Island**, is a *proprietary description*.

Locative names

An important group of descriptive names locates what is named in time or space. The general term *locative name* covers two further sub-categories, *sequential* and *spatial descriptions*. **First Island** might be a sequential name if it referred to the first island on which the namer had lived. A spatial description would lead to something like **Western Isle**. Both types of name usually relate the entity being named to something else in time or space, and whatever this is will often form part of the name. A house is **Moorside**, for instance, or a family is named **Green** because the eponymous ancestor lived next to the village green.

If 'First Island' was chosen with the meaning 'first in quality' in mind rather than the first island occupied by the namer, or perhaps the first island one would come across when coming from the mainland, it would fall into a different class. It would still, in my view, be a descriptive name, but clearly the description would now be one of spiritual and not physical qualities and reflect subjective opinion, not fact. **Happy Island** would be another *subjective description*, bearing in mind that another namer might well describe the same place as **Sad Island**.

There is a high degree of subjectivity too in *metaphorical description*, though two namers both starting from the same premise: 'What is to be named looks like x, so **X** can be its name' could easily arrive at the same result. Many of our surnames began as metaphorical descriptions. A vain man reminded people of a peacock, so **Peacock** he became.

Florence Nightingale, whose surname is an example of metaphorical description. It was given originally to someone who had a sweet voice.

What has been said so far by no means covers the whole range of possible sub-categories for descriptive names. Others will occur as we deal with different kinds of names in later chapters. A vast number of names begin as descriptions of one kind or another of what is being named, though it might be more accurate to say 'began'. Such names tend to be the older names, such as first names and surnames, place names and river names. In nomenclatures where completely new names are still being generated—as in trade names—converted names come into their own.

Converted names

By *converted names* I mean those which are converted from non-descriptive words or phrases, often for *commendatory* purposes. **Greenland**, for example, was not meant to be descriptive. It was meant to suggest a pleasant place. Often it is hoped that the suggestion inherent in the name will somehow rub off on to what is being named. When parents began to bestow flower names on their daughters they hoped that **Rose**, **Daisy** and the like

Daisy, once a popular flower name for girls.

would inherit some of the beauty and delicacy of those flowers. The same kind of thinking inspired American parents to name their son **Cash**. When parents so badly want something for their child that they will saddle him with a name like that, one can be fairly sure that they will fight for many years to see that he gets it. The name itself will have no influence on the matter, but it will not be surprising if the desired result is achieved nevertheless.

We see immediately that converted names tell us more about the namer than what is being named. A common human characteristic is the wish 'to be different', and this often causes extraordinary names to come into being. What these *whimsical conversions* have in common, in fact, is their very extraordinariness. One is justified, therefore, in grouping together such names for the desert island as **Fiddlesticks** and **Red Knickers**. The namers would argue that such names are more easily remembered because they are unusual, and that this is why they have been chosen. A surprising number of names like this, though, occur outside the entertainment and commercial worlds where a name that does succeed in attracting attention is making money. House-namers are especially prone to trying to prove by the name on the gate that unusual people live there.

Punning conversions have linguistic point to them, but again they do not describe what is being named. **Well-I'll-Be!**, **Exile**, **Docile**, **The Aisle**, **Missile**, etc., would be typical punning names for the island, since it is common in names of this type to play on the generic that is present or implied. Names like these, displaying the namers' ingenuity, are good fun for everyone when they are applied to something unimportant, such as a beach-hut. Unfortunately there are always a few parents around who are insensitive enough to make their children the victims of their onomastic wit. The NSPCC was once asked to prosecute a father who was widely publicising the absurd name he had inflicted on his son, but they declined to do so. More and more evidence comes to light each year, though, that a stupidly chosen first name can have serious consequences on a person's psychological development. When such a name is deliberately chosen it is a blatant case of inflicting mental cruelty on a child.

Quotation conversions provide us with another sub-category. A suitable name for the island might be **Sceptred Isle**. As one might expect, quotation names are often found in literature, as with the titles of novels like **For Whom the Bell Tolls** and **The Power and the Glory**. Some conversion names are particularly difficult to understand because they describe neither what is being named, nor do they seem to say anything about the namer. We can call them *tag conversions*, and they fulfil the bare requirement to identify an entity while giving as little extra information as possible. Number names and code names might seem to be of this type, but I do not consider those to be of primary origin, which is what we are discussing for the moment. A tag conversion name for the island would be something like **It**.

Invented names

Names that look as if they are neologisms or arbitrary collections of letters may in fact be quite normal as far as their primary origin is concerned. But whereas a name like **Elsi** remains a generic description (as an island name) that happens to be spelt backwards, names like **Islandette**, **Islandama** and **Minisle** would be true inventions. They would also be typical of such names in their very awfulness.

As might be expected, many invented names can be found in science-fiction novels. Jack Vance is fond of giving his characters such names as **Jheral Tinzy** or **Skebou Diffiani**, and other writers have invented a mass of suitable-sounding names for the inhabitants of various planets.

Fictional inventions can be nearer home. One of the most successful names of this kind was **Shangri-La**, invented by James Hilton in his novel *Lost Horizon* as the name of a Utopian city in the Himalayas. President Roosevelt later transferred the name to his retreat in the Catoctin Mountains during the Second World War, which may have helped to make it more widely known, but the 1937 film version of *Lost Horizon*, in which Ronald Coleman starred, was mainly responsible. Shangri-La occurs very often as an English house name, and it has even gone on to become a word, with the general sense of 'paradise'.

Several popular first names began life as fictional inventions. **Pamela**, which was meant by its inventor, Sir Philip Sidney, to be pronounced with a long 'ee' sound in the middle, came into existence in the sixteenth century but has only become popular in the last fifty years or so. **Lorna** was R. D. Blackmore's contribution to our stock of first names, and **Wendy** came along even more recently in J. M. Barrie's play *Peter Pan*. **Thelma** and **Mavis** were both the inventions of Marie Corelli, but after a short spell of popularity they appear to have faded into the background.

In industry invented names are often used for items that need to be identified within the trade, but not necessarily by the public. These may resemble words, but they are just as likely to be *code names* consisting of letters or groups of letters and numbers. Some might object to calling these names at all, but something that is identified as **ZT434** *is* named just as surely as if it were called **Harry**. Both names can be written and spoken easily.

It will be obvious that I am using *code name* in a special sense. I distinguish personally between arbitrary collections of letters which form code names and groups of initial letters which form *initial names* or *acronyms*. Any name which uses both letters and numbers, whether in a systematic or arbitrary way, I classify as a code name. *Number names*, which consist only of numbers, I treat quite separately later in this chapter.

Link names

With descriptive, converted and invented names we have been dealing with primary origin. With *link names* we move towards secondary origin. What happens is that a name or group of names that already exists is used as a basis for the new name. Other words or elements are often added. For instance, if I were to base an island name on my first name, Leslie, I might arrive at **Isleslie** or **Lesisle**.

Names like **John** and **Daniel**, which appear to us to be single names, were originally link names. John is a much shortened form of a phrase in Hebrew which meant 'Jehovah has favoured'. Daniel was once another Hebrew phrase with the meaning 'God has judged'. Thus the child being named took God's name as part of his own.

Long after John had become fossilised as a single name, 'John's son' became the further link name **Johnson**, which in turn became a single name. **Johnsonville** in Texas (named after its first Postmaster, incidentally, not L.B.J.) shows Johnson in its turn being used in a link. The **Johnsonville Old Timers**, if such a group happened to exist, would simply be forming a new link name based on Johnsonville. This would remain a link name even if expressed acronymically as **J.O.T.**, and further linking, building into a name like the **J.O.T. Cycling Club**, would be perfectly feasible.

The characteristic of a link name is this adding of something to all or part of an existing name. When John is simply borrowed from the common stock of first names and applied to a child, it is being transferred, not linked. When Johnson is passed on as a family name from one generation to another it is being transferred again. The linking process took place when the names were first formed.

Blends

When parts of two or more names are joined together to form a new name it is a *blend*. In former times it was common for parents in a Germanic tribe, who might have names like **Gerhard** and **Hildegund**, to use parts of their own names in order to name their sons **Hildeger**, **Gundeger** or **Gunthard** and their daughters **Gunthilde**, **Gerhilde**, **Harthilde** or **Hartgund**. In modern times British householders frequently blend parts of the family's names to form a house name.

Blending only occurs when the name parts are actually joined, as when a **Patricia** and an **Alan** call their island **Patalan**. The linking elements need only be single elements, such as initials, and other words may be included or not. **Apholme** would be a possible blended house name for a couple named Patricia and Alan.

Link names often occur in clusters. The existence of the Thames tributary, the **Brent**, leads to the place name **Brentford**. Many trade names in the area incorporate 'Brent' as an element, especially where the businesses think it an advantage to emphasise that they are locally based. One might, incidentally, postulate an *etymological link name*. It would be etymologically fitting for a girl born in the Brent Valley to be named **Bridget**, since it derives from the same source as 'Brent' and both mean 'the exalted one' (hinting at river worship in the case of the river name).

To return to the desert island, if the name you chose for it contains even a single letter that is deliberately included as a reminder of another name, and if it contains another element such as 'isle', it is a link name. If you used a name that already exists in exactly the same form, with no alterations or additions, you used a transferred name.

Number names

The idea of linking and transferring names is easy to grasp, but there is one special set of names that is frequently transferred which may not seem so simple. This is the set of consecutive integers which we normally refer to as 'numbers'. In other words, if you called the island **Eleven**, because that happens to be your lucky number, you gave it a number name.

If I say that there are seven days in a week I am using the number seven. I am talking about the concept of quantity. But if I decide to identify the days in the week by calling them **One**, **Two**, **Three**, **Four**, **Five**, **Six** and **Seven**, then each of these becomes a *number name*.

In some nomenclatures, such as first names, there is a common stock of names waiting to be used. Number names are a kind of free-floating set of names that can be used in any of the thousand and one nomenclatures that need to be established temporarily or permanently. There is a strong prejudice against using them for anything that has human connections, and people themselves feel rather insulted if identified in this way. Yet number names are among the most efficient we have, and they have some great advantages over other names. For instance:

- they positively identify a unique entity—natural duplication and transfer do not arise *within* a given nomenclature;
- they have a highly convenient shorthand form which is recognised internationally. This is something that is shared by relatively few words, such as 'equals' ($=$), 'minus' ($-$), 'per cent' ($\%$);
- they are usefully descriptive in the sequential information they give about what is being named;
- they follow a regular, simple pattern of formation which is readily understood.

A frequent complaint is that number names have no meaning, that they are 'soul-less'. This is not true of some numbers. Seven, thirteen, twenty-one and the like have a great deal of 'meaning' for countless people. For those who are numerologically inclined there is of course a 'meaning' in every number.

Nevertheless, Gus Lobrano of *The New Yorker* was obviously voicing a widely felt dislike of number names when he told J. Bryan III of his great epic: *How Twenty-Third Street Got Its Name.*

> Alderman Dooley announces: 'Next business, naming one of our streets. Any suggestions, fellows? I can tell you this much: the street below it is **Twenty-second** and the street above it is **Twenty-fourth**. Does that help any?'

Alderman Minetti jumps to his feet: 'I got it! I got it! How about callin' it **Twenty-thoid**?'

Cries of: 'Ya-a-a-ay! Way to go, Minnie!'

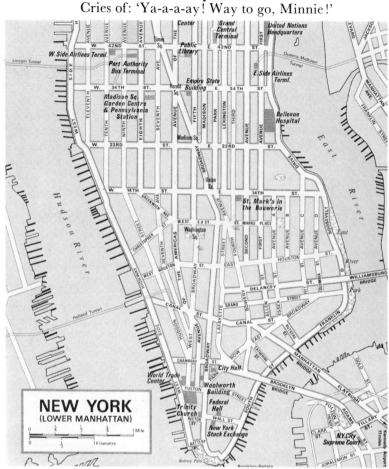

The streets of **New York**.

By contrast, E. Stewart Fay has stoutly defended New York's *functional* street names, as he calls them, in his book about London's street names, *Why Piccadilly?* His view, which on the whole I share, is that existing names should be kept, but that sensible use of number names on newly developed estates or in new towns would have more point to it than an arbitrary collection of names drawn from all sources.

Perhaps the eventual solution, which would cater for those who demand functional efficiency and those who want the greater romance of ordinary names, is suggested in many English suburban streets, where houses frequently have both number names and verbal names. All of us, too, have both kinds of name, since various institutions prefer to identify us by number names. The computer that calculates my pay knows me as **1199062**, and I am quite happy to acknowledge this particular pseudonym —or 'numbernym', as I should perhaps call it.

That is not to say that I would like only 1199062 to identify me on the cover of this book. For all its imperfections, the names that I bear because of parental whim and historical accident seem more appropriate, but this is only due to social convention. Noël Coward has already indicated the way things could go. When Lawrence of Arabia had become an airman he wrote him a letter that began 'Dear **338171**, or may I call you **338** . . .'.

The full advantages of number names can be demonstrated by substitution. It is a convention that we identify the pages of a book by number names. When a different kind of name is substituted, as on this page, we realise what we have lost. This page I have called **George**, in honour of my father, but if I were to name every page in honour of relations and friends, much as that might please them, where would it leave my readers? Imagine being asked to refer to page **Ethel** or **Nicole**. Alphabetical order might help, but that would still be clumsy compared to numerical sequence.

This example is meant to seem absurd, but the fact is that in an average town we tolerate a system of street names that is even more ridiculous. A few street names give vague help in locating the streets concerned, as when all the streets named after poets or admirals are grouped on the same estate, but one might argue that this is only a help to a minority of well-educated residents. Think of the time lost—the time you yourself have lost—searching for streets whose names have given you no help at all. We could probably change all that and devise number name systems that would effectively relate streets to each other in any given town, but we will not do it, of course. Nor are we likely to interfere with the charmingly haphazard situation that exists with our first names and surnames, our place names and trade names. With typical human stubbornness we will insist not only on retaining the disorder but will go on adding to it. We will allow simple efficiency to reign only in unimportant nomenclatures such as the pages of a book.

A move towards acceptance of number names will only be made when they are admitted to be names by people who are instinctively verbal rather than numerical. For me they are names which happen to have a number form: for most people they remain mere numbers. Those who are aware of society's dependence on numbers used quantitatively will smile at the '*mere* numbers', yet even they would probably insist on keeping their old-fashioned verbal names. The latter are occasionally disguised number names in any case. Such is the case with **Quentin** ('fifth') and **Octavia** ('eighth').

Not all number names are chosen for obvious sequential reasons. The trade name **4711**, for instance, was chalked on the wall of the original factory in Cologne by French soldiers, who were unable to cope with names written in German script. Even without this incident in the Napoleonic Wars, which demonstrated how in times of emergency number names come into their own, it would still have been a transferred name. Its use for the eau de Cologne has shown that a number name can be given all the 'soul' or 'meaning' that a normal name is said to have. One might add that, with its historical significance, its convenience for advertising purposes, its use of elements widely thought to be lucky and its novelty, its choice was by any standards a minor stroke of genius.

Some commercial number names.

The namers

Many readers who paused to name the island no doubt transferred to it a verbal rather than a number name. Place names and the like are usually transferred for sentimental reasons, and the choice of such names tells us more about the namer than what is being named. But every name tells us something about the namer. There are those who feel obliged to show possession by proclaiming 'This is mine' when they bestow a name. There are those whose plain, matter-of-fact outlook on life is reflected in obvious names, simple descriptions of shape or prominent features, for instance. There are the poets, who will have searched for a beautiful name to demonstrate their own aesthetic taste.

One would expect a trained psychologist to see in a group of names chosen by the same person certain basic attitudes revealing themselves. Perhaps one day a name test will take its place beside the ink blots. Names mirror the namers—which is one of the reasons they fascinate.

To sum it up, then, I have said that all names by primary origin are either *descriptive, converted* or *invented. Link names* are half-way between new names and *transferred names*. Some of the categories and sub-categories I have mentioned in this chapter are well established, but many are new. The trouble with most existing categories is that they have been devised for one nomenclature only. There is a need for universal categories and sub-categories, and these I have tried to supply. As we go on now to look at some important nomenclatures in more detail, let us hope that these categories will enable us to draw attention to the chief characteristics of each system and make comparisons between them.

Chapter 4
First Names First

It seems to be a universal habit, and one as old as language itself, for human beings to name one another. The regular pattern today among the English-speaking peoples is for a child to be given at least two names at birth, a *first name* and a *middle name*. Of these the first name is normally by far the more important, and not just because it is the descendant of the original single personal name with which our remote ancestors were content. It is our first name that most of us will respond to throughout our lives and come to look upon as part of ourselves. It is therefore natural for us to ask such questions as:

> where did our first names come from?
> what did they originally mean?
> which names do we make most use of today?
> why do parents choose one name rather than another?
> how should we ourselves choose a name for a child if we are given that responsibility?

What is a first name?

We shall be attempting to answer all the above questions in the next three chapters, but the question: 'What is a name?', which we earlier tried to deal with in general terms, needs a more specific answer when we come to the **Catherine/Katharine** kind of problem. Are we to treat such spelling variants as one name, or should we separate out each variant and refer to it as a new name? There is also the matter of diminutives. As everyone knows, names like **Margaret** have given rise to pet forms such as **Madge**, **Peggy**, **Greta**, **Maisie** and the like. Should all these be considered as separate names?

As we begin to answer such questions we see the widely differing viewpoints of the historically based names student and the student who is more interested in the sociological and psychological aspects of names. For the etymologist Catherine and Katharine were originally the same name, as were Margaret and all its diminutive forms. Since he is concerned with origins the etymologist takes all forms of a name in his stride provided he can explain why they occur.

But from another point of view the change of a single letter in a name is quite enough to differentiate it from all others. No one would convince a **Francis** that his name was the same as **Frances**, although an etymologist would be justified in bracketing them together. My own etymological training is instantly forgotten when someone writes my name as **Lesley** rather than **Leslie**. I do not easily forgive those who change my sex with careless orthographic surgery. The change from **Stephen**, say, to **Steven** may appear to inflict less damage, but no doubt those who bear one form of the name object to being given the other.

There is no simple answer to this problem: What is a first name? The etymological criterion obviously cannot be the only one to be applied by a researcher who is investigating such things as name frequencies. Apart from causing a mix-up of the sexes it would lead some etymologists to treat **Jennifer**, **Winifred** and **Genevieve** as one name, which would be ridiculous. Nor can he make a judgment on purely phonetic grounds, for some boys' names sound exactly like their female counterparts. Yet the spelling criterion, while obviously the easiest to apply, would also seem to be misleading. There are cases where a very general uncertainty exists about the correct spelling of a name, perhaps for good reasons. The Somerset House records show, for instance, that British public opinion is almost exactly divided as to whether **Tracy** is spelt in that way or as **Tracey**. The same records show that **Steven** is gradually catching up on **Stephen**, as it is in Australia, and may eventually become the normal form.

In cases such as **Tracy/Tracey** I find it hard to believe that parents are thinking of two names and carefully choosing between them. In my view they are choosing *a* name which happens to have genuinely variant spellings. I believe, therefore, that a modern researcher must fall back on his instinct as a native speaker and weigh up the relative importance of etymological, phonetic and orthographic factors. He must then decide in each case whether he is dealing with one or more names.

Evonne Goolagong, the Australian tennis player, who has made another spelling of **Yvonne** well known.

I once heard a father tell a registrar what name he wanted to give his daughter. He then surprised both the registrar and me by writing the name down as **Evon**. But it was the father who was surprised, not to say incredulous, when the registrar pointed out that the name was usually spelt **Yvonne**. He insisted on spelling it his way. All of us were thinking, it seems to me, of the same name, which is why I would personally bracket these two widely differing spellings as one name. I would also treat **Laurence** and **Lawrence** as one, though I admit that when another registrar recorded my son's name in the latter form my instinctive reaction was to tell her that she had written down the wrong name.

As for diminutives, it is clear that they eventually reach a point where they achieve full name status in their own right. If a girl is given the name **Elizabeth**, but her family and friends subsequently come to call her **Betty**, we could describe Betty as a link nickname. A report by the United

States Social Security Commission in 1972, however, showed that Betty was being given with great frequency as an independent first name, something that happened in England in the 1920s. The report also mentioned both **William** and **Willie** as recording very high scores, and **Frank** was recorded as a popular name. One feels a little sorry for the bearers of these diminutives turned names. The Elizabeths and Williams are given room for manœuvre. They get a bonus, as it were, in the form of a set of accepted nicknames, and no one will raise an eyebrow if they later decide to be known as **Lizbeth**, **Liza**, **Bill**, **Will** or **Willie**. Children who are definitively labelled Betty or Willie are far more restricted.

A single first name, then, like some words, can occasionally have more than one 'official' spelling: perhaps because it started out in one language and eventually came to English-speakers both in its original form and in that of another language; perhaps because two or more forms of it were fossilised at a time when spelling was by no means standardised; perhaps because it is a new name that has not yet settled into one spelling; perhaps because some parents think that a different spelling will add a touch of novelty; perhaps because of a parent's or registrar's ignorance. In the following chapters I shall be grouping names by their main spellings, indicating variations only when opinion seems to be genuinely divided. When diminutives are used as names in their own right I shall treat them as such.

Middle names

Before looking at the more common first names in detail, however, we must say something about middle names. Firstly, it is statistically normal these days for children throughout the English-speaking world to be given one first name and one middle name. Two or more middle names are more usual than no middle name. While there is legally no upper limit on the number of middle names that may be given, most parents draw the line after four.

Enoch Powell and Harold Wilson, both of whom have dropped their first names in favour of their middle names.

It has been the convention until very recently to give boys a 'safe', traditional first name and to be slightly more daring with the middle name, but to do the reverse with the girls. In the past many parents, having allowed their romantic fancy to run riot with their daughter's first name, felt that they must be more sober with the middle name. 'If she doesn't like X,' they would say, mentioning some exotic invention that they happened to have come across, 'she can always use her middle name.' There are signs that boys are now being treated in a similar way.

Relatively few people, however, do in fact drop their first names and make daily use of their middle names. There are well-known exceptions to this rule, such as the British statesmen *James* **Harold Wilson** and *John* **Enoch Powell**, both of whose first names were long ago put aside, but most people's middle names serve only to pin-point identification on official forms or, in the case of Americans, to provide the essential middle initial.

Two American correspondents whose parents were thoughtless enough, as they humorously put it, not to provide them with middle names have commented to me in the past about the difficulties thus created. J. Bryan III (who at least has an interesting personal-name modifier) reports that his fellow countrymen absolutely insist on giving him a middle

initial, and almost any seems to do. Mike Martin became M. Martin NMI ('No Middle Initial') when he joined the Army, and to avoid this disgrace he later legally adopted the middle initial **W**. The 'W' was, like the **S** in Harry S Truman, a letter name rather than an initial, not standing for any particular name. Mike was happy with his 'W' until his driving-licence arrived with his name written as Michael **W (only)** Martin.

Harry S Truman. The 'S' is an initial name, complete in itself.

In some areas, such as Scotland, it is a custom for the wife's maiden name to become the child's middle name. The surnames of noble families in particular have long been used as first or middle names, so the precedent is there. Camden, writing in 1605, remarked that many were worried about what was then a new trend, thinking it would cause great confusion if surnames mixed with first names, but we managed to absorb names like **Sidney**, **Howard**, **Neville** and **Percy** without difficulty. More recent transfers from surname to middle- or first-name status include **Scott**, **Cameron**, **Grant** and **Campbell**—the Scottish influence being very noticeable. Such names often begin with very restricted use, used as middle names only where there is a family connection. After a probationary period as middle names they are promoted to first names. General recognition follows when they are used as first names by those who have no family reason for doing so.

It is always important to distinguish between first names and middle names. Historically it was first names, as individual personal names, which came first, to be followed in the Middle Ages by surnames, a large number of which were themselves derived from first names. Middle names, occupying a highly ambiguous area between the two more important nomenclatures and borrowing heavily from both of them, have been with us from the seventeenth century only. In terms of their social and psychological importance they are also totally overshadowed by the names that surround them. Middle names constitute what is almost a separate nomenclature, useful for minor purposes such as official identification, pacifying relations who want their names to live on, or perhaps genuinely acting as tokens of respect to namesakes. First names have the vibrancy which comes from daily use: middle names, and perhaps rightly so, are more like family heirlooms, necessary to preserve if only in the attic. The metaphor may be apt in another way. We have spoken of the middle-name arena as a proving ground for new names, but it is used to put old names out to pasture. **John**, **George**, **Henry**, **Jane**, **Louise**, **Mary**, **Claire**, **Elizabeth**, **Frances**, **Ann**(e) and **Margaret** currently appear to fall into that category as far as readers of *The Times* are concerned. According to the Birth Announcements column **Ann** or **Anne** was given only nine times as a first name during 1971, for example, but in the same year it was given seventy times as a middle name. A survey based on the records at Somerset House, carried out by C. V. Appleton, confirms that most of these names had fallen out of favour with the general public that year, but **Jane** was making an effort to hold her own, while **Claire** and **Louise** were making definite gains. We shall be commenting later on the difference in onomastic taste revealed by different surveys.

The central stock of first names

Having established our definitions of 'first name' and 'middle name', we may now turn to the question of how many first names there are in what might be called 'the central stock'. There is nothing to stop parents in the English-speaking countries giving *any* name to a child as its first or middle name, but in practice the vast majority of parents make very great use in any one year of a relatively small number of names. In 1900, for example, the **Smiths** in England and Wales made really significant use of only 120 boys' names and 160 girls' names. In 1971 they made equally significant use—and by this we mean nine families out of ten made use—of 125 boys' names and 175 girls' names. In the case of the boys, about thirty 'new' names, such as **Barry**, **Craig** and **Darren**, had appeared by the 1970s but twenty-five others had been left aside. The latter included names like **Edmund**, **Herbert**, **Horace** and **Percy**. Similarly, girls' names such as **Deborah**, **Janice**, **Joanne** and **Karen** were among the seventy or so names 'new' to the 1970s. The fifty-five names that had fallen by the wayside included **Annie**, **Winifred**, **Nellie** and **May**.

There is evidence of this central stock of names on all sides. In a supplement to the Registrar-General's Report for Scotland, 1958, the first names given to 52,882 boys and 50,204 girls that year were fully analysed. Every *spelling* of a name was counted as a separate name, whereas I would certainly have bracketed such pairs as **Ian/Iain**, **Brian/Bryan**, **Alastair/Alistair**, **Ann/Anne**, **Lynn/Lynne**, **Carol/Carole**, **Teresa/Theresa**.

The Central Stock of Boys' Names

The following names for boys appear to be those mainly being used by English-speaking parents in the early 1970s. Brief indications are given as to the source, language of origin and original meaning of each name, but many explanations can only be offered tentatively.

Aaron Biblical; Hebrew or Egyptian; origin unknown.

Adam Biblical; Hebrew; 'red skin (or earth)'.

Adrian Papal; Latin; 'of the Adriatic'.

Alan Norman; Celtic, origin unknown.

Albert Germanic; Old English/German; 'noble bright'.

Alexander Historical; Greek; 'defending men'.

Alfred Royal; Old English; 'elf counsel'.

Alistair (most popular modern spelling) Translated; Gaelic form of *Alexander*.

Andrew Biblical; Greek; 'manly'.

Anthony Saint; Latin; origin unknown. **Antony** earlier and historically more correct.

Ashley Surname/place name; Old English; 'ash wood or clearing'.

Austin Saint; Latin *augustus*; 'venerable, consecrated'.

Barry Descriptive(?); Gaelic; based on 'spear'.

Benedict Saint; Latin; 'blessed'.

Benjamin Biblical; Hebrew; 'son of the south', i.e. 'the right hand'.

Bernard Germanic; Old English/German; 'brave as a bear'.

Bradley Surname/place name; Old English; 'broad clearing'.

Brendan Saint; Gaelic; origin uncertain.

Bret(t) Surname; Old French; 'a Briton'.

Brian Historical; Celtic; origin uncertain.

Cameron Surname; Gaelic; 'crooked nose'.

Carl Anglicised **Karl**; German form of **Charles**.

Charles Historical; Germanic; 'a man'.

Christian Commendatory; Latin; 'Christian'.

Christopher Saint; Greek; 'bearing Christ'.

Clifford Surname/place name; Old English; 'ford by a slope'.

Clive Surname (Historical); Old English; 'dweller by the cliff'.

Colin Diminutive; Latin *columba* ('dove') or from **Nicholas**.

Conrad Saint; Old German; 'bold counsel'.

Craig Surname; Middle English; 'dweller by the crag'.

Dale Surname; Old English; 'dweller in the dale'.

Daniel Biblical; Hebrew; 'God has judged'.

Darren Surname(?); origin uncertain.

Damian Saint; Greek; based on 'to tame'.

David Saint; Hebrew; 'friend'.

Dean Surname; Old English; 'dweller in a valley'. Also Latin; 'son of the dean'.

Derek Germanic; Old German; 'ruler of the people'.

Desmond Surname; Gaelic; 'man from south Munster'.

Dominic(k) Saint; Latin; 'of the Lord'.

Douglas Surname; Gaelic; 'dark blue' (originally a river name).

Duncan Surname; Gaelic; 'brown warrior'.

Edward Royal saint; Old English; 'happy guardian'.

Edwin Royal; Old English; 'happy friend'.

Eric Danish; Old Norse; based on 'ruler'.

Francis Saint; Latin; 'a Frenchman'. **Frank**, the diminutive, is as popular.

Frederick Germanic; Old German; 'peaceful ruler'.

Gareth Literary; Welsh form of **Gerontius**; 'old man'.

Gary Diminutive; from *Gareth* or *Gerard*.

Gavin Literary; Celtic or Germanic; probably from **Gawain**.

Geoffrey Norman; Old German; based on 'peace'.

George Saint; Greek; 'farmer'.

Gerald Norman; Old German; 'spear rule'.

Gerard Norman; Old German; 'firm spear'.

Giles Saint; Greek; 'young goat'.

Glen(n) Surname; Gaelic; 'dweller in the valley'.

Glyn(n) probably derives from this name.

Gordon Surname (Historical); Gaelic; 'great hill'.

Graham Surname; Old English; origin disputed.

Grant Surname; Old French; 'great'.

Gregory Saint; Greek; based on 'to be watchful'.

Guy Norman; Old German; origin uncertain.

Harvey Surname; Old French; 'battle worthy'.

Howard Surname; Old German; 'heart brave', also 'high warden', also 'ewe-herder'.

Ian Translated; Gaelic form of *John*.

Ivan Translated; Russian form of *John*.

James Saint; Latin; form of **Jacob** 'heel' (Hebrew).

Jamie Diminutive; Scottish form of *James* and **Jimmy**.

Jason Biblical; Greek; possibly translation of Hebrew name, but taken to mean 'healer'.

Jeremy Biblical; Hebrew form of **Jeremiah**, based on 'Jehovah'.

Joel Biblical; Hebrew; 'Jehovah is God'.

John Biblical; Hebrew; 'Jehovah has favoured'.

Jonathan Biblical; Hebrew; 'Jehovah has given'.

Joseph Biblical; Hebrew; 'Jehovah added'.

Julian Saint; Latin; form of **Julius**, possibly 'downy (beard)'.

Justin Saint; Latin; 'just'.

Karl German form of *Charles*.

Keith Surname; Celtic; 'wood'.

Kenneth Saint; Royal; Gaelic; usually taken to be 'handsome'.

Kevin Saint; Celtic; as *Kenneth*.

Laurence Saint; Latin; 'of Laurentum'. **Lawrence** occurs.

Lee Surname; Old English; 'dweller by the wood or clearing'.

Leslie Surname/Place name; Gaelic; possibly 'garden or court of hollies'.

Luke Biblical; Greek; 'of Lucania'.

Malcolm Saint; Gaelic; 'servant or disciple of St. Columba'.

Marcus Roman; Latin form of *Mark*. **Marc** is also becoming popular.

Mark Biblical; Latin; possibly connected with *Mars*.

Martin Saint; Latin; 'of Mars'.

Matthew Biblical; Hebrew; 'gift of Jehovah'.

Michael Biblical; Hebrew; 'who is like the Lord'.

Nathan Biblical; Hebrew; 'gift'.

Neil Irish; Gaelic; 'champion'.

Nicholas Saint; Greek; 'victory of the people'.

Nigel Latinised form of *Neil*.

Noël Descriptive; French; for a child born on 'Christmas Day'.

Norman Germanic; Old English/German; 'northman'.

Oliver Norman; Old French; 'olive tree', but numerous other possibilities.

Owen Literary; Welsh; taken to be from Latin *Eugenius*, 'well-born'.

Patrick Saint; Latin; 'a nobleman'.

Paul Biblical; Latin; 'small'.

Peter Biblical; Greek (translation of Aramaic); 'stone'.

Philip Biblical; Greek; 'lover of horses'.

Raymond Norman; Old German; 'wise protection'.

Reuben Biblical; Hebrew; 'renewer'.

Richard Norman; Old German/English; 'stern ruler'.

Robert Norman; Old English/German; 'bright fame'.

Robin Diminutive of *Robert*.

Rodney Surname; Old English; 'Hroda's island'.

Roger Norman; Old English/German; 'fame-spear'.

Rohan Surname; Gaelic; origin uncertain.

Ronald Scottish form of **Reginald**; Old English; 'powerful might'.

Ross Surname; Gaelic; 'dweller at the promontory'.

Roy Descriptive; Gaelic; 'red'.

Rupert Royal; Old German form of *Robert*

Russell Surname; Old French; 'red'.

Samuel Biblical; Hebrew; 'name of God'.

Scott Surname; Old English; 'a Scot'.

Shane from **Sean**; Irish form of *John*.

Shaun Translated; Irish form of **Sean** = *John*.

Simon Biblical; Hebrew form of **Simeon**, 'obedient', but in Greek *Simon* is 'snub-nosed'.

Spencer Surname; Old French; 'dispenser of provisions'.

Stephen Biblical; Greek; 'crown'. Also as **Steven**.

Stuart Surname; Old English; 'steward'. Also as **Stewart**.

Terence Roman; Latin; origin unknown. Frequently in form **Terry**.

Thomas Biblical; Aramaic; 'twin'.

Timothy Biblical; Greek; 'honoured by God'.

Toby Biblical; Hebrew; form of **Tobias**, 'Jehovah is good'.

Tony Diminutive of *Anthony*.

Travis Surname; Middle English; 'a toll-collector'.

Trevor Surname; Welsh; 'big village'.

Troy Surname/Place name; Old French; 'from Troyes'.

Vernon Surname; Old French; 'alder tree'.

Vincent Saint; Latin; 'conquering'.

Warren Surname; Old French; 'from La Varenne'.

Wayne Surname; Old English; 'wagon-maker'.

William Norman; Old German; 'will helmet'.

Some additional boys' names

Abel	**Cyril**	**Horace**	**Oscar**
Abraham	**Darryl**	**Hugh**	**Percy**
Adlai	**Denis**	**Hugo**	**Perry**
Algernon	**Drew**	**Humphrey**	**Piers**
Ambrose	**Dudley**	**Isaac**	**Quentin**
Amos	**Dylan**	**Ivor**	**Ralph**
Anatole	**Ebenezer**	**Jack**	**Randolph**
Angus	**Edgar**	**Jasper**	**Roderick**
Archie	**Edmund**	**Jerome**	**Roland**
Arnold	**Egbert**	**Joshua**	**Rory**
Arthur	**Eli**	**Kent**	**Royston**
Asa	**Elmer**	**Lars**	**Rudolph**
Aubrey	**Elvis**	**Lemuel**	**Rufus**
Aylmer	**Elwin**	**Leon**	**Saul**
Barnabas	**Enoch**	**Leonard**	**Seamus**
Bartholomew	**Ernest**	**Lester**	**Sebastian**
Basil	**Eustace**	**Lionel**	**Selwyn**
Bertram	**Evan**	**Louis**	**Sidney**
Boris	**Fabian**	**Lucian**	**Silvester**
Boyd	**Felix**	**Magnus**	**Stanley**
Bramwell	**Ferdinand**	**Marvin**	**Theobald**
Bruce	**Gabriel**	**Maurice**	**Theodore**
Caspar	**Gideon**	**Max**	**Tyrone**
Cecil	**Gilbert**	**Melville**	**Victor**
Cedric	**Gilchrist**	**Melvyn**	**Wallace**
Chester	**Godfrey**	**Miles**	**Walter**
Clarence	**Hamish**	**Nathaniel**	**Wilbur**
Clement	**Harold**	**Noah**	**Wilfred**
Conan	**Hector**	**Norris**	**Winston**
Crispin	**Henry**	**Orson**	**Winthrop**
Cuthbert	**Herbert**	**Orville**	**Zachary**

The Central Stock of Girls' Names

Abigail Biblical; Hebrew; 'father rejoiced'.

Adèle Norman; Old German; 'noble'. French form of **Adela**.

Alexandra Royal; Greek; from *Alexander*, 'defending men'.

Alice Literary; Old German; 'nobility'. Contraction of *Adalheidis* = **Adelaide**.

Alison Literary; French; diminutive of *Alice*.

Amanda Literary; Latin; 'lovable'.

Andrea feminine form of *Andrew*, 'manly'.

Angela Saint; Greek; 'messenger'.

Anita Diminutive; Hebrew; Spanish pet form of *Ann*.

Ann Biblical; Hebrew; form of **Hannah**, 'God has favoured me'. French form **Anne**; Latin form **Anna**.

Annabel Derivative(?); possibly for Latin **Amabel**, 'lovable'.

Annette Diminutive; Hebrew; French pet form of *Ann*.

Antonia Saint; Latin; Italian feminine form of *Anthony*.

Arabella Derivative(?); possibly for Latin **Amabel**, 'lovable'.

Barbara Saint; Greek; 'foreign'.

Belinda Literary; Old German; origin uncertain.

Beverley Surname/Place name; Old English; 'beaver stream'.

Bridget Saint; Celtic; 'the high one'.

Camilla Literary; Etruscan(?); origin uncertain.

Carla feminine form of *Carl*, from *Charles*, 'a man'. **Carol(e)** is another form of the name.

Caroline Royal; Germanic; Italian feminine form of *Charles*.

Catherine Saint; Greek; usually said to be 'pure'. This spelling most popular, but **Katharine**, **Katherine**, **Catharine**, etc., are frequent.

Charlotte Royal; Germanic; French feminine form of Italian **Carlo**, *Charles*.

Cheryl Diminutive(?); possibly form of *Charlotte*.

Christina Saint; Latin; 'Christian'. **Christine** is the English form.

Claire Saint; Latin; 'bright, clear'. This French form of the name is most popular, but Latin **Clare** is also frequent.

Danielle French feminine form of *Daniel*, 'God has judged'.

Dawn Literary; conversion of the word 'dawn'.

Deborah Biblical; Hebrew; 'a bee'. The pet form **Debbie** is now used as an independent name. **Debra** is found.

Denise French feminine form of **Denis**; Greek; 'of Dionysos'.

Diane Literary; Latin; name of the moon goddess in form **Diana**. **Dianne** occurs now, by analogy with *Leanne*, etc.

Donna Italian; 'lady'.

Elaine Literary; Greek; French form of *Helen*.

Eleanor Royal; Greek; another form of *Helen*.

Elizabeth Biblical; Hebrew; 'oath of God'.

Ellen English form of *Helen*.

Emily Literary; Latin; 'to excel'. **Amelia** is usually taken to be another form of it.

Emma Royal; Old German; 'whole, universal'.

Estelle Literary; possibly from **Esther**, 'star'.

Fiona Literary; Gaelic; 'fair, white'.

Frances form of *Francis*, 'a Frenchman'.

Gail Diminutive of *Abigail*.

Gaynor Historical; a form of **Guinevere**.

Gemma Italian 'gem'.

Georgina feminine form of *George*, 'farmer'. Also from **Georgia Anna**.

Geraldine Literary; from surname *Fitzgerald*, 'son of *Gerald*'.

Gillian English form of **Juliana**, from *Julian*.

Harriet feminine form of *Henry*, 'home ruler'.

Hayley Surname/Place name; possibly 'high clearing'.

Hazel from the tree name.

Heather from the plant. The Latin **Erica** also occurs.

Heidi German diminutive of *Adelaide*.

Helen Saint; Greek; 'the bright one'.

Henrietta Royal; another feminine form of *Henry*.

Jacqueline French feminine form of **Jacques** = *Jacob*, 'heel'.

Jane form of *Joanne*. **Jayne** often occurs. **Janet**, **Janice** and **Janine** are diminutive forms.

Jean another form of *Jane*. **Jeanette** occurs as diminutive.

Jennifer originally Cornish form of *Guinevere*. See *Gaynor*.

Jessica Biblical; Hebrew; 'God beholds'.

Jill form of **Juliana**.

Joanne Biblical; Hebrew; form of *John*, 'Jehovah has favoured'. This spelling far more popular than original **Joanna**.

Jodie form of *Judith*.

Josephine French feminine form of *Joseph*, 'Jehovah added'.

Joy from the word, when 'virtues' were popular.

Joyce Saint; Celtic; origin uncertain. Formerly a man's name.

Judith Hebrew; 'a Jewess'. **Judy** is also used.

Julie feminine form of *Julian* 'downy (beard)'. This spelling more popular than earlier **Julia**. **Juliet**, a diminutive, occurs.

Justine French feminine form of *Justin*, 'just'.

Karen Danish form of *Catherine*.

Kate and **Katie** Diminutive forms of *Katharine*, see *Catherine*. **Kathleen** was originally Irish form of the same name. **Katrina**, for earlier **Katrine**, represents Scottish form.

Kay Diminutive of names beginning with 'k'.

Kelly Surname/Place name; of various origins, mainly Irish; 'descendant of Ceallach'. **Kelley** and **Kellie** occur.

Kerry perhaps from Irish place name. **Kerri** and **Kerrie** also occur.

Kim Literary; Kipling's *Kim* is from *Kimball*, a surname of various origins. Thence transfer to feminine name.

Kirsten Scandinavian form of *Christine*. **Kirsty** is the Scottish form.

Kylie (Australia); Aboriginal; 'boomerang'.

Laura feminine form of *Laurence*.

Leah Biblical; Hebrew; 'cow'. **Lea** also occurs.

Leanne recent blend of *Lea* and *Anne*? Possibly reshaping of **Leonie**, feminine form of **Leo**, 'lion'.

Leigh and **Lee** are currently being used as boys' and girls' names. *Lee* seems to be male form in England, but female form elsewhere. From surname *Lee* or reshaping of *Lea* from *Leah* when a girl's name?

Lesley feminine form of *Leslie* and now far more frequent as a girl's name.

Linda short form of names like *Belinda*. **Lynda** now occurs.

Lindsey Surname/Place name; 'Lincoln island'.

Lisa Diminutive of *Elizabeth*.

Lorna Literary; from the title of the Marquesses of Lorne.

Lorraine Form suggests place name ('kingdom of Lothair') which is also surname, but may be reshaping of *Laura Ann(e)*.

Louise French feminine form of **Louis**, 'renowned battle'. **Louisa** also occurs.

Lucy Saint; Latin; form of **Lucia**, feminine of **Lucian**.

Lynn Diminutive of *Linda*. **Lynne** also occurs.

Mandy pet form of *Amanda*.

Margaret Saint; Greek; 'pearl'.

Marie French form of *Mary*. **Maria** also occurs, originally the Latin form. **Marion** is a diminutive of the name.

Mary Biblical; Hebrew; 'wished for child'. **Miriam** is the same name.

Maureen Diminutive; Irish; from **Maire** = *Mary*.

Maxine Diminutive; French; from **Maximilian**, a blend of *Maximus* and *Aemilianus*, two Roman names.

Megan Diminutive; Welsh; from *Margaret*.

Melanie Saint; Greek; 'black'.

Melinda Literary; Latin and Old German; literally 'honey snake', i.e. 'sweetly wise'.

Melissa Literary; Greek; 'a bee'.

Melody the word converted to name use.

Michaela feminine form of *Michael*, as is the far more popular **Michelle**.

Miranda Literary; Latin; 'worthy to be admired'.

Nadine French form of a Russian name meaning 'hope'.

Nancy a pet form of **Ann(e)**.

Naomi Biblical; Hebrew; 'pleasant one'.

Natalie Saint; Latin; 'Christmas Day'.

Natasha Diminutive; Latin; Russian pet form of *Natalie*.

Nicola Italian feminine form of *Nicholas*. **Nicole** is the French form.

Nina Diminutive; Russian pet form of *Ann(e)*.

Pamela Literary; Greek; 'all sweetness'.

Patricia Feminine form of *Patrick*, 'a nobleman'.

Paula Feminine form of *Paul*, 'small'.

Pauline Saint; Latin; feminine form of *Paul*, 'small'.

Penelope Literary; Greek; of uncertain origin. **Penny** is the diminutive.

Philippa Royal; Greek; feminine of *Philip*, 'lover of horses'. The diminutive **Pippa** is popular.

Polly Diminutive; from *Mary* through *Molly*.

Rachel Biblical; Hebrew; 'a ewe'. **Rachael** also occurs.

Rebecca Biblical; Hebrew; 'a snare'.

Robyn Diminutive; feminine form of *Robin*, from *Robert*, 'bright fame'.

Rosalind Literary; Old German; 'horse serpent'.

Rosemary Blend of *Rose* and *Mary*.

Ruth Biblical; Hebrew; origin uncertain.

Sally Diminutive of *Sarah*.

Samantha Aramaic(?); 'listener'.

Sandra Diminutive of *Alexandra*, from Italian *Alessandra*.

Sarah Biblical; Hebrew; 'princess'.

Sharon Biblical; Hebrew; 'plain'.

Sheila Translated; Irish form of **Cecilia**, 'blind'.

Shelley Surname/Place name; Old English; 'wood or clearing on a bank'.

Shirley Surname/Place name; Old English; 'bright clearing'.

Simone Feminine form of *Simon*.

Sonia Literary; Greek; Russian diminutive of *Sophia*.

Sophie Royal; Greek; 'wisdom'. Also **Sophia**.

Stephanie Feminine form of *Stephen*, 'crown'.

Susan Biblical; Hebrew; 'lily'. Fuller form is **Susannah**. **Susanne** and **Suzanne** also occur.

Sylvia Literary; Latin; 'wood'.

Tammy and **Tamsin** Cornish diminutives of **Thomasina**, from *Thomas*, 'twin'.

Tanya Diminutive of **Tatiana**, name of Russian saint.

Tara Place name(?); famous Irish hill mentioned in Moore's *Irish Melodies*.

Teresa Saint; Greek; 'reaper'. Also as **Theresa**.

Tina Diminutive of *Christina*.

Tracey/Tracy Very early examples diminutives of *Teresa*. Recently from surname, in turn from French place name.

Trudy Diminutive of names like **Gertrude** and **Ermintrude**.

Valerie Saint; Latin; Roman family name.

Vanessa Literary; blending parts of *Esther Vanhomrigh*. Invented by Jonathan Swift.

Vera Literary; Russian; 'faith'.

Victoria Royal; Latin; 'victory'. **Vicki** and **Vicky** are now popular.

Vivienne Literary; the lady of the lake: origin uncertain.

Wendy Literary; from 'friendy-wendy' in baby-talk. (J. M. Barrie.)

Yvonne Feminine of **Yves**, 'yew'.

Zoe Saint; Greek; 'life'.

Some additional girls' names

Amber	Cindy	Glenda	Martha
Amelia	Clarissa	Hilary	Martine
Audrey	Corinna	Holly	Monique
Bernadette	Cynthia	Ingrid	Narelle
Bettina	Deirdre	Irene	Priscilla
Bianca	Doreen	Joan	Roberta
Brenda	Eileen	Larissa	Rosina
Bridie	Eve	Lois	Stella
Bronwyn	Evelyn	Lucille	Sybil
Cecilia	Faye	Madeleine	Tamara
Celia	Gabrielle	Marjorie	Tiffany
Charmaine	Gaye	Marilyn	Verity

Even with each of these counted as a separate name, the hundred most frequently used boys' names accounted for 49,674 occurrences, or 94 per cent of the total. The top hundred girls' names accounted for 41,552 occurrences—83 per cent of the total. These are the important facts to bear in mind. One must not be misled, when one learns that 909 different names were given to the boys and 1,448 to the girls, into thinking that all these names were evenly distributed. Unique names (in that year) were given to 426 boys and 712 girls. These single-occurrence names were not listed, but one may gain some idea of what they must have been like by considering a few of the names that were given more than once. For boys they included **Ajinder**, **Aldo**, **Arshad**, **Bhenjatar**, **Erich**, **Franciszek**, **Grigor**, **Luigi**, **Mushtaq**, **Parvaiz**, **Prasanna**, **Rino**, **Shamsher**, **Sukhdev**, **Vigapale** and **Wahid**. Among the girls' names were **Balinder**, **Balkis**, **Buduh**, **Cherry**, **Ghislaine**, **Gormelia**, **Gurmet**, **Juedish**, **Kari**, **Kuldip**, **Mumtaz**, **Nasrin**, **Permla**, **Suntoky** and **Zane**.

Most of the above were clearly given by non-Scottish parents who happened to be living in Scotland in 1958. A great many of the names that occurred only once were no doubt similar, and were not indicative of Scottish parents indulging in imaginative flights of fancy. All in all it is quite safe to say that the central stock of first names being used in Scotland in 1958 consisted of no more than 100 different names for boys and possibly 120 for the girls.

The Scottish analysis is one of the most comprehensive in existence, but it reflects the first naming habits of a people rather renowned for their conservative behaviour. The same is generally said of readers of *The Times*, whose choice of first names as evidenced by the Birth Announcements column has been carefully logged each year since 1947 by Mr. John Leaver, a founder-member of The Names Society.

The number of names concerned in this yearly survey is obviously far fewer than for the whole of Scotland in 1958. In 1971, for instance, the first names of less than 4,000 boys and girls were announced, but the survey is important in other ways. Because it reflects the naming habits of a socially important group the result of the survey is always widely publicised both in Britain and abroad. The evidence it provides of how the 'top people' are naming their children may well influence many other parents, gradually affecting general fashions. Finally, the survey has caused researchers to begin similar surveys in other regions and countries, which means that there is now a good deal of information available that was not there before.

Mr. Leaver counts every spelling as a separate name, so that **Alastair**, **Alistair**, **Alaistair** and **Alasdair** are split up as in the Scottish report. In 1971 **Catherine** also occurred as **Catharine**, **Katharine**, **Katherine**, **Katheryn** and **Kathryn**. Once again, then, allowance must be made for this when saying that 292 different first names were used in 1971 for the boys, and 406 for the girls. There are also the many non-English readers of *The Times* who insert birth announcements there, which may account for the appearance during the year of names such as **Bahman**, **Dov**, **Dimitri**, **Fabrice**, **Gianni**, **Ilija**, **Misha**, **Mekaal**, **Massimiliano**, **Okechuku**, **Tariq** and **Wilhelm** for the boys. Among the girls' names were **Ayshe**, **Demelza**, **Firoozeh**, **Guanaelle**, **Imelda**, **Josella**, **Krisztina**, **Paola**, **Seonaid**, **Thamaras**, **Ullvi** and **Zahra**. There were also obvious conversions, however, such as **Fern**, **Holly**, **Liberty**, **Pleasant** and **Saffron**.

The respective top twenties in *The Times*, 1971, accounted for 1,039 of the boys' names (53 per cent) and 763 of the girls' names (42 per cent). All the signs are present, therefore, that once again a relatively small stock of names was mainly being used. At the bottom end of the popularity scale, 180 of the boys' names and 267 of the girls' names occurred only once or twice during the year. This is not to say that the latter were all weirdly spelt versions of more ordinary names or were foreign. Many were well-established names that just happened not to appeal to readers of *The Times* that year. **Barry**, **Clive**, **Donald**, **Douglas**, **Dennis**, **Ernest**, **Eric**, **Frederick**, **Gareth**, **Gregory**, **Hector**, **Harold**, **Ivor**, **Jack**, **Laurence**, **Norman**, **Noël**, **Roger**, **Victor** and **Walter** were all among the very low-scoring boys' names. Only slightly above them was **Stephen/Steven**, with five occurrences between the two spellings. Similarly, girls' names such as **Anthea**, **Ada**, **Angela**, **Barbara**, **Cecily**, **Denise**, **Elaine**, **Gail**, **Geraldine**, **Heather**, **Hazel**, **Josephine**, **Linda**, **Lydia**, **Lesley**, **Nancy**, **Phoebe** and **Sheila** made only guest appearances during the year, but still did better than **Joyce**, **Joan**, **Pamela**, **Wendy**, **Dorothy** and the like which were not given as first names at all. Among the names that were recorded in quite significant numbers, on the other hand, were **Oliver** and **Rupert** for the boys, **Natasha** and **Polly** for the girls, names which one would expect to be among the low-scorers were it not for the mysterious forces of fashion.

First-name fashions must obviously be our next topic, but let us first emphasise that apart from those surveys already mentioned, many others show the same tendency for parents to make use of a small central stock of names in any one year. Surveys drawn from other national and regional British newspapers, such as *The Daily Telegraph*, *The Yorkshire Post*, *The Scotsman*, *The Manchester Evening News* and *The Derby Evening Telegraph*; from Australian newspapers such as the *Sydney Morning Herald* and *The Sun*; from school registers and parish registers all show the same trend. In 1970 Mrs. Anne Kirkman conducted on behalf of The Names Society a regional survey of first names, comparing the names used during the same period in twelve areas of Britain.

In all analyses a central stock of names soon reveals itself, and we can note that:

- the names within the central stock change slightly year by year,
- the names may differ from region to region,
- there are always more girls' names in the central stock than boys' names.

Chapter 5
Fashionable Names

We are all aware that there are fashions in first names, and there is plenty of concrete evidence available to show that most names are subject to fashion's whims. The three major name surveys already referred to provide many examples, since all three contain name counts which show how roughly the same groups of parents have chosen different names at different times. The Scottish Registrar-General, for instance, issued his statistical supplements in 1858, 1935 and 1958. From these we see that thirteen of the top twenty boys' names in 1858 were still at the top a hundred years later, **John**, **James** and **William** having remained in first three places throughout. Names like **Hugh**, **Duncan**, **Samuel**, **Archibald**, **Angus** and **Walter**, however, had fallen from favour, though still registering considerable scores in 1958. The new names that had come into the top rank were **Brian**, **Alan**, **Michael**, **Kenneth**, **Gordon**, **Stephen** and **Derek**.

Such changes hardly speak of sudden or violent fashionable currents at work. They might seem rather to be evidence of the Scots' ability to resist social changes. But in England and Wales too, until very recently, boys' names were far less influenced by fashion than girls' names.

Of the Scottish girls' names, **Margaret**, **Elizabeth** and **Mary** had also held out for a hundred years to retain first three places in 1958, though not quite in the same order as in 1858. But below these three names, only **Catherine**, **Helen**, **Jane** and **Janet** had managed to remain among the leaders for a century. Newcomers such as **Ann(e)**, **Susan**, **Fiona**, **Carol**, **Jacqueline**, **Patricia**, **Christine**, **Elaine**, **Maureen**, **Sandra** and **Caroline** had all appeared, and of these **Patricia** was the only one to have been in the top twenty since 1935. It is clear that even Scottish parents look for a certain amount of novelty when they name their daughters.

'The Times' survey

John Leaver has been tabulating *The Times*' statistics since 1947, but it was only in 1962 that he began to record occurrences of first names as well as first and middle names combined. Nevertheless his analysis of individual names, year by year, is most interesting. In the records to which he has generously allowed me full access one sees names like **Dominic**, **Matthew** and **Rupert** steadily rising in popularity since 1947, while **Toby**, **Jason** and **Luke** make spectacular entrances in the 1970s. Far more girls' names reflect the upward swing of fashion since 1947. They include **Annabel**, **Amanda**, **Alexandra**, **Anna**, **Alice**, **Charlotte**, **Claire**, **Emily**, **Emma**, **Georgina**, **Harriet**, **Jessica**, **Kate**, **Lucinda**, **Lucy**, **Louise**, **Nicola**, **Rachel**, **Rebecca**, **Sophie** and **Sarah**. Some of these, however, have already begun to fade away again. Names for the 1970s, as far as *The Times'* readers are concerned, appear to be **Antonia**, **Natasha** and **Tamsin**.

To what extent the preferences of *The Times'* readers reflect the preferences of England and Wales as a whole may be judged by the tables given on pages 65 and 67. The Somerset House figures given there are based on a massive analysis made by Mr. C. V. Appleton. He has examined how the Smiths in England and Wales have named their children at roughly twenty-five year intervals since the first full year of the records. The changes in the order of names show us accurately enough the effects of fashion on a wide variety of names. To support his long-term survey, Mr. Appleton also made a yearly analysis from 1921 on of the five most popular boys' and girls' names used by the Smiths. I reproduce these figures on pages 60 and 61. They enable us to see what happens to certain names in finer detail.

Are the Smiths typical of the country as a whole in their naming habits? This question must naturally be asked, and Mr. Appleton made yet another survey, given on page 69, which provides the necessary proof that for all practical purposes they are. There are also enough Smiths born each year to furnish a good cross-section of the names being used. Since 1925 an average of 10,000 Smith children a year have been born, and roughly one child in seventy in England and Wales bears this name.

Other evidence of name fashions

Some interesting information about first name fashions before the Somerset House records began occurs in a poem by Charles Lamb, which was first published in 1809. Putting himself in the place of a little girl who has been offered the chance to choose a name for her sister, he writes:

> Now I wonder what would please her,
> **Charlotte**, **Julia** or **Louisa**?
> **Ann** and **Mary**, they're too common;
> **Joan**'s too formal for a woman:
> **Jane**'s a prettier name beside;
> But we had a **Jane** that died.
> They would say, if 'twas **Rebecca**,
> That she was a little Quaker,
> **Edith**'s pretty, but that looks
> Better in old English books.
> **Ellen**'s left off long ago:
> **Blanche** is out of fashion now.

None that I have named as yet
Are so good as **Margaret**.
Emily is neat and fine.
What do you think of **Caroline**?

How I'm puzzled and perplexed
What to choose or think of next!
I am in a little fever
Lest the name that I shall give her
Should disgrace her or defame her.
I will leave Papa to name her.

The problem would probably not have existed had it been a boy that had to be named, neither would there have been any question of names that were in or out of fashion. Boys' names changed very little because a great many fathers thought like Mr. Dombey in Dickens's *Dombey and Son*: 'He will be christened **Paul** . . . of course. His father's name, Mrs. Dombey, and his grandfather's.'

Victorian and Edwardian name brooches provide further evidence of past name fashions.

What must have been another common method of preserving the same male names is seen in Fielding's *Tom Jones*: 'the little foundling to whom he had been godfather, giving his own name of **Thomas**', and yet another in Goldsmith's *The Vicar of Wakefield*: 'Our oldest son was named **George**, after his uncle, who left us ten thousand pounds.'

But Goldsmith, who was writing in 1765, goes on to give further evidence of the different attitudes that parents had when it came to naming girls—different attitudes which in turn led to changing fashions:

> 'I intended to call her after Aunt **Grissel**, but my wife, who . . . had been reading romances, insisted upon her being called **Olivia**. In less than another year we had another daughter, and now I was determined that **Grissel** should be her name; but a rich relation taking a fancy to stand godmother, the girl was, by her directions, called **Sophia**, so that we had two romantic names in the family, but I solemnly protest I had no hand in it.'

The Vicar may protest about his daughters' names, but at least he allowed them. It would have been quite another matter had his wife tried to interfere with the onomastic tradition that was taken for granted in the naming of his son.

A lot of evidence about attitudes to first names and reasons for naming must be buried in our literature. It would make a fascinating research topic to collect the material together.

First name sources

First name fashions in the still more distant past are closely linked to the opening up of new sources for names. The Normans, for instance, brought their own distinctive personal names with them when they came to England in the eleventh century. These quickly replaced most of the Old English names that had been used for centuries, names like **Ethelbert** and **Leofwin**. It was the aristocracy who first named their sons **William**, **Richard**, **Robert**, **Hugh**, **Ralph** and the like, but what is perhaps surprising is the way the peasants so quickly followed suit.

This aping of the Norman upper classes was paralleled in the twelfth and thirteenth centuries by the influence of the Church. Biblical and saints' names such as **John**, **Peter**, **James**, **Michael**, **Philip**, **Simon**, **Paul**, **Luke** and **Mark** became widely popular, no doubt having been praised and recommended from the pulpit. The new trend also influenced girls' names, and it was now that **Mary**, **Joan**, **Agnes**, **Catherine**, **Margaret** and **Ann(e)** became common.

These religious names did not simply swell the potential stock of English first names, so that parents could call on them occasionally. Although a wide variety of names was used, it is clear that the situation was the same then as today—a few names were especially favoured and accounted for a very high percentage of all occurrences. The scriptural names joined the favourite Norman names at the top of the popularity poll, so that a documentary count of men's names in the fourteenth

The Top Five First Names for Boys, 1921–1971

(based on the Smiths in England and Wales)

	1	2	3	4	5
1921	JOHN	WILLIAM	GEORGE	JAMES	RONALD
1922	John	William	George	Ronald	James
1923	John	William	George	Ronald	James
1924	John	William	George	Ronald	James
1925	John	William	George	James	Ronald
1926	John	William	George	Ronald	KENNETH
1927	John	William	George	Ronald	Kenneth
1928	John	William	Ronald	George	Kenneth
1929	John	William	George	Ronald	Kenneth
1930	John	William	Ronald	George	PETER
1931	John	William	Ronald	Peter	George
1932	John	Ronald	William	Peter	BRIAN
1933	John	Peter	Ronald	William	Brian
1934	John	Brian	Peter	William	Ronald
1935	John	Brian	Peter	Ronald	MICHAEL
1936	John	Brian	DAVID	Peter	William
1937	John	Brian	David	Peter	Michael
1938	John	Brian	David	Peter	Michael
1939	John	Brian	David	Michael	Peter
1940	John	David	Brian	Peter	Michael
1941	John	David	Michael	Brian	Peter
1942	John	David	Michael	Peter	Brian
1943	John	David	Michael	Peter	ALAN
1944	David	John	Michael	Peter	Alan
1945	John	David	Michael	Peter	ROBERT
1946	John	David	Michael/Peter		Robert
1947	David	John	Peter	Michael	Alan
1948	David	John	Michael	Peter	Alan
1949	David	John	Michael	Peter	Robert
1950	David	John	Peter	Michael	Alan
1951	David	John	Michael	Peter	STEPHEN
1952	David	John	Michael	Stephen	Peter
1953	David	Stephen	John	Michael	Peter
1954	David	Stephen	John	Peter	Michael
1955	Stephen	David	Michael	John	Peter/PAUL
1956	Stephen	David	Michael	Paul	Peter
1957	Stephen	David	Paul	Michael	Peter
1958	Stephen	David	Paul	Michael	John
1959	Stephen	David	Paul	Michael	Peter
1960	Stephen	David	Paul	Michael	MARK
1961	Stephen	David	Paul	ANDREW	Mark
1962	David	Stephen	Paul	Andrew	Mark
1963	David	Andrew	Stephen	Mark	Paul
1964	Paul	David	Andrew	Mark	Stephen
1965	Paul	David	Andrew	Stephen	Mark
1966	Paul	Andrew	David	Mark	Stephen
1967	Andrew	Paul	David	Mark	Stephen
1968	Mark	Paul	Andrew	David	Stephen
1969	Paul	Andrew	Mark	Stephen	David
1970	Mark	Paul	JASON	Andrew	Stephen
1971	Mark	Stephen	Paul	Jason	Andrew

The Top Five First Names for Girls, 1921–1971

(based on the Smiths in England and Wales)

	1	2	3	4	5
1921	JOAN	MARGARET	MARY	DOROTHY	IRENE
1922	Joan	Mary	Dorothy	Margaret	DORIS
1923	Margaret	Joan	Mary	Dorothy	Doris
1924	Margaret	Joan	Mary	JOYCE	Dorothy
1925	Joan	Mary	Joyce	Margaret	Dorothy
1926	Joan	Joyce	Margaret	Mary	Dorothy
1927	Joan	Margaret	Joyce	Dorothy/Mary	
1928	Joan	Margaret	Mary	JEAN	Joyce
1929	Joan	Margaret	Jean	Joyce	AUDREY/DOREEN
1930	Margaret	Jean	Joan	Doreen	Mary
1931	Margaret	Jean	Joan	Mary	Doreen
1932	Margaret	Jean	Joan	BARBARA	Joyce
1933	Margaret	Jean	Joan	SHEILA	Mary
1934	Margaret	Jean/Joan		PATRICIA	Sheila
1935	SHIRLEY	Margaret	Jean	Joan/Patricia	
1936	Margaret	Shirley	Sheila	Patricia	Jean
1937	Margaret	Jean	Patricia	MAUREEN	Sheila
1938	Margaret	Patricia	Jean	Barbara	Maureen
1939	Margaret	Patricia	Barbara	ANN	Jean
1940	Margaret	Patricia	Ann	Jean	VALERIE
1941	Margaret	Patricia	Ann	Valerie	Jean
1942	Patricia	Margaret	Ann	Jean	Valerie
1943	Margaret	Patricia	Valerie	CAROL	Ann
1944	Margaret	Patricia	Carol	CHRISTINE	JANET
1945	Margaret	Carol	Patricia	Christine	Ann
1946	Patricia	Margaret	Carol	Christine	SUSAN
1947	Susan	Margaret	Carol	Patricia	Christine
1948	Susan	LINDA	Margaret	Patricia	Christine
1949	Susan/Linda		Christine	Patricia	Margaret
1950	Susan	Linda	Christine	Margaret	Carol
1951	Susan	Linda	Christine	Margaret	Janet/Patricia
1952	Susan	Linda	Christine	Carol	Patricia
1953	Susan	Linda	Christine	Janet	Carol
1954	Susan	Linda	Christine	Carol	Janet
1955	Susan	Linda	Carol	Christine	Janet
1956	Susan	Linda	Carol	Janet	Christine
1957	Susan	Carol	Christine/Linda		Janet
1958	Susan	JULIE	Carol	KAREN	Linda
1959	Susan	Julie	Karen	Linda	Carol
1960	Karen	Susan	DEBORAH	Julie	Carol
1961	Deborah	Julie	Karen	Susan	JACQUELINE
1962	Karen	Deborah	Julie	Susan	Jacqueline
1963	Karen	Deborah	Julie	Susan	TRACEY
1964	Tracey	Julie	Deborah	Susan	Karen
1965	Tracey	Deborah	Julie	Karen	Susan
1966	Tracey	Deborah	Karen	Susan	Julie
1967	Tracey	Deborah	Julie	Karen	HELEN
1968	Tracey	Deborah	Julie	Karen	ALISON
1969	Tracey	SHARON	Karen	Deborah	JOANNE
1970	Tracey	Joanne	Sharon	NICOLA	LISA
1971	Tracey	SARAH	Joanne	Sharon	Nicola

century has shown that **Henry**, **John**, **Richard**, **Robert** and **William** were in themselves able to account for 64 per cent of the men. More exotic names were also used at this time and one finds girls' names such as **Hodierna**, **Italia** and **Melodia**.

Supplementary evidence about the popular medieval first names comes from a study of modern surnames, many of which simply indicated originally that a man was **Harry**'s son (**Harris**), **Alexander**'s son (**Sanders**), etc. Apart from those names already mentioned, **David**, **Thomas**, **Nicholas**, **Gilbert**, **Martin**, **Maurice**, **Adam** and **Stephen** were obviously much used. Surnames are less helpful with girls' names, but they nevertheless point to numerous women named **Eleanor**, **Isabel** and **Matilda** in addition to those mentioned above.

Camden, writing at the beginning of the seventeenth century, commented on 'new' names that were then appearing. These were the famous Puritan names, such as **Free-Gift**, **Reformation**, **Earth**, **Dust**, **Ashes**, **Delivery**, **More-Fruit**, **Tribulation**, **Discipline**, **Joy Again**, **From Above**, **Thankful**, **Praise-God** and **Live Well**. A few fanatical ministers were probably responsible for persuading parents to use these names, which no doubt seemed a good idea within the religious communities. But when the outside world realised what was going on there was a great howl of laughter. The playwrights of the time in particular fell upon the names with glee, for the Puritans had been trying to put them out of business. In Ben Jonson's **Bartholomew Fair** is a typical example of their ridicule:

> *Quarlous:* O, I know him! a baker, is he not?
> *Littlewit:* He was a baker, sir, but he does dream now, and see visions: he has given over his trade.
> *Quarlous:* His Christian name is **Zeal-of-the-land**?
> *Littlewit:* Yes, sir; Zeal-of-the-land Busy.
> *Winwife:* How! what a name's there!
> *Littlewit:* O, they all have such names, sir: he was witness for **Win**, here, and named her **Win-the-Fight**: you thought her name had been **Winifred**, did you not?

The more sensible Puritans themselves objected to such excesses, signs of the extreme behaviour which led the public, partly inspired by their victims' cropped heads, to turn the very letters of 'Puritan' into 'a turnip'. Names like **Lament**, **Helpless** and **Obedience** (this for a girl) disappeared quite quickly, as did the many names like **Zelophehad** which the Puritans took from the Old Testament. Nevertheless, our stock of first names was permanently increased by the less objectional Puritan discoveries of this period. **Faith**, **Prudence** and the like lived on. As for the Old Testament, not every name that it contained was a strange-looking tongue-twister. It provided such currently popular names as **Samuel**, **Benjamin**, **Joseph**, **Jacob**, **Daniel**, **Sarah**, **Susan** and **Sharon**. All these were quietly introduced by those who wished the Bible's influence to be ever present in their lives, but who were able to exercise a little linguistic discretion at the same time.

Some of the names the Puritans themselves objected to because they had no religious significance had come from yet another social influence—classical literature. When the vocabulary of the English language itself was being inflated almost daily by borrowings from Latin and Greek, it was natural that first names common to those languages should likewise be taken over. If anything it is surprising that so few were borrowed. Camden mentions the use of names like **Diana**, **Cassandra** and **Venus**. **Cynthia**, **Delia**, **Corinna**, **Sylvia** and **Anthea** were similarly learned names, and we must not forget **Alexander**, the most famous Greek name of all. It became the most popular classical name to enrich our name stock.

The search for novelty being what it is, a great many other languages have been plundered since the seventeenth century, but in more individualistic ways. The origins of the central stock of first names (page 48 on) show the variety of sources. The use of surnames as first names has already been commented on, and one other major trend that deserves mention is the formation of feminine link names. These take a male name as the base and become such names as **Alfreda**, **Roberta**, **Philippa**. Some of these are now so thoroughly established as girls' names that their origin is overlooked, but in the present social climate we shall presumably see less formations of this type in the future.

I have been speaking about the main *sources* of English first names rather than their primary origins, which is quite another matter. The origin of a name is rarely known by parents when they are choosing one for their child, and it has little to do with a name's popularity or use. This is true now, and I am sure it was so in the past. **William** was taken over not because of its original meaning in Old German, where it was a compound of 'will' and 'helmet', but because it had the right social associations in the eleventh and twelfth centuries. **Sarah** was likewise brought in later not because of its Hebrew meaning, 'princess', but because it had the sanction of Old Testament usage and adapted easily to our general linguistic system. **Paul** was not and is not used because it meant 'small' in Latin: it is rather used in spite of its origin.

The point needs to be emphasised because year after year new books appear which supposedly deal with first names. In fact they merely repeat what is often highly doubtful etymological conjecture as if that was the important information everybody needed. Most of us, it is true, reach the stage sooner or later when we want to know as much as possible about our names, including the likely origins, but we should keep the historical explanations very firmly in perspective.

First name origins

When we do turn to them we quickly see the five kinds of origin discussed in Chapter 3. These are:

Descriptive names

which include generic descriptions such as **Charles**, 'a man', **Thomas**, 'a twin', and direct descriptions such as **Adam**, 'of red complexion',

The Top Fifty First Names for Boys

England and Wales (The Smiths) Indexes of Births

1838	1850	1875	1900	1925
1. William	1. William	1. William	1. William	1. John
2. John	2. John	2. John	2. John	2. William
3. Thomas	3. George	3. George	3. George	3. George
4. George	Thomas	4. Thomas	4. Thomas	4. James
5. James	5. James	5. James	5. Charles	5. Ronald
6. Henry	6. Henry	6. Henry	6. Frederick	6. Robert
7. Joseph	7. Charles	7. Charles	7. Arthur	7. Kenneth
8. Charles	8. Joseph	8. Frederick	8. James	8. Frederick
9. Robert	9. Robert	9. Arthur	9. Albert	9. Thomas
10. Edward	10. Samuel	10. Joseph	10. Ernest	10. Albert
11. Samuel	11. Edward	11. Albert	11. Robert	11. Eric
12. Richard	12. Frederick	12. Alfred	12. Henry	12. Edward
13. Alfred	13. Alfred	13. Walter	13. Alfred	13. Arthur
14. Frederick	14. Richard	14. Harry	14. Sidney	14. Charles
15. Benjamin	15. Walter	15. Edward	15. Joseph	15. Leslie
16. David	16. Arthur	16. Robert	16. Harold	16. Sidney
17. Daniel	17. Benjamin	17. Ernest	Harry	17. Frank
Walter	18. David	18. Herbert	18. Frank	18. Peter
19. Edwin	19. Edwin	19. Sidney	19. Walter	19. Dennis
20. Isaac	20. Albert	20. Samuel	20. Herbert	20. Joseph
21. Francis	21. Francis	21. Frank	21. Edward	21. Alan
Peter	22. Daniel	22. Richard	22. Percy	22. Stanley
Stephen	Sidney	23. Fred	23. Richard	23. Ernest
Sidney	24. Harry	24. Francis	24. Samuel	24. Harold
25. Arthur	Philip	25. David	25. Leonard	25. Norman
26. Adam	26. Isaac	26. Percy	26. Stanley	26. Raymond
Edmund	27. Herbert	27. Edwin	27. Reginald	27. Leonard
28. Matthew	Peter	28. Alexander	28. Francis	28. Alfred
29. Mark	29. Alexander	29. Peter	29. Fred	29. Donald
30. Elijah	Frank	Tom	30. Cecil	Reginald
Jacob	Matthew	31. Benjamin	31. Wilfred	31. Roy
32. Enoch	32. Stephen	Harold	32. Horace	32. Derek
Job	Tom	33. Daniel	33. Cyril	Henry
Jonathan	34. Elijah	Isaac	34. David	34. Geoffrey
Joshua	35. Jacob	35. Edgar	Norman	35. David
Philip	Jonathan	Matthew	36. Eric	Gordon
Reuben	37. Edmund	Philip	37. Victor	Herbert
38. Alexander	Hugh	38. Stephen	38. Edgar	Walter
Nicholas	Joshua	39. Andrew	39. Leslie	39. Cyril
Ralph	Josiah	Sam	40. Bertie	40. Jack
41. Andrew	Reuben	41. Christopher	Edwin	41. Richard
Eli	42. Amos	Oliver	42. Donald	42. Douglas
Herbert	Eli	Willie	43. Benjamin	43. Maurice
Jonas	Ralph	44. Bertram	Hector	44. Bernard
Michael	45. Andrew	Horace	Jack	Gerald
46. Hugh	Christopher	Leonard	Percival	46. Brian
Jeremiah	Horace	Ralph	47. Clifford	47. Wilfred
Josiah	Israel	48. Alan	48. Alexander	48. Francis
Lewis	Moses	49. Reginald	49. Bernard	Victor
Patrick	Seth	Wilfred	Redvers	50. Anthony

		'The Times'	'The Sun' (Australia)
1950	1971	1971	1971
1. David	1. Mark	1. James	1. Andrew
2. John	2. Stephen	2. Edward	2. David
3. Peter	3. Paul	3. Richard	3. Jason
4. Michael	4. Jason	4. Thomas	4. Matthew
5. Alan	5. Andrew	5. Nicholas	5. Paul
6. Robert	6. David	6. Matthew	6. Michael
7. Stephen	7. Darren	7. Charles	7. Peter
8. Paul	8. Richard	8. Jonathan	8. Mark
9. Brian	9. Michael	9. William	9. Stephen
10. Graham	10. Robert	10. Alexander	10. Christopher
11. Philip	11. Simon	Andrew	11. Scott
12. Anthony	12. Christopher	12. Christopher	12. Darren
13. Colin	13. Matthew	13. David	13. Craig
14. Christopher	14. Ian	14. Benjamin	14. Anthony
15. William	15. Gary	Simon	15. Simon
16. James	16. Nicholas	16. Mark	16. Brett
17. Keith	17. John	17. John	17. Glenn
18. Terence	Philip	Timothy	18. Adam
19. Barry	19. Anthony	19. Oliver	19. Timothy
Malcolm	James	20. Daniel	20. Robert
Richard	21. Martin	Michael	21. Dean
22. Ian	22. Stuart	22. Peter	22. Stuart
23. Derek	23. Kevin	23. Robert	23. Shane
24. Raymond	24. Peter	24. Philip	24. Sean
25. Roger	25. Neil	25. Rupert	25. John
26. Geoffrey	26. Craig	26. Toby	26. Justin
27. Kenneth	Jonathan	27. Julian	27. Bradley
28. Andrew	28. Graham	28. Adam	28. Nicholas
29. Trevor	Shaun	Alistair	29. Cameron
30. Martin	30. Adrian	Anthony	30. James
31. Kevin	31. Alan	31. Guy	31. Damian
32. Ronald	32. Wayne	32. Henry	32. Gregory
33. Leslie	33. Lee	Jeremy	33. Daniel
34. Charles	34. Colin	Patrick	34. Richard
George	35. Dean	Paul	35. Brendan
36. Thomas	36. Carl	36. Justin	36. Geoffrey
37. Nigel	37. Adam	37. Duncan	37. Jamie
Stuart	38. Justin	Ian	38. Benjamin
39. Edward	39. Geoffrey	39. George	39. Travis
40. Gordon	Timothy	40. Dominic	Adrian
41. Roy	41. Daniel	Robin	41. Wayne
42. Dennis	42. Brian	Samuel	42. Gavin
43. Neil	43. Jamie	43. Francis	43. Grant
44. Laurence	44. Nigel	Jason	44. Philip
45. Clive	45. Edward	Joseph	45. Ashley
Eric	46. Gavin	46. Giles	Rodney
47. Frederick	Thomas	Luke	47. Troy
Patrick	48. Russell	Martin	48. Rohan
Robin	49. Barry	49. Adrian	49. Martin
50. Donald	50. Julian	Sebastian	50. Dale
Joseph	Trevor		

The Top Fifty First Names for Girls

England and Wales (The Smiths) Indexes of Births

1838	1850	1875	1900	1925
1. Mary	1. Mary	1. Mary	1. Florence	1. Joan
2. Sarah	2. Elizabeth	2. Elizabeth	2. Mary	2. Mary
3. Elizabeth	3. Sarah	3. Sarah	3. Alice	3. Joyce
4. Anne	4. Ann(e)	4. Annie	4. Annie	4. Margaret
5. Jane	5. Eliza	5. Alice	5. Elsie	5. Dorothy
6. Eliza	6. Jane	6. Florence	6. Edith	6. Doris
7. Hannah	7. Emma	7. Emily	7. Elizabeth	7. Kathleen
8. Emma	8. Hannah	8. Edith	8. Doris	8. Irene
9. Harriet	9. Ellen	Ellen	9. Dorothy	9. Betty
10. Ellen	10. Martha	10. Ada	Ethel	10. Eileen
11. Margaret	11. Emily	11. Margaret	11. Gladys	11. Doreen
12. Martha	12. Harriet	12. Ann(e)	12. Lilian	Lilian
13. Maria	13. Alice	13. Emma	13. Hilda	Vera
14. Susannah	14. Margaret	14. Jane	14. Margaret	14. Margery
15. Louisa	15. Maria	15. Eliza	15. Winifred	15. Jean
16. Alice	16. Louisa	16. Louisa	16. Ellen	16. Barbara
Catherine	17. Fanny	17. Clara	17. Lily	17. Edna
18. Caroline	18. Caroline	18. Martha	18. Ada	18. Gladys
19. Charlotte	19. Charlotte	19. Harriet	19. Emily	19. Audrey
20. Emily	20. Susannah	20. Hannah	20. Violet	20. Elsie
Susan	21. Frances	21. Kate	21. Rose	21. Florence
22. Isabella	22. Catherine	22. Charlotte	Sarah	Hilda
23. Rebecca	23. Amelia	23. Ethel	23. Nellie	Winifred
24. Frances	24. Lucy	Lucy	24. May	24. Olive
25. Fanny	25. Clara	Rose	25. Beatrice	25. Violet
26. Matilda	Esther	26. Lily	26. Gertrude	26. Elizabeth
27. Esther	27. Betsy	27. Agnes	Ivy	27. Edith
28. Amelia	Isabella	28. Minnie	28. Mabel	Ivy
29. Lucy	Matilda	29. Fanny	29. Maud	29. Phyllis
30. Sophia	Sophia	30. Caroline	30. Eva	30. Peggy
31. Betsy	Susan	31. Amy	31. Jane	31. Evelyn
Jessie	32. Eleanor	Jessie	32. Agnes	32. Iris
Lydia	33. Rebecca	33. Eleanor	33. Evelyn	33. Annie
Phoebe	34. Anna	34. Maria	34. Frances	34. Rose
Rachel	35. Rachel	Catherine	Kathleen	35. Muriel
36. Anna	36. Agnes	36. Gertrude	36. Clara	36. Beryl
Helen	37. Julia	37. Isabella	37. Olive	Ethel
Julia	Rose	38. Maud	38. Grace	Lily
39. Eleanor	39. Kate	39. Laura	Jessie	Sheila
40. Clara	Nancy	Lilian	Catherine	40. Alice
Nancy	Phoebe	41. Amelia	41. Emma	41. Constance
42. Agnes	42. Annie	Esther	42. Nora	Ellen
Betty	Lydia	43. Beatrice	43. Louisa	43. Patricia
Selina	Ruth	44. Bertha	Minnie	44. Gwendoline
45. Dinah	45. Priscilla	45. Susannah	45. Lucy	45. Sylvia
Hester	46. Roseanna	46. Henrietta	46. Eliza	46. Nora
47. Rhoda	47. Jemima	Nellie	47. Amy	Pamela
Ruth	48. Grace	Rebecca	Daisy	48. Grace
49. Naomi	Henrietta	49. Lydia	49. Ann(e)	49. Jessie
Priscilla	Lavinia	Mabel	50. Kate	50. Mabel
Rosetta			Phyllis	

1950	1971	'The Times' 1971	'The Sun' (Australia) 1971
1. Susan	1. Tracey	1. Catherine	1. Nicole
2. Linda	2. Sarah	2. Sarah	2. Michelle
3. Christine	3. Joanne	3. Emma	3. Lisa
4. Margaret	4. Sharon	4. Victoria	4. Kylie
5. Carol	5. Nicola	5. Lucy	5. Catherine
6. Jennifer	6. Lisa	6. Elizabeth	6. Joanne
7. Janet	7. Julie	7. Rebecca	7. Jodie
8. Patricia	Karen	Sophie	8. Fiona
9. Barbara	9. Michelle	9. Anna	9. Melissa
10. Sandra	10. Rachel	10. Alexandra	10. Karen
11. Pamela	11. Deborah	11. Clare	11. Amanda
Pauline	12. Alison	Fiona	12. Tracey
13. Jean	13. Claire	13. Amanda	13. Sharon
14. Jacqueline	Catherine	14. Jessica	14. Tania
Kathleen	15. Amanda	15. Rachel	15. Kellie
16. Sheila	Victoria	16. Charlotte	16. Julie
17. Valerie	17. Samantha	Nicola	17. Rachel
18. Maureen	18. Susan	18. Eleanor	18. Kim
19. Gillian	19. Helen	Emily	Samantha
20. Ann(e)	20. Rebecca	Helen	Megan
Mary	21. Angela	21. Annabel	21. Leanne
22. Marilyn	22. Louise	Caroline	22. Susan
23. Elizabeth	23. Emma	23. Joanna	23. Simone
24. Lesley	24. Jane	24. Antonia	24. Rebecca
25. Catherine	25. Caroline	25. Camilla	25. Jennifer
26. Brenda	Jacqueline	Susannah	26. Natalie
27. Wendy	27. Kerry	27. Harriet	27. Andrea
28. Angela	28. Paula	28. Alison	28. Alison
29. Rosemary	29. Donna	Louise	29. Sarah
30. Shirley	30. Andrea	30. Kate	30. Jacqueline
31. Diane	31. Elizabeth	Mary	31. Narelle
32. Joan	32. Wendy	32. Philippa	32. Elizabeth
33. Jane	33. Dawn	Samantha	33. Danielle
Lynn	34. Tina	34. Jennifer	34. Kerrie
35. Marion	35. Kelly	Laura	35. Katrina
36. Janice	Lorraine	36. Abigail	36. Carolyn
37. Elaine	Teresa	Alice	37. Suzanne
Heather	38. Diane	Natasha	38. Melinda
39. June	Jennifer	39. Frances	Debra
40. Eileen	40. Linda	Georgina	40. Christine
41. Doreen	41. Ann	Henrietta	41. Donna
Judith	42. Elaine	Juliet	Louise
Sylvia	43. Justine	Polly	Jane
44. Denise	44. Hayley	Ruth	44. Vanessa
Helen	45. Mandy	Tamsin	45. Melanie
Yvonne	46. Fiona	Vanessa	46. Emma
47. Dorothy	47. Gillian	47. Melanie	47. Janine
Hilary	Julia	Miranda	48. Sally
Joyce	Sally	49. Michelle	49. Linda
Julia	50. Janet	Penelope	50. Robyn
		Tara	

Algernon, 'with whiskers or moustaches', **Crispin**, 'with curled hair', **Cecil**, 'blind'. Activity descriptions occur, such as **George**, 'a farmer', as do provenance descriptions: **Francis**, 'Frenchman'.

Sequential description led to names like **Septimus**, 'seventh', and **Decimus**, 'tenth'. **Original** and **Una** probably came into being as descriptions of first children, and **Natalie** and **Noël** were certainly temporal descriptions for children born or baptised on Christmas Day. Many names may have been either morally descriptive—**Agnes**, 'pure', **Agatha**, 'good'—or were commendatory conversions.

Converted names

include those which seem to have reflected parental reaction to the birth. **Abigail**, 'father rejoiced', is an instance, as are **Benedict**, 'blessed', **Amy**, 'loved'. Commendatory conversions such as **Felicity** and **Prudence** merge with what were almost certainly descriptive names applied first as personal names to adults and subsequently transferred to children. Many Germanic names appear to be of this type, but **Cuthbert**, 'famous bright', **Robert**, 'fame bright', **Bernard**, 'stern bear' and the like may often have originated as blends, making use of standard name elements.

Invented names

have mostly been introduced by writers. They include **Fiona**, **Lorna**, **Mavis**, **Miranda**, **Pamela**, **Thelma**, **Vanessa**, **Wendy**.

Link names

were frequently formed with **Jehovah** as an element, as in **John**, **Joan**, **Joseph** and many others. **God** occurs in names like **Elizabeth**, 'oath of God'. Other names could be the basis, as with **Malcolm**, 'a disciple or servant of St. **Columba**'. Diminutive links were common, and some have been established as first names in their own right for so long that the link has been forgotten. **Colin**, from **Nicholas**, is probably of this type. Feminine links such as **Louise** from **Louis** were also very frequent.

Transferred names

have often been surnames which were themselves transferred place names. Examples are **Clifford**, **Graham**, **Keith**, **Leslie**, **Percy**. River names that have ultimately become first names by a long process of transfer include **Douglas**, **Alma** and more recently, **Brent**.

We must remember, of course, that we can speak about primary origin only when a name first comes into being. The immediate origin of most first names has been transfer for the last several hundred years. This is another reason why we should now go on to consider such points as:

> What causes somes names to come into or go out of fashion at a particular time?
> What motives inspire parents to choose certain names for their children rather than any others.

Obviously it is not possible to give specific answers here, but parents definitely follow main trends in their naming habits, and it is to these that we can now turn.

Comparative Use of Typical First Names in England and Wales, 1971

	Live Births	Paul	David	Mark	Sarah	Tracey	Joanne	Top Names
1. Smith	11,253	265	219	276	182	220	176	Mark/Tracey
2. Jones	9,398	220	230	219	185	136	59	David/Sarah
3. Williams	6,272	150	174	169	102	102	80	David/Sharon
4. Taylor	4,902	125	97	151	81	68	102	Mark/Joanne
5. Brown	4,807	109	111	101	68	90	75	Stephen/Tracey
6. Davies	4,586	103	65	109	87	76	74	Mark/Sarah
7. Evans	3,720	92	122	66	63	65	61	David/Tracey
8. Thomas	3,408	98	101	91	65	41	28	David/Sarah
9. Wilson	3,144	88	75	96	57	58	55	Mark/Tracey
10. Roberts	3,068	64	94	91	47	49	45	David/Tracey
11. Johnson	3,054	82	61	92	54	56	42	Mark/Tracey
12. Wright	2,650	65	62	44	52	47	39	Paul/Sarah
13. Robinson	2,640	69	66	88	55	54	61	Mark/Joanne
14. Thompson	2,617	91	67	76	43	45	52	Paul/Joanne
15. Edwards	2,537	58	81	71	50	43	29	David/Sarah
16. White	2,514	61	66	56	45	32	41	David/Sarah
17. Walker	2,500	60	54	69	50	45	41	Mark/Sarah
18. Hughes	2,470	55	58	60	35	40	43	Mark/Nicola
19. Hall	2,361	9	63	46	37	33	39	Stephen/Joanne
20. Green	2,358	56	63	54	37	44	52	David/Joanne
21. Clarke	2,341	58	57	10	42	45	41	Stephen/Tracey
22. Lewis	2,330	53	66	59	41	35	42	David/Joanne
23. Harris	2,309	79	58	65	40	29	35	Paul/Michelle
24. Jackson	2,248	71	52	58	36	38	21	Paul/Lisa
25. Turner	2,116	58	50	49	38	33	44	Paul/Joanne
26. Wood	2,071	51	46	46	34	44	44	Paul/Tracey
27. Morris	2,056	41	57	33	31	32	29	David/Lisa
28. Moore	2,019	35	43	20	31	32	35	Stephen/Nicola
29. Cooper	2,001	53	55	45	46	34	28	Stephen/Sarah
30. Martin	1,999	65	43	11	38	42	31	Paul/Tracey
	101,749	2,484	2,456	2,421	1,772	1,708	1,544	

Chapter 6
Naming the Baby

I shall be summarising in this chapter the results of a research project I carried out early in 1973. I was asking parents who had named a child in the previous year to tell me what conscious motives prompted their choice. Those that were mentioned can be arranged under a variety of sub-headings.

Fashion

A great many parents mentioned the question of which names were currently fashionable, for this had affected their choice of names one way or the other. Parents who had chosen **Philippa** for their daughter, for instance, said that they had 'a major desire to avoid modern excesses of vulgarity and trend following'. It was perhaps an accident that 'vulgarity' occurred in such close context with 'trend following', but it should be emphasised that the two are not connected. Vulgarity presumably refers to a name's respectability, which I shall be discussing later. As for trend following, it is doubtful whether the majority of parents are really aware of what the trend is until several years after it has begun. When it becomes generally known which names are being used a great deal, there is ample evidence to show that most people hastily move away from them. This is true, at least, of names that have not had a high following for several generations. There is a fear that such names will not stand the test of time and that they will therefore 'date' a child.

Jason appears to be the outstanding example of such a name at the moment. Nearly 20,000 boys were given this name in 1971 in England and Wales alone. It came in for a great many negative comments from my correspondents, many of whom said things like: 'I shall scream if I hear of another Jason.' There was a general feeling that the name was working class, a word which some writers equate with 'vulgar'. Others scoffed at it because of its television associations.

I believe there are working-class names, just as there are middle-class names, but Jason is *not* marked in this way. It clearly appealed to a wide range of social levels. I also believe that some names are 'vulgar', but by my definition these are names which are totally unsuitable for use as first names which are given by publicity-seeking parents. Jason clearly does not fall into this class, either. The television question is too non-sensical to take seriously. However, I shall be extremely surprised if **Jason** continues to be as popular in the next few years as it has recently been. Parents are perfectly justified in wanting a name that sounds right for the time, but most of them want their child to have as much indivi-duality as possible. They will not like the thought of his being in a class-room with half a dozen other boys bearing the same name.

A less dramatic swing of fashion than that which affected Jason can have a positive influence on a name, however. As one parent wrote about **Matthew**: 'Probably a few years ago I would never have dreamt of using this name, but simply for the fact that it has become popular one gets used to the sound of it and eventually likes it.'

This comment hints at another parental fear—that they will choose a name which is completely out of fashion. The majority of parents pro-bably make a conscious attempt to steer between the two extremes. 'It isn't very common,' wrote a mother who had chosen **Timothy** during 1972, 'but it is not too unusual.' Other parents chose **Jessica** because it was 'not particularly fashionable, so wouldn't date her'. The parents of **John** considered the name 'not gimmicky, not easily dated'.

But if this conscious motivation is admirable in itself, how effectively do most parents achieve their aim? They tend to base their ideas about which names are popular and which names are not on their own social circle, which is a shaky base indeed. There are signs of an awakening interest in **Timothy** and **Philippa**, for instance, which could turn them very quickly into the trendy names the parents wished to avoid. As for Jessica, it definitely *was* fashionable at the beginning of the 1970s with readers of *The Times*. Most surprisingly of all, John, which seems to be a name that could not possibly be accused of dating a child, may well do so by the end of the century. It has suffered such an amazing decline on all sides that it is likely to become a rare name for future generations. Even now a John who is beginning school is likely to be the only boy of that name in the class—something which would have been out of the question a few years ago.

Social class associations

This is not the place to discuss the subtleties of what makes people 'working class' or 'middle class', or whether the labels can still be used meaningfully. Most of my correspondents clearly felt that there are still recognisable social strata in Britain and that the classes of people have different tastes in most things, including names.

First name evidence seems to give this theory some support. In 1971, for example, sixty-seven Smith children were given the first name **Craig**. The name did not appear that year in *The Times*' Birth Announcement columns at all. **Rupert**, on the other hand, was bestowed on twenty-seven sons of readers of *The Times*. Six times as many Smith boys were named that year, but only two were called Rupert. On the basis of such evidence I believe that one can say that at the beginning of the 1970s, Rupert was a middle-class name in Britain, while Craig was not.

Parents can certainly be influenced when choosing a name by their assessment of a name's social standing. Of **Benjamin** one parent wrote: 'It also appealed to the snob in me, seeming to be a name Hampstead-type people used.' On **Louise** another writer commented: 'it sounds very sophisticated', and a third parent said of **Alexandra**: 'I like regal names', which I take to be another indirect reference to social class. According to the various name surveys, Louise *was* middle class in the 1960s, but it is now making a good showing in the Somerset House registers, a sign of far more general popularity. Benjamin and Alexandra are still confined to middle-class parents. One possible reason for the slight flurry of interest in Benjamin recently may be the portrayal of Dustin Hoffman of a character of that name in the film *The Graduate*.

Dustin Hoffman as **Benjamin**, in *The Graduate*, and Peter Wyngarde as **Jason** King. The popularity of the names Benjamin and Jason was almost certainly influenced by the portrayals of these fictional characters.

Not all names, needless to say, suggest one social class rather than another. When the associations are there, they can change drastically with the passing of time. **Abigail** went out of fashion completely because it had become almost a synonym for a lady's maid. It now seems to be coming back into fashion at the other end of the social scale. If it follows a normal course it will make its way slowly down the social grades until it fades away again, waiting for the whole mysterious process to bring it back to the top.

Euphony

The sound of a first name when placed alongside the surname is a common factor considered by parents. **Paul**, **Mark**, **Joanne** and **Tracey** may be popular generally, but as the birth registers reveal very clearly, there is an avoidance of such combinations as **Paul Hall**, **Mark Clarke**, **Mark Martin**, **Joanne Jones** and **Tracey Thomas**. **Jason** has never caught on with the **Jackson** family, for similar reasons.

Sometimes parents fall in love with the sound of an individual name. One parent commented on **Bronia** that 'it has an interesting sound', and another said of **Bryony**: 'short musical sound and the combination of an abrupt start and a subtle ending'. The reference by one mother to 'the beautiful name **Berengaria**' was presumably another comment on euphony.

The 'sound' of a name is sometimes pleasant not because of its linguistic form, but rather because of the associations that are instantly brought to mind as it is uttered. In *Don Juan* Byron probably has both ideas in mind when he wrote:

> I have a passion for the name of **Mary**,
> For once it had a magic sound to me . . .

Initials

There is the famous example of Colin Cowdrey to prove that parents can name a child deliberately to create a certain set of initials (MCC in his case for the Marylebone Cricket Club). Parents usually make a final check when they have a particular name in mind to make sure that the first name and surname initials will not make an embarrassing combination, and it is in this primarily negative way that initials influence the choice of a name.

Colin Cowdrey, whose full initials are **M.C.C.**

Other surname influences

As we shall see when we come to discuss surnames in detail, there is a central surname stock just as there is a central first name stock. Some parents try to balance first names with surnames, the usual with the unusual or vice versa. In choosing **Guinevere**, for example, the **Day** family had in mind that this was 'a name to complement her surname', and **Jemima** was chosen as 'a fairly unusual name to go with **Brown**'. Another correspondent began by saying that they had had to find 'something unusual, because her surname is **Smith**'. This seems to be sensible thinking in principle, but all the evidence is that the majority of people with common surnames choose equally common first names.

Another factor that concerns the surname is the latter's meaning, or potential meaning when placed beside a first name. One comes across occasional instances of **Ann Teak**, **Iris Tugh**, **Handsome Mann**, **Orange Lemon** and the like, but one can safely say that the majority of parents are careful to avoid such combinations. Some may come about later by marriage. There is a recorded instance of a **Rose** family who named their daughter **Wild**, thinking that they had hit on a beautiful combination. She later married a gentleman called **Bull**.

Respectability

This is felt to be conferred on a name when it has been in existence for some centuries, though parents who are concerned with such a point often use euphemistic expressions such as 'traditional' or 'old-fashioned' rather than 'respectable'. We are not necessarily talking about the use of a name by one social class rather than another here. We are talking about the choice of **Sarah**, say, rather than **Tracey**—both of them immensely popular over a wide social range—simply because Sarah has been in use as an English first name for centuries whereas Tracey has not.

Whether for practical considerations, such as the difficulties that can be caused for the bearer of a relatively unfamiliar name, for historical nicety, or simply for the usual reasons of snobbishness, one detects in many letters from middle-class parents a strong reaction against modern first names such as **Craig**, **Darren**, **Scott**, **Shane**, **Warren** and **Wayne** for the boys, **Beverley**, **Cheryl**, **Gaynor**, **Hayley**, **Kelly**, **Kerrie**, **Lorraine**, **Mandy** and **Tracey** for the girls. **Lee/Leigh** should also be included in both lists.

Originality

A small number of parents want their children to bear unique names, but not necessarily absurd ones. They invent new names, convert words into names or transfer names from other sources. In 1971, for instance, there were Smith children who received the names **Bevron**, **Bina**, **Blossom**, **Brookie**, **Charisma**, **Crystal**, **Dahlia**, **Damask**, **Junior**, **Marina**, **Queen**, **Sandy**, **Star**, **Vernal** and **Zee**. In 1925 a child was named **Uname Smith**, which was not, one hopes, the joke it appears to be.

The arguments for original names are that they avoid associations with other people who have borne the name and really do identify an individual. But very great care must be taken by parents who tread this dangerous path. Several studies by psychologists have shown that people who have names that are considered to be decidedly unusual or odd by those around them can experience great difficulties in their normal social relationships. This can apply to well-established, but very outmoded names as well as invented ones, for Harvard students classed **Ivy**, **Rosebud**, **Hope**, **Patience**, **Cuthbert**, **Reginald** and **Egbert** as 'odd' a few years ago. Another age-group in another place would naturally compile quite a different list of odd names and perhaps accept most of these as perfectly normal.

Sexual characteristics

Parents frequently mention that certain names are particularly masculine or feminine and that this has affected their choice. Most of our first names give clear indications of a child's sex, and it is obviously felt to be important to preserve this situation. **Leslie** and **Lesley** are both fading away rapidly in the popularity charts, perhaps because of this sexual confusion. I would expect both **Lee** and **Leigh** to drop away if more boys as well as girls are given the name.

I also detect in many letters the belief that a strong, masculine name will make a boy into a 'real man', while a soft, feminine name will somehow produce a 'lovely lady'. I emphasise that these are letters being written by young parents in the 1970s. Ideas about the sexual roles clearly do not change overnight.

Religion

The parents' religious beliefs sometimes influence the choice of first names. There are plenty of Christian first names available, so parents have a wide choice. The recent upsurge of **Christian** itself as a first name for the Smiths presumably reflects religious motivation, but with first names one can take nothing for granted.

Origins

A few parents take account of a first name's origin when choosing a name for their child, but this tends to be a confirmatory rather than a deciding factor. If parents already have an inclination towards a certain name for other reasons, they are pleased to discover that it originally meant something favourable, as most of our first names did. But the parents of at least one boy who wrote to me were primarily influenced by the origin of the name they chose. Of **Selwyn** they wrote: 'an old English name meaning "house friend" . . . we liked its meaning'.

Personal associations

A name's associations with other people provide one of the most important reasons for choosing it or not choosing it. There can be both private and public associations. Where the latter are concerned I think it is essential to distinguish immediately between the situation that exists when a name is simply brought to the public's attention because of a famous person, and that where conscious commemorative use is made of a name. **Tracey**, as far as one can judge, was first publicised when Jean Simmons chose it for her daughter. I believe she had Spencer Tracy in mind, which would make it a conscious commemorative use.

Spencer Tracy, who may indirectly have influenced the popularity of the name **Tracy/Tracey** for girls.

The name having appeared in print, it seems to have been spotted by young parents searching for a name. Here are some basic facts about the name's use. In 1956, when Jean Simmons's daughter was named, no Tracy or Tracey Smith was registered at Somerset House. In 1957, 15 little Smith girls were given the name. The same number received it in 1958. In 1959 the number increased to 27, and by 1960 it was 49. A year later 105 girls became Tracy/Tracey Smith, and in 1962 this number rose yet again to 157. In 1963 the name accounted for 192 Smith girls, and in 1964 it reached an amazing score of 291. Over 200 Smith girls have been named Tracy or Tracey every year since then. Between 1956 and 1964 the total number of Smith births, it is true, rose by 25 per cent (it has been falling steadily since then), but that obviously does not account for the increase in Traceys.

From being a virtually unknown name, therefore—though Tracey had much earlier been used as a pet form of **Theresa**—this newcomer has in the space of less than twenty years attached itself to some 200,000 girls in England and Wales. One wonders how often the parents concerned had Jean Simmons's daughter, or Spencer Tracy, in mind when they chose the name **Tracey** for their daughter.

With **Shirley** in 1935, however, and with several of the 'new' names popular in 1970–71, I think we do have a conscious link by most namers with individuals, either real or fictional, bearing the name. In Shirley's case, this led to a fall as rapid as its rise. It remains to be seen whether **Jason** and the others will suffer a similar fate.

Specific commemorative use of names, as we have seen, was normal for the naming of boys until the present century, with members of the family rather than public figures being honoured. A very large number of first names are still chosen in honour of friends and relations, particularly, it would seem, among the 'upper' classes. Such names are sometimes what Ian Hay once called 'sprats to catch testamentary whales'. But private or public associations of a name can just as frequently act against it. We all know of parents who reject names because they have known somebody unpleasant who bore it. A public taboo also operates against names like **Adolf**, not that this particular name was popular *before* the 1930s in the English-speaking world.

Hitler and Oscar Wilde, who helped to prevent the names **Adolf** and **Oscar** from becoming popular.

Fictional associations

The Vicar of Wakefield remarked that his daughters' names came from romances. Literary characters still provide an immediate motivation for the choice of some names. I have often thought, looking at the names being used by readers of *The Times* especially, that it would be interesting to extract the names of characters that are in the books set for the Ordinary Level G.C.E. examinations in English six or seven years previously and make a comparison. Jane Austen's *Emma* is certainly much read in English classes, and one or two correspondents have mentioned its influence when they came to name their children.

Television creates its own fictional characters or gives new life to old ones. Once again it serves the double function of making names familiar in a general way and associating them with specific characters. Names chosen with fictional characters in mind are particularly interesting, it seems to me. The namer is thinking of a person who has never at any time existed, and wants the son or daughter to grow up to be like that person.

A large number of **Jasons** and **Samanthas** must have begun life in recent years with these impossible hopes pinned to them.

Associated characteristics

A combination of several of the factors so far mentioned leads to the strange phenomenon of people believing that everyone who bears a certain name will have certain characteristics. Laurence Sterne made superb fun of this idea in his eighteenth-century novel *Tristram Shandy*, expounding a 'philosophy of nomenclature' which was seized upon later by R. L. Stevenson in an essay of that name. More recently Roger Price and Leonard Stern have made suitable fun of the whole idea in their booklet *How Dare You Call Me That!* In the Introduction they say: 'Once you give a baby a name society begins to treat it as if it has the type of personality the name implies, and the child, being sensitive, responds consciously or unconsciously and grows up to fit the name.' The authors go on to give their own ideas about the public associations of a large number of names. A sample: '**Angus** is a giant who smiles a lot and looks as if he might have been at Bannockburn. Be careful shaking hands with Angus. He'll dislocate all bones up to the elbow.'

There is a modicum of truth in this name-characteristics theory. If a large number of people from the same social group were asked to describe a **Cuthbert** or an **Agnes**, a **Fred** or a **Rita**, they might well show some kind of agreement in what they said. They would be drawing upon information stored in their minds about the social class, age and profession of people they had met who bore these names. It is also partly true that when two girls who both started life as **Elizabeth** or whatever have become **Liz** in one case and remained Elizabeth in the other by the time they reach their twenties, the two forms of the name may reflect to some extent their different personalities.

Some names, then, do have generally accepted associated characteristics, and these can influence parents' choices. It is hard to say where associated characteristics end and personal associations begin on occasions. Did Jerry Lewis choose **Wilbur** as the name for a silly person because of characteristics that he felt were already associated with it, or is the name now associated with Lewis's portrayals?

In our own society it is of course impossible to pin down seriously these 'meanings' of names, which can be positive or negative, which can vary from person to person, region to region, and which are constantly mutating with the passing of time and the arrival of new social influences. The researcher can only conceal himself behind academic camouflage and talk about the onomastic *Zeitgeist*, a certain feeling in the air which most people seem to sense.

In some other societies, however, far more specific beliefs exist and the effect of those beliefs can to a certain extent be measured. G. Jahoda, for example, has made an interesting study of Ashanti day names (whereby children are named according to the day on which they are born), and the characteristics associated with each name. He discovered that a child born on a 'bad' day was more likely to end up in the juvenile court than a child whose name advertised the fact that he had been born on a 'good' day. The bad day name would cause others to act towards its bearer in a certain way, and this would affect his personality.

Verbal associations

Many of the names that have been common in the past have come to have verbal associations. Everyone is familiar with expressions like: 'every **Tom**, **Dick** or **Harry**', 'simple **Simon**', 'a **Jack** of all trades'. Simon seems to have overcome its unpleasant associations recently, but the first name popularity tables indicate that some names are hampered by such idioms. The American use of 'the john' for the lavatory can hardly have helped the name **John**, and may have contributed to its recent spectacular downfall. Wise parents remind themselves of any verbal associations that may exist by checking a potential name in a good dictionary before finally deciding on it.

Numerical associations

For a few parents a name has a numerical value which is important. Usually, each letter is assigned a number and a name can thus be totalled. If the total is something like 34 these digits may again be added to produce a single key number, 7. Each single number is thought to have special attributes, and these are applied to anyone bearing a name that adds up to that total.

I have been assured by a numerologist that my own full name works out quite well from a numerical point of view. I assume that parents who believe in this theory make a complete numerical check on any name they have in mind for their child and are influenced by the results.

What must be said about numerology, and all other forms of name magic, such as the rearrangement of the letters in a name to form other words, is that they have survived a long time. Pythagoras began the number idea in the sixth century BC and other forms of onomancy were believed in long before that. The ancient Romans held what was probably a very common belief by that time, that *nomen est omen*—one's name is an omen of one's future.

Objectively speaking, most of us would want to dismiss all such ideas as empty superstitions, but I wonder whether we have any reason to be complacent? If we have named our children with a vague thought at the back of our minds about the names we have chosen being particularly masculine or feminine, being of good taste and at the right social level, being the same as someone we have known because we have a quiet hope that our children will come to resemble the namesakes, then surely we were very close indeed to believing in a little name magic ourselves?

Other associations

Place names such as **Florence** and **Kent** have been used as first names because of a wish to commemorate the place of birth. American twins were given the names **Okla** and **Homa** for a similar reason. **Tulip** was chosen by the singer Tiny Tim to remind him of the song that made his fortune: 'Tip-toe through the tulips.' A more general transfer from a song in recent times is seen with **Michelle**, which the Beatles undoubtedly set on its way. It is also possible that the affectionate regard in the public's mind for the late Maurice Chevalier extended to his song 'Louise', and that the popularity of that name stems in part from the song.

Some songs that have influenced first names. Tiny Tim named his own daughter **Tulip**, because of his success with 'Tip-toe Through The Tulips'. The other songs helped to make the names concerned generally popular at the time.

On the other hand one family wrote to explain that they had called their daughter **Louise** because 'this is the name of one of our cats, whom we love very much'. Transfers can be made from any source and for any reason, with no harm being done if the result is that the child receives an appropriate name. Most parents clearly consider it safer, however, to stay with names that are already accepted as first names, rather than draw on a wide range of other nomenclatures.

Nationality

Parents often want to proclaim their child's nationality in its name. Scottish, Welsh and Irish parents are especially fond of doing this—and I am speaking here of those who choose to do so. If one lives in Scotland, Wales or Ireland one is naturally exposed to a rather different central stock of first names and may pick a name from it without thinking of its national markings.

Some names have regional rather than natural associations. **Jennifer** was for a long time a mainly Cornish name, and parents who chose **Yorick** for their son in 1972 told me it was because the name suggested the West Country.

Diminutive forms

The variant forms of a name are usually considered by parents, since it is accepted that many names are rarely used in their full forms by a child's friends. If parents do not like the usual diminutives and short forms they may well avoid a name altogether.

I have already commented on the difference between these formalised nicknames and names like **Jim** or **Bob** when the latter are bestowed as the legal names. With the development of the latter, it is possible that at some time in the future someone bearing a name like **Richard** will always remain Richard, since **Dick** will be looked upon as a completely separate name and not a diminutive.

Incidents at birth

Incidents that occur at or close to a child's birth often influence the name that is given to it. One little girl was called **Caroline** because 'she was born in the middle of a power cut, and as the power came on "Sweet Caroline" was being played on the radio'. A boy likewise became **James** because of 'a song, "St James' Infirmary" which my husband was playing just before I went to hospital'. I have also been told of a girl who was called **Sirene** because she was born during an air-raid and the siren was heard soon afterwards.

Perhaps one should include here the mother who 'had a dream two weeks before she was born that I had a baby girl and that we had named her **Jessica**'. This dream name was duly given to the daughter. Names that relate to the time of birth are also incident names in their way. **Noël**, **Avril**, **April**, **June** and **Natalie** are well established for this purpose. One parent wrote to say that **Octavia** was chosen partly because of an October birth, an interesting example of an incidental link name.

There is also a kind of verbal incident name. In *The Forsyte Saga* is a well-known example, when Annette looks down at her newly born daughter:

> *'Ma petite fleur!'* Annette said softly.
> *'Fleur,'* repeated Soames: **'Fleur**! We'll call her that.'

A little girl who was called **Surprise** also owed her name to a verbal incident. The process seems to be an apt one for nicknames, but rather dangerous as a means of selecting the all-important first name.

Description

A **Serena** received her name, according to a correspondent, because a friend of the family described her as 'so serene'. A **Daniel** received his name in 1972 'because he looked like a judge'. The choice of a first name for descriptive reasons is rare, however. The majority of names are decided on before birth, and it is recognised that a baby's appearance is hardly likely to remain that way for long.

Sibling influence

It should not be forgotten that a particular child may not be given a name because a brother or sister already bears it. Nevertheless, some families have been known to give all their sons the same name, and others like all the names of their children to begin with the same letter. Many parents consider whether a name they are thinking about for a later child will 'match' the names already in use in the family.

Spelling and pronunciation

The rarer names may cause pronunciation problems. Looking through the birth registers, for instance, I wonder myself how I would pronounce **Annarenia**, **Deion**, **Gyda** and the like. Parents sometimes try a name out on friends to see whether the pronunciation causes difficulty.

The spelling situation is far worse. Even very common names appear in strange forms, such as **Henery**, **Jonothon**, **Katheryne**, **Markk**, **Neal**, **Rebekah**, which shows that people can find them difficult. One advantage of the more familiar names, though, as many parents are aware, is that those who bear them will probably not have to go through life painfully spelling out their first names every time they meet someone new.

Some conclusions

As the above notes are meant to illustrate, naming a baby can be a complicated affair. For parents who have yet to make a choice I have tried to provide help in the diagram at the end of the book. The golden rule that should always be observed was hinted at by Charles Lamb in the poem quoted earlier about choosing a name. 'I wonder what would please *her*,' he said. It was the right thing to wonder. When you choose a name for a baby you are acting on the child's behalf and doing something that is of great importance for its future. You are not simply satisfying a personal whim.

The responsibility is rather frightening, and it is all too clear that a minority of parents are not capable of exercising that responsibility properly. One can sometimes see the arguments in favour of an official bureau that would vet and advise on the choice of first names, a function which the more enlightened registrars unofficially perform already. In view of the undoubted psychological damage that can be caused to children by the bestowal of absurd names, such a bureau would have to have powers of veto. Naturally there would be no question of all names needing approval, but doubtful cases could be submitted by registrars. Children are legally protected from parental cruelty when it takes a physical form: why should they not be protected from mental cruelty?

For the unfortunate fact is that one would be justified in establishing yet another sub-heading in our survey of factors that affect the choice of a child's first name. We could call it 'Parental egotism', or 'Look at me—the namer.' The mostly serious considerations I have described above play no part at all in the naming process for these parents. The sole consideration becomes: how much attention can I attract to myself by naming my child in an unusual way?

While one can find some excuse for the parents who give their children a large number of 'normal' names—because they may genuinely believe that a child will thus have a wide choice of names that he can use later in life—it is difficult to forgive those parents who go in for other excesses. I labour the point because we *do* forgive them. Journalists gleefully report on their idiocies in column-fillers, and we smile and pass on.

But let us not end this brief survey of the whole first name situation on a sour note. First names are usually little volumes of social history in themselves as well as evocations of friends and loved ones. They provide a fascinating study, and if your appetite has been aroused, you will find suggestions for continuing the investigation in the further information section of this book. We shall not be putting first names entirely to one side, but it is time now to look at their normal companions—surnames.

Chapter 7
The Family Name

There was a time in Britain when no one had a hereditary surname. The Norman Conquest of 1066 is a convenient point at which we can note the appearance of the first family names, but the Normans certainly did not bring a fully developed surname system with them. It was not yet their conscious policy to identify a family by one name, but the idea was soon to occur to them. There is every sign that it would also have occurred spontaneously to the people they conquered, but the Norman example no doubt helped speed things along.

Before we turn to modern surnames, let us look at the situation that existed in Britain before the eleventh century. Our remote ancestors had single *personal names* which were quite enough to distinguish them in the small communities in which they lived. Personal names were either well-established name elements, or permutations of such elements. These in turn usually referred to abstract qualities such as 'nobility' and 'fame'. A new single-element name, or a new permutation, was given to every child, so that everyone in the community had a truly personal name. Natural duplication must have caused the same name to come into being simultaneously in different communities, but names were not deliberately re-used.

Some of the Anglo-Saxon personal names later made the change to become first names such as **Alfred**, **Audrey**, **Cuthbert**, **Edgar**, **Edmund**, **Edward**, **Harold** and **Oswald**. Many more of them survived long enough to form the basis of modern surnames. **Allwright**, for example, was once a personal name composed of *aethel* and *ric*, or 'noble' and 'ruler'. **Darwin** was *deor wine*, 'dear friend', and **Wyman** was *wig mund*, 'war protection'.

Scandinavian names

When the Danes and later the Norwegians invaded England and settled in large numbers, they naturally brought their own names with them. Still more important, they brought their own ideas about naming. The Scandinavian personal names sometimes resembled those of the Anglo-Saxons, so that both Old Norse *Harivald* and Old English *Hereweald* could lead to **Harold**, while similar pairs led to **Oswald** and **Randolph**. Many truly Scandinavian names survive today in surnames, though not usually in an easily recognisable form.

But it was the Scandinavian method of naming, rather than the names themselves, that eventually had the biggest effect on the English naming system. Among the Anglo-Saxons, personal names that had been made famous by distinguished ancestors had always been honoured by *not* using them for descendants. The Scandinavians, however, readily duplicated their personal names in different generations of the same family. It was also their common practice to name a son after a famous chief or a personal friend. They believed, as Sir Frank Stenton has explained, that 'the soul of an individual was represented or symbolised by his name, and that the bestowal of a name was a means of calling up the spirit of the man who had borne it into the spirit of the child to whom it was given'.

Coins provide further evidence of Anglo-Saxon and Scandinavian personal names. Those shown here bear the names of King **Aelfrede** and King **Cnut**.

The natural result of consciously re-using the same personal names, apart from creating a far smaller central stock of names, was to make those names far less effective as identifiers of individuals. When exact identification was particularly necessary it became essential to add a second name which gave extra information about the person concerned. This did not lead to the immediate creation of surnames, but it was certainly a step in that direction.

Bynames

The new second names that came into existence at this period, at first among the Scandinavian settlers, were temporary surnames, similar to nicknames in many ways. It is useful to distinguish them as a historical phenomenon, however, from surnames or nicknames as we know them today. For this purpose they have often been referred to as *bynames*. Bynames were meant to be added to someone's personal name to help identification, but sometimes they simply replaced it completely. As substitute personal names they were probably not always to their bearers' liking. Many men must have begun life with flattering traditional names, only to become at a later date **Drunkard**, **Clod**, **Idler**, **Short Leg**, **Shameless**, **Squinter**, **Clumsy** or **Miser**. These are all direct translations of names which occur in medieval records. When these bynames were common enough to be used frequently they sometimes became true surnames at a later date. Of those mentioned above, for instance, the first three subsequently became family names, though their meanings would fortunately not now be recognised. In a modern directory they might appear as **Gipp**, **Clack** and **Sling**.

The need for a supplementary name, then, had made itself felt in England before the Normans arrived, but the Normans, even more than the Scandinavians, believed in using the same personal names over and over again. They also needed second names to identify them properly, especially in legal documents. In the Domesday Book of 1086 almost all the Norman landowners have such names. An earlier version of this survey also gives bynames for many of the former English landowners, and those Englishmen who managed to retain their lands under the new régime also have them. The Norman bynames were frequently the names of the villages from which they came or were the personal names of their fathers, but some described occupations and others personal characteristics. Many of the elements of modern surnames were thus present.

A major difference between bynames and surnames is that the former were not passed on from one generation to the next. They were meaningful names that were meant to apply to the individuals who bore them. The retention of a particular name as a family identifier may have been deliberate, but it could just as easily have happened accidentally at first. One way in which it could occur, for instance, was by the inheritance of property. If the father was known as 'of' followed by the name of his estate, the eldest son might logically take over both the estate and the name.

However it began, one can imagine how this passing of a name from one generation to the next was noted as an aspect of aristocratic behaviour —for it would certainly have begun at baronial level— and duly imitated. The officials who dealt with wills and the like must also have found what soon became a fashion of great convenience to them, and no doubt they encouraged the habit. Slowly bynames were turned into hereditary surnames, a process which spread downwards through society until even the humblest person had one. It was to be 300 years, however, before that happened. At the end of that period, the concept of the single personal name had gone for ever.

Another feature of bynames while they lasted was their linguistic status. Personal names, composed of traditional name elements, were clearly recognised as names. Bynames introduced a great many place names into the personal name system, but transfer of names between people and places had always seemed natural. This type of byname was probably readily accepted, as were the patronymic link names. The latter simply described someone as '**John**'s son' or '**William**'s son', so that the new names contained an obvious personal name element. It was the descriptive names that must have had a harder time of it. One would expect it to take longer for phrases like 'the carpenter' or 'the short one' to convert to the names **Carpenter** and **Short**. Where some activity names were concerned, two factors would help the process. One of these would be the following of the same occupation by a succession of fathers and sons, thus enabling the same byname to remain in a family for a long period and appear to be a hereditary surname.

Surnames from Old English Personal Names

Some Old English personal names have survived as surnames. The 'meaning' of these names is rather special. **Edrich**, for example, contained the elements *ead* and *ric*, the first meaning something like 'prosperity' or 'happiness', the second indicating 'power' or 'rule'. This is not to say that the name therefore means 'prosperous rule'. It may well have come about because the mother's name contained *ead* (in a name like **Edith**) and the father's name *ric* (in a name like **Kenrick**). Such names must often have been blended simply in order to show parentage. This accounts for the names where the elements seem to contradict each other. In their modern forms, many elements have more than one possible origin. *Al-* and *El-* could derive from 'elf' or 'noble', for instance. Alternative possibilities are indicated below.

Adlard noble—hard.
Alflatt elf/noble—beauty.
Allnatt noble—daring.
Alvar elf—army.
Alwin noble/old/elf—friend.
Averay elf—counsel.
Aylmer noble—famous.
Aylwin noble—friend.
Badrick battle—famous.
Baldey bold—combat.
Balman bold—man.
Balston bold—stone.
Bedloe command—love.
Brightmore fair—famous.
Brunger brown—spear.
Brunwin brown—friend.
Burchard fortress—hard.
Burrage fortress—powerful.
Burward fortress—guard.
Cobbald famous—bold.
Cutteridge famous—ruler.
Darwin dear—friend.
Eastman grace—protection.
Eddols prosperity—wolf.
Eddy prosperity—war.
Ellwood elf—ruler.
Elsey elf—victory.
Erwin boar—friend.
Gladwin glad—friend.
Godwin good—friend.
Goldbard gold—bright/beard.
Goldburg gold—fortress.
Goldhawk gold—hawk.
Goldwin gold—friend.
Goodliffe good/God—dear.

Goodrich good/God—ruler.
Goodwin good—friend.
Gummer good/battle—famous.
Hulbert gracious—bright.
Kenward bold/royal—guardian.
Kenway bold/royal—war.
Kerrich family—ruler.
Lambrick land—bright.
Leavey beloved—warrior.
Leavold beloved—power/ruler.
Lemmer people/dear—famous.
Lewin beloved—friend.
Lilleyman little—man.
Litwin bright—friend.
Lovegod beloved—god.
Loveguard beloved—spear.
Milborrow mild—fortress.
Ordway spear—warrior.
Orrick spear—powerful.
Osmer god—fame.
Oswin god—friend.
Outridge dawn—powerful.
Quenell woman—war.
Redway counsel—warrior.
Seavers sea—passage.
Siggers victory—spear.
Trumble strong—bold.
Whatman brave—man.
Whittard elf—brave.
Winbolt friend—bold.
Winbow friend—bold.
Woolgar wolf—spear.
Wyman war—protection.
Yonwin young—friend.
Youngmay young—servant.

A second factor that would have helped this group would be natural duplication. During the period we are considering, which is between 1066 and 1400, each community had its important and easily recognisable craftsmen, tradesmen, officials and other workers. It would have been natural for every village to have someone who was a smith, another who was a baker, and so on. All these medieval occupations are seen in modern surnames as we see on page 100. We must not forget, however, that with each of these names there had to come a point when their status as names was finally accepted. When it was considered quite usual for a **John Carpenter** to be a baker or follow some other trade, 'carpenter' had in one sense lost its meaning. It had acquired, however, a new kind of referential meaning and had passed through the byname stage to become a surname.

Patronyms also had to get by this hurdle, though with names of the John **Andrews** type it is very easy to see how new generations could inherit it, with those around them slightly adjusting its meaning. At first they would have said to themselves that he was the son of **Andrew**, later that he was the grandson, later still, that he was a descendant of someone called Andrew. Eventually this type of name, like the others, would no longer be interpreted at all in a literal sense, but as showing a connection with the Andrews family.

Locative bynames were easily inherited, too. A family that lived by the village green, on the hill, near the ford, or wherever, was likely to remain there for several generations. As for place names, when these indicated provenance rather than inherited property one can see how they were passed on. Even today a village community will remember for several generations that a family came from some other place.

But if one can understand how a great many bynames of different types developed into hereditary surnames, those which described an individual's physical or moral attributes are surprising. A father may rightly have been described as a drunkard, but surely this was not a suitable name for his descendants? Such names may have been another kind of patronymic to begin with, indicating 'son of the drunkard'. If they were bestowed as bynames late in the fourteenth century, by which time the majority of people had surnames, they may have been mistaken for surnames. Nevertheless, one would expect this kind of name to have survived less frequently as a surname and all the evidence points quite clearly to this being the case. The early bearers of such surnames must have occupied a very lowly social position and had no say in the matter. Later descendants who have been of higher standing have frequently rid themselves of such embarrassing family reminders.

We shall never know the exact details of how bynames became surnames, but from the beginning of the fifteenth century nearly all English people inherited a surname at birth and the word 'surname' was used with the meaning we give it today. It had been borrowed from the French *surnom*, deriving in turn from Latin *super-* or *supranomen*, and was used at first to mean simply 'an extra name', 'a nickname'. Modern French retains that meaning and translates 'surname' as *nom de famille*.

Surnames that Link with First Names

The following surnames mostly began by meaning 'son of' (later 'descendant of') or 'employee of' the person named.

ADAM	Adams, Adamson, Adcock, Addison, Addy, Adkins, Aitkins, Atkins, Atkinson.
AGATHA	Aggass, Tag.
AGNES	Annis, Annison, Anson.
ALAN	Alcock, Allan, Allanson, Allen, Alleyn.
ALEXANDER	Sanders, Sanderson, Saunders, Saunderson.
AMICE	Ames, Amies, Amis, Amison, Aymes.
ANDREW	Anderson, Andrews, Dandy.
AUGUSTINE	Austen, Austin.
BARTHOLOMEW	Bartle, Bartlet(t), Bate, Bateman, Bates, Bateson, Batkin, Batt, Batten, Batty.
BEATRICE	Beaton, Beatty, Beet, Beeton.
BENEDICT	Benn, Bennett, Benson.
CASSANDRA	Case, Cash, Cass, Casson.
CECILY	Sisley, Sisson.
CHRISTIAN	Christie, Christison, Christy.
CLEMENT	Clements, Clementson, Clemms, Clempson, Clemson.
CONSTANCE	Cuss, Cussans, Cust, Custance.
DANIEL	Daniels, Dannet, Dannson.
DAVID	Dakins, Davidge, Davidson, Davies, Davis, Davison, Davitt, Dawe, Dawes, Dawkins, Dawson, Day.
DENIS	Dennett, Dennis(s), Dennison, Denny, Tennyson.
DURAND	Durant, Durrance, Durrant.
EDITH	Eade, Eady, Eddis, Eddison, Edis.
EDWARD	Edwardes, Edwards.
ELEANOR	Ellen, Ellinor, Elson.
ELIAS	Eliot, Elliot(t), Ellis, Ellison.
ELIZABETH	Bethell.
EMERY	Amery, Emerson.
EMMA	Emmett, Empson.
GEOFFREY	Jeeves, Jefferies, Jefferson, Jeffrey, Jephson, Jepp, Jepson.
GERALD	Garrard, Garratt, Garrett, Garrod, Gerard, Jarrett, Jerrold.
GERVAIS	Gervas, Gervis, Jarvie, Jarvis.
GILBERT	Gibb, Gibbin, Gibbons, Gibbs, Gibson, Gilbart, Gilbertson, Gilbey, Gilpin, Gilson, Gipps.
GREGORY	Greer, Gregson, Greig, Grierson, Grigg, Grigson.
HAMO	Hamblin, Hamlet, Hamley, Hamlyn, Hammett, Hammond, Hamnet, Hampson, Hamson.
HARVEY	Harvie, Hervey.
HENRY	Harriman, Harris, Harrison, Hawke, Hawkins, Henderson, Hendry, Henryson, Heriot, Parry, Perry.
HERMAN	Armand, Arment, Harman, Harmon.
HUBERT	Hobart, Hubbard.

HUGH	Hewes, Hewett, Hewitson, Hewlet, Hewson, Howkins, Huggett, Huggins, Hughes, Hullett, Hullis, Hutchings, Hutchins, Hutchinson, Pugh.
HUMPHREY	Boumphrey, Humphreys, Humphriss, Pumphrey.
ISABEL	Bibby, Ibbotson, Ibson, Libby, Nibbs, Nibson, Tibbs.
JAMES	Gemson, Gimson, Jamieson, Jimpson.
JOHN	Hancock, Hankin, Hanson, Jackson, Jaggs, Jenkins, Jennings, Jennison, Johns, Johnson, Jones.
JULIANA	Gill, Gillett, Gillott, Gilson, Jewett, Jolyan, Jowett, Julian, Julien, Julyan.
KATHARINE	Catlin, Caton, Cattling.
LAURENCE	Larkin(s), Laurie, Law, Lawrence, Lawrie, Lawson, Lowry.
LUKE	Lucas, Luck, Luckett, Luckin, Lukin.
MABEL	Mabbot, Mabbs, Mapp, Mappin, Mapson, Mobbs.
MAGDALEN	Maddison, Maudling.
MARGARET	Maggs, Magson, Margerison, Margetson, Margretts, Meggeson, Meggs, Moxon, Pegson, Poggs.
MARTIN	Martell, Martens, Martinet, Martinson.
MARY	Malleson, Mallett, Marion, Marriott, Marrison, Maryat, Mollison.
MATILDA	Madison, Maudson, Mault, Mawson, Mold, Mould, Moulson, Moult, Tillett, Tilley, Tillison, Tillotson.
MATTHEW	Machin, Makins, Makinson, Matheson, Mathieson, Matson, Matterson, Matthews, Mattin, Maycock, Mayhew, Maykin.
MAURICE	Morcock, Morrice, Morris, Morrison, Morse, Morson.
MICHAEL	Michell, Michieson, Mitchell, Mitchelson, Mitchison.
NICHOLAS	Cole, Collett, Colley, Collins, Collis, Collison, Nicholson, Nickells, Nicks, Nickson, Nicolson, Nixon.
NIGEL	Neal, Neilson, Nelson.
PAGAN	Paine, Pannel, Payne.
PATRICK	Paterson, Paton, Patterson, Pattinson, Pattison.
PETER	Parkin, Parkinson, Parks, Parr, Parrot, Pears, Pearse, Pearson, Perkins, Perrin, Perrot, Peters, Peterson, Pierce.
PETRONELLA	Parnell, Purnell.
PHILIP	Filkins, Phelps, Phillips, Phillipson, Philpot, Phipps, Potts.
RALPH	Rawkins, Rawle, Rawlings, Rawlins, Rawlinson, Rawlison, Rawson.
RANDAL	Randall, Randolph, Rand(s), Rankin, Ransome.
REYNALD	Rennell, Rennie, Rennison, Reynolds, Reynoldson.
RICHARD	Dickens, Dickenson, Dickerson, Dixon, Hickie, Hicks, Hickson, Higgins, Higgs, Hitchens, Prickett, Pritchard, Pritchett, Richards, Richardson, Ricketts, Rix.
ROBERT	Dabbs, Dobbie, Dobbs, Dobie, Dobson, Hobart, Hobbs, Hobson, Hopkins, Hopkinson, Nobbs, Probert, Probyn, Robbie, Robbins, Robens, Roberts, Robertson, Robey, Robson.
ROGER	Dodd, Dodge, Dodgson, Dodson, Hodges, Hodgkinson, Hodgkiss, Hodgson, Hodson, Hotchkiss, Rogers.
SIMON	Simms, Simmonds, Simpkins, Simpson, Sims, Symonds.
STEPHEN	Stenson, Stephens, Stephenson, Stevens, Stevenson.
THOMAS	Tamlin, Tampling, Thomason, Thompson, Tombs, Tomlinson, Tompkins, Tomsett, Tonkins, Tonks.
WALTER	Walters, Waterson, Watkins, Watkinson, Watson, Watts.
WILLIAM	Gilham, Gillam, Gilliam, Mott, Wilcock, Wilcox, Wilkie, Wilkins, Wilkinson, Williams, Williamson, Willis, Wills, Wilson.

Spelling and pronunciation

Most of our surnames have, therefore, been in the family for 500 years or more, but that is not to say that the one name among many by which our ancestors finally came to be known is exactly the same as the name we bear today. The names came into existence, but they had no fixed forms. Our ancestors—and this probably includes any who were of the upper classes—were for centuries mostly illiterate. Their names were occasionally recorded by a parson or clerk when there was a birth, marriage or death in the family, and he wrote down what he heard using his own ideas about the spelling. He was obliged to do this, for though the spelling of ordinary words very slowly became standardised after the fifteenth century, there were no agreed forms for names. It was the printed books which helped to fix the words, but only a tiny proportion of names ever appeared in print.

The same name could be written down in many different ways by different clerks, and even, as the parish registers clearly show, by the same clerk at different times. A further complication was provided by regional dialects. A sound which in the personal name period could be represented by 'y', for example, became 'i' in the North and East Midlands, 'e' in the South East and 'u' in the Central Midlands and other southern counties. These changes had occurred by the beginning of the surname period. This is why, incidentally, we can connect surnames like **Dunkling** and **Dunkley** with the Lancashire place names **Dinkling** and **Dinckley**.

Sir Walter **Raleigh**, whose surname has been spelt in many different ways.

The influence of the French officials who later came to write down English names has also been felt in our surnames. They too spoke different dialects and had varying orthographic systems. All in all it is hardly surprising that what was once the same name can appear in a wide variety of modern forms. We normally refer to Sir Walter **Raleigh**, for instance, but **Rawley** probably captured the name's pronunciation more accurately. Other forms include **Ralegh**, **Raughley**, **Rauly**, **Rawleigh**, **Rawleleygh** and **Rayley**.

Almost every modern surname has its variant forms. Even the short man we referred to earlier whose byname lived on as a surname has become **Shortt** in some instances, acquiring a superfluous letter somewhere along the line. As a word this would long ago have been regularised; as a name it now remains fossilised in the form it accidentally took on.

Many names have acquired extra letters, but we should note that the initial 'ff' preserved by some families is rather different. This was a medieval scribal alternative for an 'F' and should always be written, therefore, as two small letters. One thinks of the Wodehousian baronet Sir Jasper ffinch-ffarrowmere, who was deeply upset by an enemy's parting shot: 'Furthermore, I think your name is spelt with a capital F like anyone else's.'

In some cases the spelling of a surname has remained artificially fixed while its pronunciation has changed. One finds the same lack of relationship between spelling and pronunciation in many place names. Well-known surname examples include **Cholmondeley**, 'Chumley', **Mainwaring**, 'Mannering', **Marjoribanks**, 'Marshbanks', **Beauchamp**, 'Beecham', **Featherstonehaugh**, 'Fanshaw'. With these names as with many others the pronunciation normally used by one family may differ from that preferred by another.

Irish surnames

As in England, bynames preceded surnames in Ireland. The earliest kind mentioned the name of the father, preceded by 'Mac', or that of a grandfather or earlier ancestor, in which case 'O' preceded the name. Later, names were formed by adding these prefixes to the father's byname, which could be of any of the kinds seen in England. The 'Mac' (or 'Mc', which means exactly the same) and 'O' prefixes were dropped during the period of English rule, but the 'O' especially has now been resumed by many families.

Other influences on Irish surnames include translation from Gaelic to English, abbreviation and absorption of rare names into common ones. By translation, which in many cases was demanded by the English authorities, families such as the **McGowan**s correctly became **Smith**s, but many mistranslations were made.

The Norman invasions of Ireland in the twelfth century naturally carried many of their personal names and bynames there. Some of these, in the form of surnames such as **Burke**, **Cruise** and **Dillon**, are now thought of as essentially Irish, and with good reason. Later English settlement in Ireland also caused many English surnames to become well established.

Scottish surnames

In the Scottish Lowlands surnames developed along the same lines as in England, though at a slightly later date. In the Highlands the development of hereditary surnames was held back by the clan system. Many families voluntarily allied themselves to a powerful clan or were forced to do so, and in either case they assumed the clan name as their new surname.

The power of the clan names in their day is seen in the action taken by James VI against the **McGregor**s. By an Act of Council he proscribed and abolished the name altogether, because 'the bare and simple name of **McGregor** made that whole clan to presume of their power, force and strength, and did encourage them, without reverence of the law or fear of punishment, to go forward in their iniquities'. The proscription against the name was not finally removed until 1774.

Gaelic names from the Highlands began to spread south in the eighteenth century, and later throughout the English-speaking world. Mrs. Cecily Dynes, who keeps records of the names used by parents in New South Wales, noted in 1972 'a sudden upsurge of "Mac" or "Mc" middle names'. Other typically Highland names, such as **Cameron**, are already being used as first names.

Welsh surnames

The many Welshmen who came into England in the byname period were treated like Englishmen as far as their names were concerned. A few Welsh personal names, such as **Morgan**, **Owen**, **Meredith**, thus became established as surnames centuries before hereditary surnames were normal in Wales itself. The usual custom there was for a man to be something like **Madog Ap Gryffyd Ap Jorweth**, with 'ap' meaning 'son of'. As late as 1853 the Registrar-General was able to say—using expressions that no one would dare use today—that 'among the lower classes in the wilder districts . . . the Christian name of the father still frequently becomes the patronymic of the son'.

Traces of the 'ap' system survive in names like **Price**, formerly **Ap Rhys**, and many of the original Welsh personal names have managed to live on, but the well-known preponderance in modern Wales of names like **Jones**, **Davies**, **Williams**, **Thomas**, **James**, **Phillips**, **Edwards**, **Roberts**, **Richards** and **Hughes** show all too clearly that the **John**, **David** and **William** type of first name became thoroughly established there. When formal surnames were eventually used, the traditional method of naming after the father was remembered but it was the new names that formed their base.

Surnames in America

British surnames, as we have seen, are not without their complications. When those surnames have been taken to other countries and mixed with surnames from all over the world, the situation becomes almost impossible to cope with. A glance at a list of common surnames in America, for instance, shows that there are as many **Jorgensens** as **Cliffords**, as many people called **Lombardo** as **Dickens**. It is not that these common names cause difficulty, for a 'son of **George**' is not particularly difficult to recognise even in his Danish disguise, and a 'man from **Lombardy**' is not concealed by that final '-o', but for every common name there are a dozen unusual ones brought from the same country.

Elsdon C. Smith has made a heroic attempt to cope with the difficulties in his *American Surnames* and other works, in all of which he has collated

Presidents **Washington**, **Abraham Lincoln**, **Roosevelt** and **Woodrow Wilson** portrayed as 'nameographs'.

information from a vast range of sources. His work has an added interest in that it compares surname development and types of modern surname in many countries. Not unnaturally he expands on **Smith**, which has its equivalent in many countries. Apart from the German **Schmidt** and French **Lefevre**, Gaelic **Gowan** and Latin **Faber**, it occurs as the Syrian **Haddad**, Finnish **Seppanen**, Hungarian **Kovacs**, Russian **Kuznetsov**, Ukrainian **Kowalsky**, Lithuanian **Kalvaitis**, and so on. One can see why Mark Lower, a highly entertaining writer on names in the nineteenth century, suggested that there should be a science called *Smithology* to deal properly with all aspects of this family name.

Some Celtic Surnames

The surnames of Scotland, Wales, Ireland, Cornwall and the Isle of Man have distinct characteristics, deriving as they do from Celtic languages such as Gaelic and Old Welsh. Separate dictionaries exist which deal with them in detail (see the Bibliography). Some examples of common and well-known names are given below.

Berryman 'man from St. Buryan'.

Bevan son of *Evan* (John).

Bosanquet 'dwelling of *Angawd*', a Cornish place name.

Boyd 'yellow-haired'.

Boyle 'pledge'.

Brennan 'sorrow/raven'.

Bruce from a Norman place name.

Burke probably from *Burgh*, a place name.

Burns 'dweller by the stream'.

Cameron 'crooked nose'.

Campbell 'crooked mouth'.

Cardew 'dark fort'.

Carrick 'rock mass'.

Craig 'dweller by rocks'.

Cunningham from Scottish place name, or descendant of *Con* (Ireland).

Daly 'assembly'.

Docherty 'the stern one'.

Douglas from place name, 'dark stream'.

Doyle 'dark stranger'.

Duncan 'brown warrior'.

Dyer 'thatcher' (Cornwall).

Farrell 'man of valour'.

Ferguson son of 'man choice'.

Findlay 'fair hero'.

Forbes from the place name, 'field'.

Freethy 'eager, alert'.

Gallacher 'foreign help'.

Gough 'red-faced or red-haired'.

Guinness son of *Angus*, 'one choice'.

Hamilton from place name.

Innes 'dweller on an island'.

Jago son of *James*.

Jory son of *George*.

Kelly son of *Ceallach*, 'war'.

Kennedy 'ugly head'.

Kermode son of *Diarmaid*, 'freeman'.

Kerr 'dweller by the marsh'.

Lloyd 'grey'.

McFarlane son of *Bartholomew*.

McGregor son of *Gregory*, 'to be watchful'.

McIntosh son of the 'chieftain'.

McIntyre son of the 'carpenter'.

McKay son of *Aodh*, 'fire'.

McKenzie son of *Coinneach*, 'fair one'.

McLean son of the devotee of St. John.

McLeod son of *Ljotr*, 'the ugly one'.

McMillan son of *Mhaolain*, 'the tonsured man', a religious servant.

McPherson son of the 'parson'.

Mundy 'dweller in the mine house' (Cornwall).

Munro from a place name, 'mouth of the River Roe'.

Murphy descendant of the 'sea warrior'.

Murray from the place name, 'sea settlement'.

Nance 'dweller in the valley'.

Negus 'dweller by the nut grove'.

Nolan descendant of the 'noble one'.

O'Brien descendant of *Brian*, from King Brian Boru.

O'Byrne descendant of the 'bear' or 'raven'.

O'Connor descendant of *Connor*, 'high will'.

O'Neill descendant of the 'champion'.

Opie descendant of *Osbert*.

O'Reilly descendant of the 'prosperous or valiant one'.

Pascoe 'Easter child'.

Pengelly 'dweller by the top of the copse'.

Penrose 'dweller at the top of the heath'.

Quiggin son of *Uige*, 'skill'.

Quirk son of *Corc*, 'heart'.

Ritchie son of *Richard*.

Ross from the place name.

Ryan descendant of *Rian*.

Sinclair from places called Saint-Clair in Normandy.

Stewart 'the steward'.

Sullivan part of the name means 'eye'. The other part could mean 'black', 'one', hawk', etc.

Sutherland from the place name, 'south land'.

Trease 'dweller in the homestead by a ford'.

Tremaine 'dweller in the stone homestead'.

Trevean 'dweller in the little homestead'.

Trevor from the place name, 'big village'.

Trewen 'dweller in the white homestead'.

Vaughan 'the little man'.

Wynne 'fair, white'.

JOHN F. **KENNEDY**

DONALD **CAMPBELL**

Many surnames in America have retained the form they had in other countries, but others were consciously adapted by immigrants so that English-speakers would find them easier to spell and pronounce. The Dutch name **Van Rosevelt**, 'of the rose field', became **Roosevelt**; German **Huber**, 'tenant of a hide of land', became **Hoover**, while German **Roggenfelder**, 'rye field', became **Rockefeller**. The Finnish name **Kirkkomäki** was changed to **Churchill**.

Americans in particular must therefore check their individual family histories very closely when investigating the origins of their surnames, but so too must all bearers of the less common British surnames. Reliable investigations have been made by competent scholars into at least 25,000 British surnames, including all the common ones, and this information is now to be found in standard dictionaries and reference books. These names must account for a very large number of people, for one person in eight to begin with in England and Wales bears one of the top thirty surnames listed on page 69. But beyond the central stock of names there are perhaps another 100,000 names which are far less common. To return to America, the situation is literally ten times as complicated there. Over a million different surnames were registered with the Social Security Administration in 1964.

Tracing the origin of a surname

A search for the origin of a surname should obviously begin with the main works of reference, which I list at the end of this book. Many surnames were originally place names, and works on place names should therefore be consulted as well. But the problem will probably lie in the modern form of the surname itself, which is often highly corrupt. If the reference books do not help one must investigate the family history, noting carefully the various forms of the surname that will begin to appear as one delves into previous centuries. One of these forms, or perhaps all of them considered together, may provide the necessary clue, especially when coupled with information about where the family formerly lived.

A special search of that kind will have a particular interest to the name-bearer, but it is a long, complicated and sometimes expensive procedure. Obviously it is worth making such genealogical investigations if one can afford the time or money, since one's personal family history is fascinating, but there can be no guarantee that the origin of one's surname will emerge even when the early forms of it are known. It requires an expert to interpret medieval onomastic data, and there are not that many experts around. Those that do exist are obliged to leave many names aside as unexplained and perhaps unexplainable. As for the rest of us, we must pay homage to the careful scholarly work that has been done (and which continues at such centres as the Department of English Local History, University of Leicester), and be grateful for the information so far uncovered.

Chapter 8
Class-conscious Names

Dr. Basil Cottle, in the Introduction to his *Penguin Dictionary of Surnames*, says very firmly that all surnames of British ethnic stock 'fall into only four classes'. He then describes the traditional categories, which are those based on

1. first names
2. localities
3. occupation or status
4. nicknames

These traditional categories have been followed by writer after writer, but they are woefully inadequate. R. A. McKinley usefully subdivides two of them and adds another in his *Norfolk Surnames in the Sixteenth Century*. The first name group usually refers to a father or mother relationship, but there are other surnames which indicate relationship without mentioning a name. **Neave**, for example, is 'nephew', **Eames** is 'son of the uncle'. Dr. Cottle classifies these as 'nicknames'; Mr. McKinley puts them more convincingly into a new class of *relationship* surnames. He also divides 'locality' surnames into *locative* and *topographical*, the first deriving from names of settlements such as villages, towns or larger areas, the second deriving from natural features such as hills and brooks. Finally, Mr. McKinley sets up a new category for surnames which have more than one possible origin. He includes here those whose origin is unknown.

Mr. McKinley's system is undoubtedly an improvement, but the categories mentioned have been set up with only surnames in mind. They do not allow us to see at a glance how surnames compare with other nomenclatures. Using the 'universal' classification system outlined in Chapter 3, and rearranging the information provided by a number of scholars, we can classify our surnames by origin as follows:

Descriptive surnames

Of the many subdivisions in this category the most important are *locative*, *provenance*, *activity*, *relationship*, *direct* and *metaphorical* descriptions. The locative descriptions began as crude forms of a person's address. The man who lived 'beyond the stream' became **Overy**, the 'man on the hill',

Uphill. While names like these have preserved the prepositions that were always present originally, it is more normal for them to have been lost altogether or to have left only a trace. 'At the' was *atte*, *atten* or *atter* in Middle English, so that the phrase 'at the ash tree' can appear today as **Ash**, **Nash**, **Rash** or **Tash**. Trees, woods, hills, streams, marshes, fields, valleys—any feature, natural or man-made, that could easily be seen was used in names of this kind.

Provenance descriptions could indicate where a person came from specifically, as in **Cornwallis**, 'man from Cornwall', **Walsh**, 'the Welshman', or more vaguely, as in **Southern**, 'the man from the South'. We must not forget that many transferred place names were also used to indicate provenance.

Activity descriptions are very common as surnames, and include all the obvious occupational names. But this group includes names that were bestowed because of occasional activities. The common surnames **King**, **Lord**, **Abbot**, **Pope** and the like clearly do not reflect normal occupations. They could be metaphorical descriptions, but they are just as likely to have been given to men who played these parts occasionally or regularly in the medieval pageants.

Direct descriptions include all the physical characteristics that we notice in one another. A **Long** was tall, a **Whitehead** had precisely that, a **Beard**, **Skegg** and some **Whitbreads**, 'white beard', were all bearded when it was normal to be clean-shaven. The colour of a man's hair or complexion, a physical defect or the clothes he normally wore could all lead to descriptive names such as **Blunt**, 'blond-haired', **Bossey**, 'hunchbacked' and **Shorthouse**, a wearer of 'short hose, or boots'.

The relationship descriptions mentioned by Mr. McKinley include the many names like **Parsons** and **Sergeantson** where a family or other relationship is attested. The final '-s', which also occurs in many link names, must undoubtedly indicate parenthood in many cases, phrases like 'the parson's son' having become shortened. A master-servant relationship might lie behind the names, however.

There is an interesting sub-group of *verbal descriptions*, which seem to derive from the favourite oaths and phrases of those being named. **Goodall** probably represents the street cry 'Good ale!' used by the man selling it. **Purdie**, **Purdue** and the like are clearly the popular medieval oath which we may translate as 'by God', or 'in God's name'. Verbal descriptions do not necessarily include, however, surnames which are phrasal in form but may be perfectly normal activity or other descriptions. **Knatchbull**, for example, was a man who knocked bulls on the head, a butcher, while **Shakespeare** is far more likely to have been a real spear-shaker, a soldier, than the 'Jacques-Pierre' dreamed up by one of the tribe of ingenious etymologists.

William **Shakespeare**, whose surname began as a descriptive nickname.

Subjective descriptions reflected opinions about the person rather than simple facts. If he was held in high esteem he might become **Noble**,

Hardy or **Smart**, but he could also become an **Unwin**, 'an unfriendly man', or a **Giddy**, 'one who was mad or insane'. Allied to these are metaphorical descriptions which make comparisons between the person and birds or animals. Most animals were associated with certain characteristics in the Middle Ages, as many still are today. We talk about 'foxing' someone, and perhaps address them in a friendly way as *duckie*. A **Fox** was a crafty fellow when he received his name, and the friendly personal name substitutes based on 'duck' perhaps preserve a kindly medieval attitude to this bird. **Duck** occurs as a surname, but it is impossible to say whether it was used metaphorically or metonymically—whether it described the person's nature or simply recorded that he was a breeder and seller of ducks.

A partiality for metonymic description, whereby an item associated with what is being named is used as the name itself, is well attested in other nomenclatures such as house names, and there is no reason to suppose that it is only a modern phenomenon. One must bear points like this in mind when we know the literal meaning of a name but cannot be certain why the name was chosen.

Converted surnames

There are many people who have surnames which can be classed as commendatory conversions, but these names do not belong to the main body of surnames which arose naturally hundreds of years ago. They are the deliberately adopted surnames of film stars, writers and the like, which we shall be discussing more fully in the next chapter.

Invented surnames

These now exist, but once again they do not belong in the early surname-forming period. They arise when immigrants arrive in English-speaking countries and choose a new surname, or do this for any other reason. But it would totally throw out of perspective our view of surnames as a whole to place too much emphasis on this minor group. That is true at the moment, but it will not necessarily remain so in the future. There is every reason to suppose that more and more people will abandon inherited surnames and create new ones.

Link surnames

Here belong the surnames based on personal or first names. The commonest type includes the name of the father and an element that means 'son of'. Examples are **Robertson**, **Nixon** 'Nick's son', **Jones**, 'John's son', **McDonald**, 'son of Donald', **Fitzwilliam**, 'son of William', with the prefix representing an earlier form of the French *fils*, 'son'. Diminutive and pet forms of first names occur very frequently in names of this type.

Women's names often form the basis of such names, and there can be little doubt that this frequently indicates illegitimacy at the time of naming. When Canon Bardsley drew this natural conclusion in his *English Surnames* he was assailed by the critics. They were concerned at the picture

Surnames Reflecting Medieval Life

The surnames given below are examples of the traditional 'occupational' group. Taken together they provide us with a wide-ranging picture of medieval life and activities.

Archer a professional archer, or perhaps a champion.

Arrowsmith responsible for making arrow-heads.

Bacchus a worker in the bakehouse.

Backer a baker.

Bacon he would have sold or prepared bacon.

Bailey a bailiff, a word that described (high) officials of several kinds.

Baker the bread-maker.

Barber he trimmed beards, cut hair, pulled out teeth and performed minor operations.

Barker he worked with bark for the leather trade.

Bayliss usually the son of a *Bailey*.

Baxter a female baker.

Bowman like the *Archer*.

Brasher a brazier, brass-founder.

Brewer occasionally from a place name, but usually what it says.

Brewster a female brewer.

Butcher as now, though once a dealer in buck's (goat's) flesh.

Butler chief servant who supervised the *bottles*.

Campion a professional fighter, a champion.

Carpenter as now.

Carter driver, perhaps maker, of carts.

Cartwright maker and repairer of carts.

Chamberlain once a nobleman's personal servant, but became a general factotum in an inn.

Chambers as *Chamberlain*.

Champion see *Campion*.

Chandler he made or sold candles.

Chaplin a chaplain.

Chapman at first a merchant, later a pedlar.

Chaundler as *Chandler*.

Clark(e) a minor cleric.

Coke a cook.

Collier he sold charcoal.

Cook(e) a professional cook. The extra -*e* acquired accidentally in such names or an attempt to disguise the name's meaning.

Cooper concerned with wooden casks, buckets, etc.

Cowper as *Cooper*.

Day often a worker in a dairy.

Draper maker and seller of woollen cloth.

Dyer a cloth-dyer. *Dye* was deliberately changed from *die* to avoid confusion.

Falconer in charge of the falcons, used for hunting.

Falkner, **Faulkner**, etc., as *Falconer*.

Farmer the modern meaning came after the surname. He was a tax-collector before that, 'farm' once meaning 'firm or fixed payment'.

Farrar a smith or farrier.

Fearon an ironmonger or smith.

Feather a dealer in feathers.

Fisher a fisherman.

Fletcher he made and sold arrows.

Forester a gamekeeper.

Forster sometimes a cutler, scissors-maker, or as *Forester*.

Fowler a hunter of wild birds.

Frobisher he polished swords, armour and the like.
Fuller he 'fulled' cloth, cleansing it.
Gardner, **Gardiner**, etc., a gardener.
Glover a maker and seller of gloves.
Goldsmith often a banker as well as a goldsmith.
Grave a steward.
Grieve manager of property, a bailiff.
Harper maker or player of harps.
Hayward literally a 'hedge-guard'. In charge of fences and enclosures.
Herd a herdsman.
Hooper he fitted hoops on casks and barrels.
Hunt, **Hunter**, both 'huntsman'.
Kellogg literally 'kill hog', a slaughterer.
Kemp as *Campion*.
Knight in the surname period the meaning was 'a military servant'.
Lander a launderer.
Lavender a launderer.
Leach a doctor.
Leadbeater, **Leadbetter**, **Leadbitter**, etc., worker in lead.
Leech a doctor.
Lister a dyer of cloth.
Lorimer a spur-maker.
Machin a mason, stone-worker.
Marchant a merchant.
Marshall a marshal, originally in charge of horses, rising to be a high official.
Mason a skilled stone-worker.
Mercer a dealer in silks and such-like fabrics.

Merchant a dealer, especially wholesale imports/exports.
Mills a miller.
Miller a corn-miller.
Milner as *Miller*
Mulliner as *Miller*.
Naylor a maker and seller of nails.
Page a minor male servant.
Paget a little *Page*.
Paige as *Page*.
Parker keeper of a private park.
Parson a parson, rector.
Parsons servant or son of the *Parson*.
Pepper a dealer in pepper and other spices.
Piper a pipe-player, but may include the name *Pepper*.
Plummer a plumber, lead-worker.
Potter a maker and seller of earthenware.
Proctor a 'procurator', a steward, agent, tithe-farmer.
Redman sometimes from 'reed-man', a thatcher.
Reeve a high-ranking official, a bailiff, a steward.
Saddler a saddle-maker.
Salter a salt-worker, or seller of salt.
Sargent a domestic, legal, or military servant.
Sawyer a sawer of wood.
Shepherd, **Sheppard**, etc., a shepherd.
Singer a professional singer.
Skinner a preparer of skins, a tanner.
Slater a slate-layer.
Slatter as *Slater*.
Smith a metal-worker, maker of all-important weapons and implements.

Smithers son of *Smith*.
Smythe as *Smith*.
Spencer a dispenser of provisions, a steward or butler.
Spicer a seller of spices.
Spooner a spoon-maker, or roofing-shingle maker.
Squire a knight's attendant, usually a young man of good birth.
Steele a steel-worker.
Stringer a maker of strings for bows.
Tanner a tanner of hides.
Taylor a maker of clothes, though the Normans could also 'tailor' other materials, such as stone.
Thatcher 'thatch' is linked with the Roman 'toga' and means 'to cover'.
Thrower a potter.
Tucker a cloth-worker.
Turner a wood-worker, but possibly a turnspit-operator, a translator, competitor in tournaments, etc.
Tyler maker and layer of tiles.
Vickers son or servant of a vicar.
Wainwright a wagon-maker and repairer.
Walker a cloth-worker, who trod cloth in order to cleanse it.
Waller sometimes a builder of walls, but other origins possible.
Ward a watchman, guard.
Weaver, **Webb**, **Webber**, **Webster** all mean weaver.
Wheeler a maker of wheels.
Woodward a forester.
Wright a workman who made a variety of articles.

Some Descriptive Surnames

Arlott young fellow, rogue.

Armstrong as **Strongitharm**.

Ballard a bald man.

Bass a short man.

Bassett diminutive of *Bass*.

Beard a man who was bearded when beards were not fashionable.

Belcher a man who belched or had a 'pretty face'.

Bell (sometimes) the handsome man.

Bellamy handsome friend.

Best a man who was beast-like.

Biggs son of a big man.

Black with black hair, or darkish skin.

Blackbird with a black beard.

Blake usually as *Black*.

Blundell a blond man.

Blunt as *Blundell*.

Bossey a hunch-backed man.

Bragg a brisk man, or a proud one.

Brennan (English) a man whose job was to 'burn the hand' of a criminal, or a man whose hand was branded.

Brent (sometimes) a branded man.

Brown with brown hair.

Burnett with dark brown hair, or wearer/seller of cloth of that colour. Other meanings are also possible.

Carless free from care.

Cave (usually) a bald man.

Crippen with curly hair.

Cripps as *Crippen*. Also **Crisp** and **Crispin**.

Cronk a vigorous man.

Cruikshank with crooked legs.

Curtis courteous/educated, or a wearer of short hose.

Doggett 'dog head'.

Dunn a swarthy man.

Dwelly a foolish man.

Fairchild a handsome young man.

Fairfax with beautiful hair.

Fortescue a strong shield.

Fry(e) free, generous.

Gay a cheerful man.

Giddy a madman.

Goodfellow a good companion, a **Goodman**.

Goolden with yellow hair.

Grant a tall man.

Gray or **Grey**, a grey-haired man.

Gulliver a glutton.

Hardy a tough man, courageous.

Hendy a courteous man.

Hoare a grey-haired man.

Jolliffe as **Jolly**, a cheerful man.

Keen a brave man.

Lang a tall man.

Lemon a lover.

Long a tall man.

Lovelace (sometimes) a man who loved the lasses.

Mallory an unlucky or unfortunate man.

Moody a bold man.

Moore (sometimes) swarthy as a Moor.

Noble of noble character.

Parfitt a man who was **Perfect**.

Pettit a small man.

Pratt a cunning man.

Prettyman as *Pratt*.

Proudfoot a man with a haughty walk.

Prowse a valiant man.

Quartermaine a man with 'four hands', wearing mailed gloves.

Rank a strong or proud man.

Read (usually) a man with red hair.

Reed as *Read*.

Russell as *Read*.

Savage a savage man. *Best* is the same type of name.

Shakespeare a shaker or brandisher of a lance or spear, a soldier.

Sharp a quick-thinking man.

Short a small man.

Shorthouse a wearer of short hose.

Simple an honest man.

Skegg a bearded man.

Small a thin or small man.

Smart as *Sharp*.

Smollett a man with a small head.

Snell a bold man.

Snow a white-haired man.

Sorrell with reddish-brown hair.

Strang a **Strong** man.

Swift a swift man.

Tait a cheerful man.

Thoroughgood a thoroughly good man.

Turnbull a strong man, able to turn a bull.

Wagstaffe similar to *Shakespeare*.

Whitbread (sometimes) a man with a white beard.

Whitehouse (sometimes) a man with a white neck.

Wild a man who behaved wildly.

Wise a wise man.

Worledge and **Woollage**, a distinguished man.

of medieval immorality he was painting. That was in 1875, and we are less squeamish these days about such matters. We need not go in for the tortuous excuses made by other writers to explain these names, the only reasonable alternative among them referring to the children of widows. **Moult** and **Allison** are examples of such names, with **Maud** and **Alice** the names contained in them.

Transferred names

These are surnames transferred from place names in the majority of cases, but occasionally from first names, field names, inn names and the like. The place names were used to identify landowners, but also people who had moved away from their homes in order to live elsewhere. The surname has sometimes retained the same spelling as the place name, as in **Newton**, **Morton**, **Crosby**. At other times the connection is hardly recognisable. **Burtonshaw** and **Bruckshaw** are both corrupted forms of **Birkenshaw**, for instance.

When a personal name has been taken over with no additional element it must be considered as a transferred name, though it is highly likely in many cases to have been a link name originally. As for the surnames frequently explained in the past as deriving from house or inn names, Dr. Reaney in his *Origin of English Surnames* effectively proves that many of them must come from other sources. A few surnames of this type do exist, however. Examples include **Bell**, **Rose**, **Swan** and **Vine**, but all of these can be alternatively explained.

This brings us to the question of Mr. McKinley's category of multiple-origin and unexplained names. For statistical purposes they need to be separated out, but multiple origin in itself does not constitute a separate category of origin. Such names must be referred to each of the categories to which they could belong. Perhaps we should emphasise that even when a surname has been identified in terms of the words or names which formed its base, we can never know for certain *why* the name was bestowed 500 years ago. Even a name like **Miller**, which is no doubt a simple activity description in nearly all cases, *could* have been applied as a metaphorical description, since millers were as renowned in the Middle Ages for their craftiness and dirty dealings as animals such as the fox. Statements about the reasons for giving this or that name must often be no more than intelligent guesses, and it is here that the philologist must turn to a more recent nomenclature where evidence about why the names were chosen is still available, in order to learn about the general patterns which are present in any naming system.

With our classifications made we can bring to an end this brief survey of surname history. I remind those who wish to trace the origin of their own surname that they should refer to the further information section of this book. They will find the names and addresses of societies that could help them, and details of reference books that should first be consulted. For the moment let us take it that we have our surnames, and know in general terms, at least, why we have them. Our next consideration can be: what should we do with them?

Surnames That Put a Man in His Place

A very large number of surnames originally indicated where a man lived, where he came from or where he worked. These names began as phrasal descriptions, often mentioning a specific place name. When a surname is the same as an English place name, this kind of origin is always possible. Other surnames made use of a topographical feature, such as a **Ford**, or a building, such as a **Hall**, to indicate residence or working place. The surnames below are among the most frequent of this kind.

Alston	Clifton	Fenton	Melton	Shelton	Thurston
Barton	Compton	Hampton	Milton	Skelton	Tipton
Benton	Cotton	Hilton	Morton	Stanton	Walton
Bolton	Dalton	Hinton	Newton	Stapleton	Washington
Burton	Denton	Horton	Norton	Stratton	Winston
Carlton	Dutton	Houston	Pendleton	Sutton	Worthington
Clayton	Eaton	Hutton	Preston	Thornton	Wotton

Alford	Buckley	Dudley	Kirby	Prescott	Ware
Ashby	Caldwell	Durham	Langford	Ramsey	Warren
Bentley	Churchill	Farley	Langley	Rowland	Wells
Blackwell	Clifford	Hartley	Lincoln	Shipley	Wesley
Bradford	Conway	Hastings	Mayfield	Stafford	Westbrook
Bradley	Crawford	Hatfield	Moseley	Stanford	Whitaker
Bradshaw	Crosby	Holbrook	Norwood	Stanley	Willoughby
Brandon	Davenport	Holloway	Oakley	Stokes	York

Banks	Grove	Knapp 'hilltop'	Shaw 'small wood'
Bridges	Hayes 'enclosure'	Knowles 'hilltop'	Townsend
Brooks	Heath	Lake	Woods
Castle	Hill	Lane	Yates 'gate'
Downs	Holmes 'island'	Lee 'glade'	
Fields	Holt 'thicket'	Meadows	
Green	House 'religious house'	Mills	

Another way of assigning a man to his place was to describe his nationality. Some of the following names have more than one possible origin, but all could have indicated the nationality of the man who was so named.

Brittany	**Breton, Brett, Britt, Britten, Britton.**
Cornwall	**Cornell, Cornish, Cornwall, Cornwallis, Cornwell.**
Denmark	**Dence, Dench, Dennis, Denns.**
England	**England, English, Inglis.**
Flanders	**Flament, Flanders, Fleeming, Flement, Fleming, Flinders.**
France	**France, Frances, Francis, Frankish, French, Gascoigne, Gascoyne, Gaskain, Gaskin, Loaring, Loring, Lorraine.**
Germany	**Germaine, German, Germing, Jarman, Jermyn.**
Ireland	**Ireland, Irish.**
Italy	**Romain, Romayne, Rome, Room, Roome.**
Netherlands	**Dutch, Dutchman.**
Norway	**Norman, Normand** (but also Norman French).
Portugal	**Pettengale, Pettingale, Pettingell, Portugal, Puttergill.**
Scotland	**Scollan, Scotland, Scott, Scutts.**
Spain	**Spain, Spanier.**
Wales	**Walch, Wallace, Walles, Wallis, Walsh, Walsman, Welch, Wellish, Wellsman, Welsh.**

Chapter 9
Making a Name for Yourself

A great many people have a burning ambition to make a name for themselves. Although 'name' here is used for 'reputation', the name itself remains of great importance. If it is to be widely used and remembered, other people must be able to say it and spell it easily, and it must not suggest anything undesirable or silly. At the same time, a slight dash of the unusual is welcome to provide the necessary individuality. Many of our surnames, casually bestowed centuries ago and badly treated since, do not fulfil these criteria. Bearers of such names are left with little alternative but to change them if they really are set on a public life. They must begin quite literally by making a name for themselves.

Stage names

The world of entertainment naturally comes immediately to mind. Stage names are an accepted part of the profession. Among those who have adapted their real surnames to some purpose are Dirk **Bogarde**, otherwise Derek Gentron Jules Gaspard Ulric van den **Bogaerde**; Fred **Astaire**—Frederick **Austerlitz**; Danny **Kaye**—David Daniel **Kominsky**; Jerry **Lewis**—Joseph **Levitch**; Greta **Garbo**—Greta **Gustaffson**.

Bing Crosby and **Bob Hope**. Both surnames are real, deriving from English place names. **Bing**, formerly **Bingo**, is a nickname, deriving ultimately from an American place name. **Bob** was formerly **Les**, which led to **Hope-less**, and a change of name.

The smallest possible change was made by Warren **Beatty**, formerly **Beaty**. His sister, Shirley Maclean Beaty, emerged as Shirley **Maclaine**. **Liberace** is one who retained his real surname but dropped the **Wladziu Valentino** that preceded it. Others have preferred to take more drastic action and forget the old surname completely. Well-known examples include Diana **Dors**, formerly Diana **Fluck**; Judy **Garland**—Frances **Gumm**; Kirk **Douglas**—Issur Danielovitch **Demsky**; Engelbert **Humperdinck**—Arnold **Dorsey**.

Politicians can hardly be described as entertainers, but they also need names that the public can cope with. Spiro **Agnew** understandably adapted his Greek family name, **Anagnostopoulos**, for this reason. Such changes differ from the adoption of political pseudonyms, which have been used in countries such as Russia. **Stalin**, 'steel', was chosen by **I. V. Dzhugashvili**, whose real name derived from a word meaning 'dross'. **Lenin**'s name was meant to be a reminder of political disturbances on the River **Lena**, in Siberia, though it exists as a real name, derived from **Alexander**. Lenin's real name was **Ulyanov**.

Mention of Russian names brings us back to stage names, for in certain circles, such as the ballet, they have great prestige. Those not as fortunate as Rudolf **Nureyev**, who is able to use his real name, have sometimes adopted one that has a suitably Russian-sounding flavour. Alice **Marks** became Alicia **Markova**, while Patrick **Healey-Kay** changed to Anton **Dolin**. The dignity and romanticism of such names contrasts interestingly with the names of some other dancers, who appear in the Parisian Crazy Horse Cabaret. The latter appear under such evocative names (and little else) as Pamela **Boum-Boum**, Polly **Underground** and Rita **Cadillac**.

Pen names

Writers' pseudonyms have been used far longer than stage names and often for different reasons. The desire is not necessarily to escape from an unfortunate name, but genuinely to conceal the writer's true identity. In the past it was sometimes thought that readers would be prejudiced against women writers, so many of them wrote as men or tried to conceal their sex in non-committal names, such as those used by the Brontë sisters, **Currer**, **Ellis** and **Acton Bell**. Other authors have been ashamed of their works for one reason or another and have not wished anyone to know their true identities. In modern times there are authors who would flood the market if they used their own name all the time, and a string of pseudonyms becomes necessary. A single pen name can, on the other hand, conceal the fact that several different authors are writing the stories concerned. Finally, if an author has made himself something of an authority in one area, he may feel that another name is required when he turns to pastures new.

One would expect authors to choose pen names that have linguistic point to them. **Lewis Carroll** has a suitably etymological connection with **Charles Lutwidge Dodgson**, its inventor. Lutwidge is a form of **Ludwig**, which can be directly translated as Lewis. Charles is **Carolus** in Latin, and Carroll simply adapts it slightly. The nineteenth-century

Some People Who Made a Name for Themselves

Anouk Aimee Françoise Sorya

Julie Andrews Julia Elizabeth Wells

Pier Angeli Anna Maria Pierangeli

Mary Astor Lucille Langehanke

Lauren Bacall Betty Pepske

Eva Bartok Eva Sjöke

Jack Benny Benjamin Kubelsky

Irving Berlin Israel Baline

Sarah Bernhardt Rosine Bernard

Scott Brady Gerald Tierney

Dora Bryan Dora Broadbent

Richard Burton Richard Jenkins

Rory Calhoun Francis Timothy Durfin

Phyllis Calvert Phyllis Bickle

Eddie Cantor Edward Israel Isskowitz

Jeannie Carson Jean Shufflebottom

Jeff Chandler Ira Grossel

Lee J. Cobb Lee Jacoby

Claudette Colbert Claudette Chauchoin

Gary Cooper Frank J. Cooper

Lou Costello Louis Cristillo

Constance Cummings Constance Halverstadt

Tony Curtis Bernard Schwarz

Vic Damone Vito Farinola

Bebe Daniels Virginia Daniels

Bobby Darin Robert Walden Cassotto

Doris Day Doris Kappelhoff

Yvonne de Carlo Peggy Yvonne Middleton

Marlene Dietrich Maria Magdalene Von Losch Dietrich

Douglas Fairbanks Julius Ullman

José Ferrer José Vincente Ferrer Otero y Cintron

Gracie Fields Grace Stansfield

W. C. Fields William Claude Dukinfield

Bud Flanagan Robert Winthrop

Mitzi Gaynor Francesca Mitzi Marlene de Charney von Gerber

Sam Goldwyn Samuel Goldfish

Cary Grant Archibald Leach

Nadia Gray Nadia Kujnir-Herescu

Kathryn Grayson Zelma Hedrick

Joyce Grenfell Joyce Phipps

Jean Harlow Harlean Carpenter

Rex Harrison Reginald Carey Harrison

Laurence Harvey Larushka Skikne

Susan Hayward Edythe Marriner

Hy Hazell Hyacinth Hazel O'Higgins

Audrey Hepburn Edda Hepburn van Heemstra

William Holden William Beedle

Judy Holliday Judith Tuvim

Leslie Howard Leslie Stainer

Rock Hudson Roy Fitzgerald

Tab Hunter Art Gelien

Burl Ives Burl Icle Ivanhoe

Al Jolson Asa Yoelson

Boris Karloff William Pratt

Buster Keaton Joseph Francis Keaton

Veronica Lake Constance Keane

Hedy Lamarr Hedwig Kiesler

Dorothy Lamour Dorothy Kaumeyer

Mario Lanza Alfred Cocozza

Wilfrid Lawson Wilfrid Worsnop

Gypsy Rose Lee Louise Hovick

Peggy Lee Norma Egstrom

Herbert Lom Herbert Charles Angelo Kuchacevich ze Schluderpacheru

Sophia Loren Sofia Scicolone

Dean Martin Dino Crocetti

Tony Martin Alvin Morris

Virginia Mayo Virginia Jones

Ethel Merman Ethel Zimmerman

Ray Milland Reginald Truscott-Jones

Carmen Miranda Maria de Carmo Miranda de Cunha

Marilyn Monroe Norma Jean Baker
Anna Neagle Marjorie Robertson
Kim Novak Marilyn Novak
Ivor Novello Ivor Davies
Merle Oberon Estelle O'Brien Merle Thompson
Maureen O'Hara Maureen Fitzsimmons
Jack Palance Walter Palanuik
Cecil Parker Cecil Schwabe
Jean Parker Mae Green
Mary Pickford Gladys Smith
Jane Powell Suzanne Burce
Chips Rafferty John Goffage
Ted Ray Charles Olden
Debbie Reynolds Mary Frances Reynolds
Cliff Richard Harold Webb
George Robey George Edward Wade
Ginger Rogers Virginia McMath
Roy Rogers Leonard Slye
Mickey Rooney Joe Yule
Romy Schneider Rosemarie Albach-Retty
Randolph Scott Randolph Crane

Mack Sennett Mickall Sinott
Moira Shearer Moira King
Tommy Steele Tommy Hicks
Connie Stevens Concetta Ingolia
Gale Storm Joseph Cottle
Jacques Tati Jacques Tatischeff
Robert Taylor Spangler Arlington Brough
Terry-Thomas Thomas Terry Hoar-Stevens
Mike Todd Avrom Goldenborgen
Sophie Tucker Sophia Abuza
Lana Turner Julia Turner
Rudy Vallee Hubert Prior Vallee
Odile Versois Militza de Polikoff-Baidarov
Erich von Stroheim Hans Erich Maria Stroheim von Nordenwall
Anton Walbrook Adolf Wohlbruck
Jean Wallace Jean Wallasek
Jack Warner Jack Waters
John Wayne Marion Michael Morrison
Clifton Webb Webb Parmelee Hollenbeck
Shelley Winters Shirley Schrift
Jane Wyman Sarah Jane Fulks

Gary Glitter and **Alvin Stardust**. Both singers were known by other stage-names (**Paul Raven** and **Shane Fenton**) before a further change of name helped them to success.

writer **Ouida** looks as if she transferred her name from the city of that name in Morocco, but she herself explained it as a natural linguistic development. It represented her own attempt as a child to pronounce her middle name, **Louise**.

Aliases

These last examples once again retain a definite link with the real name, which many people who adopt a new name consider to be necessary. Traces of name magic are revealed here, for this hints at a deep-rooted belief that one's real name is somehow part of one's real self, and that complete abandonment of it will have evil consequences. Criminal records support this contention strongly, for an analysis of aliases that have been used shows that the adopted surnames normally have the same initial, number of syllables and basic sound as the originals. What appears to be a totally new name is more often drawn from the namer's immediate onomastic environment. It will be the mother's maiden name or the surname of a close friend, or a name transferred from a street or place that has strong personal associations. The link with the real past is maintained.

As we have seen, immigration into an English-speaking country can be another reason for name change and here again an attempt is often made to link with the original name. The Ukrainian Vasyl **Mykula** who became William **McCulla** showed one way of doing it. Other Russian-English pairs are **Prishchipenko—Price**, **Chernyshev—Chester**, **Grushko—Grey**. Direct translation, e.g. of German **Müller**, French **Meunier**, Hungarian **Molnar**, Dutch **Mulder** into English **Miller** achieves a similar result.

Maiden names

But by far the commonest reason for a surname change is marriage. Here, of course, there is no question of a woman consciously choosing a new name; she is simply re-exposed to the complex of accidental factors that gave her a surname in the first place. As for the name that has been so much a part of her life for many years, she finds that it becomes a mere maiden name. It is instantly reduced to at best middle-name status, and perhaps even less.

The implications of this marital name change have been much commented on, but although one reads at regular intervals of women who insist on using their maiden names after marriage, no general protest seems to be made. Suggestions that both husband and wife should take on a new name at marriage—perhaps blending parts of their surnames—are not taken very seriously. The blocking up of both surnames with hyphens between them has unfortunate connotations of pretentiousness, apart from leading to some very unwieldy combinations. Perhaps the problem will only be solved if we finally abolish hereditary surnames altogether. They are already superfluous in many ways. If we were allocated an individual number name at birth and used that for all official purposes, we could probably get by very well with one other personal name.

Other surname changes

Meanwhile, however, a large number of ordinary people who are not seeking public fame or trying to conceal their identities, change their surnames every year. They make use of a very simple legal process to rid themselves of a name which for one reason or another is an embarrassment to them. Who can possibly blame the Mr. **Bugg** who became a **Howard**, or the gentlemen called **Bub**, **Holdwater**, **Poopy**, **Piddle**, **Honeybum**, **Leakey**, **Rumpe** and **Teate** who quietly dropped these surnames a century ago? Curiously enough, they *were* criticised at the time, though the criticisms were directed at the names they adopted, thought to be too high and mighty for ordinary citizens.

Personally, I can only wonder why more people do not follow the sensible example set by these name-changers. Why on earth do *I*, for example, put up with **Dunkling**, which is frequently converted into **Dumpling** by the hard-of-hearing or malicious? I have had its replacement standing by for years, an easy-to-spell, easy-to-say, pleasant-sounding name with the most respectable literary and other associations, and not, to my knowledge, at present attached to any other family. If I do not adopt it, is it because—not being an actor by nature—I would not be able to live out my life behind an onomastic disguise? Or am I conceited

enough to think that I can overcome the natural disadvantages of my name and win through anyway? Perhaps it is simply that what is totally familiar ceases to be unusual. Then again, what is unusual for one person may seem quite normal to the next. I was surprised to see, for example, in a list of names which are all real, and which the American writer clearly considered to be strange, the name of Sir Alec **Guinness**.

Sir Alec Guinness, who has made his real name famous. He is not connected with the family of brewers.

Ideas about what is unusual also change with the passing of time. At one time somebody named **Petard**, which derives from a word meaning 'to break wind', would presumably have wanted to change it: today his friends might simply associate him vaguely with a passage in *Hamlet* and he would not feel under attack. A **Belcher**, on the other hand, was quite happy when others interpreted his name as *bel chiere*, 'pretty face'. The forgetting of this early meaning has left him sadly exposed.

Other men are quite happy with their names until they reach adulthood and take up a profession. They then fall victim to the inevitable comments about their being **Berriman** the undertaker, or **D. Kaye**, the dentist. Partnership names such as **Reid** and **Wright** for Belfast printers, and **Doolittle** and **Dally** for estate agents are also much commented on, though they do have the advantage of attracting publicity.

If you are seriously thinking of changing your surname you would do well, for your descendants' sake, to begin it with a letter near the front of the alphabet. The custom when groups of people are gathered together for any purpose of working through them in alphabetical order has had a serious effect on people named **Young** and the like, psychologists tell us. They are constantly made to feel insignificant because they are dealt with last. Another consideration in this modern world is an international one. In Europe, certainly, there will be in the future far more mixing of English-speaking people with others who speak French, German, Italian and the like than ever before. It will be necessary to remember that what is simple in one language may cause great difficulty in another. When Mr. **Heath** was in France he found that his seemingly uncomplicated name was a severe obstacle for the French.

Psychological effects of surnames

If you are *not* thinking about a surname change, perhaps you should be. At the very least you should make an honest evaluation of your surname to see whether it is a definite hindrance to you, or whether it will be so for your children. As an adult you may be well aware that your surname is totally irrelevant in any evaluation of your total worth as a human being, but your children will spend many important years in a group where there is no such awareness. Studies such as that made by Christopher Bagley and Louise Evan-Wong ('Psychiatric Disorder and Adult and Peer Group Rejection of the Child's Name') prove beyond all reasonable doubt that children who consider a surname derisive will transfer their feelings about the name to the person who bears it. The attitude of his class-mates is likely to reinforce a child's negative opinion of himself, which will have been influenced by his own assessment of his name.

A point not pursued in the above-mentioned article is that if children evaluate unusual names, they presumably evaluate *all* names. How does a **Smith** child react, one wonders, when he realises that he has a very common name? It could conceivably lead him to think that he must be a very ordinary person. And what effect does it have on a child who discovers that he happens to possess a rather distinguished name? I can personally recall, as a child, envying a boy in the class *because of his name*, which happened to be **Nelson**. Surely I am not the only one to have known such feelings? And was the young Nelson so self-confident and assured partly because of his name?

I am not advocating a change of surname as a way of adjusting a person's psychological balance, or as a way of instantly improving his self-image. It appears to be a belief of the Kabalarians, founded in 1926 by Alfred J. Parker and based in Vancouver, that the one will automatically lead to the other. An article in *The Province*, December 1972, gives several examples of name changes advised by this organisation. They include **Jennifer Lulham** to **Alannah Matthew**, **Dorothy Rayner** to **Dhorea Delain**, **Marian Birch** to **Natallia Hohn**.

The very existence of the Kabalarians, and their ability to attract adherents, proves that a belief in the association of name with character can be carried into adult life. The name-changers clearly believe that mystic qualities of the new name will rub off on to them. They speak in the newspaper article of immediate and beneficial results of taking on a new name, and in this one can readily believe. But one can believe, too, that it boosts a normal person's morale to be well groomed and dressed. The effects of the new name will last no longer than the effects of make-up if the underlying attitude is wrong.

A short course in the history of first names and surnames, built into the normal school curriculum, would certainly help to adjust children's attitudes to their own and one another's names. Such a course, perhaps designed as a project, would have many other educational advantages, particularly relating to history. But a major aim of teachers would have to be the instillation of a common-sense attitude about both first names and surnames. They are an interesting, not to say fascinating, social custom, but they have nothing whatever to do with a person's character. This realisation is just as vital for the adult name-changers. If they decide to change their names in order to change their public image, just as they might decide to change their hair-style or clothes, then by all means let them change them with that in mind. What they must not believe is that they are actually changing themselves.

Name change, or a straightening out of attitudes by parents and teachers—these are two possible solutions to a problem that certainly exists. There is a third. In Britain the idea is accepted on the whole that a school uniform is useful for removing signs of individual family status. Perhaps the concept of a school name should also be considered. Children entering secondary school could choose from a list of possibly neutralised names, e.g. colour names, and retain these for their school lives. However strange such an idea might seem, it is in this direction, or so it seems to me, that those few psychological studies so far made clearly point.

The name-makers

But to return to those adults who are considering changing their name: where should they turn for guidance? Should they begin, for instance, with the most practised and prolific name-makers in our society, the writers of fiction? Novelists as name-makers provide an interesting study. The writers still occasionally fall back on the literary convention of type-names, the **Shallow** of Shakespeare or the Mrs. **Slipslop** of Fielding, but when they do so the characters concerned are usually personifications of abstract ideas rather than ordinary people. At their best, novelists have a feeling for a name's associated characteristics—for surnames have these just as first names do—and use a name that works below the conscious level to achieve the desired result. Dickensian characters such as **Pickwick** and **Scrooge** seem to be perfectly named. One wonders whether Pickwick appealed to the author because it partly echoed his own name, or did he simply see the name somewhere and jot it in his notebook, as he frequently did with names. Scrooge seems to be a made-up name, based on the word 'screw' as in the sentence used by Thackeray: 'I must screw and save in order to pay off the money.'

But authors are not always objective in their naming. They often seem to have a liking for particular sounds, and they return to these again and again. Thackeray clearly fell in love with the surname **Crump**, which actually exists and originally meant 'stooping'. He used it for three different characters. He has another character named **Crampton**. Dickens, as it happens, has a **Crumpton** and a **Crupp**. Both Dickens and Thackeray made use of **Crawley** as a character name, and between them they cover a wide range of other names beginning with 'Cr-'. Those they omit are accounted for by Sir Walter Scott, George Eliot, Jane Austen, Thomas Hardy, John Galsworthy and Anthony Trollope, all of whom begin the surnames of more than one character with these letters. Perhaps they pay a subconscious tribute to the first fictional character in English literature, **Robinson Crusoe**, but they may be revealing what a linguist might call their 'phonaesthetic preference'.

An analysis of any writer would probably reveal quite quickly his particular likes in this respect. Graham Greene, for example, has characters called **Rank**, **Rolt** and **Rowe**, **Rennit**, **Rimmer** and **Robinson**. If we ourselves were faced with the problem of naming a series of characters in different books we too would no doubt fall into some kind of pattern. If we tried to make a name for ourselves we would make use again of our linguistic preferences. This would be something to beware of, for it would be subjective. There is no point, surely, in changing one's name unless one is totally objective about it. The name would be meant to appeal to other people, not oneself.

Namesakes

Which surnames *do* please people? There have been no studies made that I am aware of which could answer that question. The names of popular people presumably have a head start on others, but it would be an error for anyone to turn himself into a namesake. I can think of nothing more depressing than having to answer the constantly repeated question: 'Not *the* **James Stewart**? (or whoever) with 'No', or a wan smile.

Some people evidently enjoy being namesakes. The Jim Smith Society was founded in 1969 and has annual gatherings in America. One object of the society, according to a letter from its founder, James H. Smith, Jr., of Camp Hill, Pennsylvania, is to seek 'background information about acts of heroism by Jim Smiths'. Such as founding a Jim Smith Society, perhaps. I gather that a lot of fun is had by all concerned at the annual meetings, and perhaps we shall see more societies of this type in the future.

Becoming a partial namesake of someone famous might be an answer to the name-change problem. A little glory will rub off, possibly, and one will avoid the jokes. Reflected glory of a kind has been turned to commercial advantage in recent years by the firms which supply coats of arms. What happens here is that a coat of arms which has been awarded to a family is treated as being attached to the surname rather than the family concerned. In fact, a coat of arms in its 'undifferenced' form can be used only by the head of the family to which it was granted. Other members of the family use it too, but incorporate cadency marks. A man cannot sell his coat of arms or give someone else permission to use it, so there is absolutely no question of another family, which happens to have the same name, having the right to use it. This does not deter a great many people from displaying in their homes someone else's coat of arms with the shared family name written beneath it. There is little doubt that many people confuse coats of arms with clan tartans as far as usage is concerned, though the firms concerned usually explain the situation fairly clearly in the small print of their advertisements.

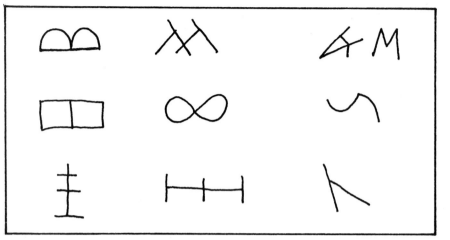

A primitive kind of heraldry is seen in the 'personal marks' of seventeenth-century farmers who could not write, but had to sign documents frequently. Those shown (from left to right) were used by Bartholomew Martin, William Rowbottom, George Males, Thomas Dust, William Bagley, Francis Seaton, John Craythorn, John Austin, senior, John Austin, junior.

Perhaps no harm is done, other than to the occasional outraged head of a family who sees his personal property being trampled on, as it were. He might console himself with the thought that those meaningless little plaques are exerting a little name magic, enabling some anonymous people to feel somehow more dignified and content with the names they bear. If name magic is to continue having an influence, even in our apparently civilised society, it might as well have some positive effects as well as negative.

I have talked at some length about changing names, but my main object has been to stimulate a few thoughts about the meaning in modern times of the surnames that we inherit. Changing one's name is easy from a legal point of view, but it is understandable that many people are reluctant to do it. Those of us who put up with what we have must console ourselves with the thought that a change might not bring about the desired result in any case. Our bright new name might be brushed aside in favour of a nickname, and nicknames are not always complimentary as we shall see in the next chapter. Or perhaps our new names would simply fail to convince. Mr. A. A. Willis makes this point in a story he passed on to me about a gentleman named **Brown** who applied to change his name to **Smith**. He was asked why he wanted to make this change, as he had changed his name only six months previously from **Gorfinckel** to **Brown**. His reply was: 'Becos ven pipple say to me: "Vot vas your name before it was Smith?" I vant to be able to say: "It was Brown—so there."'

Chapter 10
Eking Out Names

With his first name, middle name and surname it might seem that the average person was adequately identified, but far from it. We are all given additional names for official purposes—mostly number names or code names—and most of us acquire an unofficial extra name as well. We use the term 'nickname' to describe the latter, which is usually friendly. The word 'sobriquet', which we borrowed centuries ago from the French, is also useful. It describes a name which is decidedly unfriendly, meant to cut a person down to size. The etymology of the word seems to hint at a 'taming', for the original meaning was 'a chuck under the chin', as when a horse is reined in.

'Nickname' itself simply means 'an additional name', with no bias towards a good or bad name and no indication as to whether a person, place or thing is involved. The word derives from the expression 'an eke name', which later became 'a nekename'. This is the 'eke' we use when we say that we must 'eke out our supplies'. Traced back far enough it probably links up with the Latin word *augere*, which is the root of words such as 'augment'.

This explanation of 'nickname' is fairly modern, by the way. Dr. Johnson thought it must derive from the French *nique*, which means a gesture (but not a name) of mockery. Harry Long, a nineteenth-century writer on names, appears to have connected it with the German *nicken*, which means 'to nod', for he explains it as 'a name given with a contemptuous nick of the head'. Long also explained 'sobriquet' wrongly, but he can perhaps be forgiven because of his fine comment that nicknames and sobriquets are 'biographies crowded into a word'.

To-names

We have already separated out bynames as a special kind of nickname, acting as a temporary surname. There is another special kind of personal nickname which is sometimes called a *to-name*. This is an extra name that becomes necessary for identification purposes in communities where many people bear the same surname. John McPhee, for example, in his book about the Scottish island of Colonsay (*The Crofter and the Laird*) describes the substitute surnames taken on by the McNeills and McAllisters.

Many of them are known by place names, of which there is an ample supply. Only 138 people lived on the island when McPhee was there, but there were 1,600 recorded place names—with the most minor landmarks being counted as places.

Another system is for a husband and his wife to borrow each other's first names. **Peter McAllister** is known as **Peter Bella**, his wife as **Bella Peter**. Such a system might be very useful at an ordinary social gathering, such as a cocktail-party, and it would certainly add a touch of charm. The more usual kind of patronymic nickname is seen in **Mary Calum Coll**, Calum being the lady's father, Coll her grandfather. **Donald Gibbie** is the son of Gilbert, but his cousin is **Angus the Post**.

Welsh nicknames

This last example naturally reminds us of Wales, where the commonness of **Jones** traditionally necessitated nicknames. An article in *The Times* (December 1970) by Trevor Fishlock, however, claimed that names like **Jones the Meat**, **Flat Nose Jones**, **Jones King's Arms**, **Jones Popbottle** and **Jones the Bread** were fast disappearing. In modern times people know fewer of their neighbours than they did in the older communities, and there is less need to distinguish between individuals. One hopes that the folk-wit displayed in the names will be recorded before it is too late. **Dai Piano**, for instance, was not the musician his nickname might suggest. He was for ever cadging cigarettes and saying that he had left his own at home on the piano. **Amen Jones** and **Jones Hallelujah** were men who responded over-enthusiastically in chapel.

Sartorial as well as verbal habits could provide nicknames, as in **Jones Spats** and **Harry Greensuit**. A favourite food or drink could lead to names like **Jones Caerphilly** and **Dai Brown Ale**. The phrasal equivalents of activity surnames—**Jones the Milk**, **Eddie Click-Click** (for a photographer)—were found everywhere, as were locative names—**Jones Cwmglo**, **Jones Craig-Ddu** (from farms), **Will Plough**, **Huw Railway Inn** (from public houses).

In any community where surnames failed to distinguish individuals, nicknames were formerly added or substituted. In the nineteenth century the shopkeepers in towns like Peterhead would write down the *fee-names* of their customers. Their account-books reveal names like **Buckie**, **Beauty**, **Bam**, **Biggelugs**, **The Smack**, **Snuffers**, **Toothie**, **Doodle**, **Carrot** and **Nap**. The novelist Henry Treece has described Black Country nicknames that were applied to the many **Fosters** and **Wilkes**. A character in *The Rebels*, himself nicknamed **Bacca Chops** because of his habit of chewing plug tobacco, remarks on **Ode Mouldyhead**, whose hair grew in patches, **Ode Foxy**, **Gentleman**, **Whackey**, **Dragon**, **Bullet**, **Brick End** and **Soft Water Jack**.

In the case of royal nicknames, a similarity of first names may be one of the reasons that brings them into being. The kings took on a sequential surname, **The First**, **The Second**, etc., but their subjects usually replaced this with a descriptive nickname. **Richard Lionheart** was more fortunate than **Richard the Coxcomb** and **Richard the Boar**.

Some Famous Nicknames

The Admirable Crichton, a Scottish scholar who gained his Master of Arts degree at the age of fourteen.

Beau or **Buck Brummel**, patronised by George IV until Brummel's 'Who's your fat friend?' remark deliberately insulted him.

Bloody Mary Queen Mary, daughter of Henry VIII, who persecuted the Protestants.

Blue Beard Possibly meant to refer to Giles de Retz, Marquis of Laval.

Boney Napoleon Bonaparte.

Bozzy James Boswell.

Capability Launcelot **Brown**, who always saw 'capabilities' in the gardens he looked at.

Conversation Richard **Sharpe**, a critic.

Crum-Hell One of the nicknames of Oliver **Cromwell**, whose name was pronounced Crum-ell in his own time. Also known by names such as the **Almighty Nose**, **King Oliver.**

Dizzy Benjamin Disraeli.

Elocution John **Walker**, author of a pronouncing dictionary and teacher of elocution.

Farmer George George II, said to have the dress, manners and tastes of a farmer, and to have referred more to his farming problems than matters of State when opening Parliament.

Goldy Oliver Goldsmith.

Hotspur Henry Percy, son of the Earl of Northumberland, so named because of the fiery temper he could not control.

Iron Duke The Duke of Wellington. An iron steam-boat named after the Duke was known as the *Iron Duke*. The nickname was later jokingly applied to the Duke himself.

Ironside Edmund II, from his iron armour.

King Coll Colley Cibber.

King of Bath or **Beau Nash**, who managed social events at Bath.

Lionheart Richard I, for his courage, though one writer tells of his plucking out the heart from a lion.

Man in the Iron Mask The great historical mystery man in France. Guessing his identity is as much a sport as deciding who wrote Shakespeare's plays for him. A summary of the theories appears in Frey's *Sobriquets and Nicknames*.

Merry Andrew Andrew Borde, Physician to Henry VIII.

Merry Monarch Charles II.

Old Harry and **Old Nick** are the best-known nicknames of the devil, who is also known as **Auld Clootie**, **Auld Hangie**, **Nickie-Ben**, **Old Scratch**, etc.

Old Hickory Andrew Jackson, because he was as tough as old hickory.

Old Rough and Ready Zachary Taylor, twelfth President of the USA.

Prince of Showmen Phineas Barnum.

Railway King George Hudson of Yorkshire, but also applied to William Vanderbilt.

Rob Roy Robert Macgregor, later Campbell, the Robin Hood of Scotland.

Sixteen-String Jack John Rann, a highwayman renowned for his stylish dress, especially the eight tags on each side of his breeches which gave him his name. Hanged in 1774.

Stonewall Thomas **Jackson**, so called after another general remarked that he was standing there in front of the enemy like a stone wall.

Swedish Nightingale Jenny Lind, later Jenny Goldschmidt, the singer.

Tumbledown Dick Richard Cromwell, son of Oliver.

Turnip-Hoer George I, who talked of planting turnips in St. James's Park.

The Unready Ethelred II, who was without 'rede' or counsel.

The Venerable Bede, ecclesiastical historian of the eighth century.

Virgin Queen Elizabeth I.

Water Poet John Taylor, who worked as a Thames waterman.

The Georges likewise varied from **The Turnip-Hoer** and **Farmer George** to **Augustus** and **George the Greater**. In France the eighteen kings called Louis naturally attracted nicknames. **Baboon**, **The Foolish**, **The Universal Spider**, **The Fat** and **The Indolent** were among the less complimentary, but one or two were rather better favoured. The last Louis had a nickname which is impossible to translate, punning on his liking for oysters (*des huîtres*) and his sequential surname, 18 (*dix-huit*).

Other reasons for nicknames

It would be foolish, however, to imply that personal nicknames are always to-names, given because they are genuinely needed for identification purposes. They arise for a number of other reasons, reflecting such human habits as ornamenting what is plain, being clever, showing dislike or affection, being funny, being secretive, showing group membership. Most of these reasons could be applied to the use of slang, with which nicknames have a great deal in common.

A desire for linguistic ornamentation is seen in daily speech, not just in the books of the creative writer. Not that every speaker is a creator of slang or nicknames, any more than he is a painter or musician. It is usually impossible to say who does create new words or names. Somehow they seem to appear and are used, probably by those who particularly wish to show that they are in the know, that they share a special knowledge.

Family members naturally share a special knowledge of one another, and this may well extend to nicknames. They are frequently bestowed on children by the parents, though more often by the father than the mother, it would seem. A teacher friend discovered recently that his ten-year-olds were known at home as **Crunchy**, **Boo**, **Squitface**, **Popsy Dinkums**, **Woo**, **Moonbeam**, **Muff** (girls), and **Dilly**, **Dump**, **Hug**, **Longlegs**, **Luscious Legs**, **Bigpants** (boys). It is much rarer for children to have a nickname for either parent, but Angus Wilson, in his *Anglo-Saxon Attitudes*, may be reflecting a real-life situation known to him when he makes **Thingy** the mother's nickname.

Other nicknames connected with children are those that arise at school. Children invariably seem to nickname one another and their teachers, sometimes following intricate paths to arrive at the final name. The point is illustrated in a letter from Mr. James B. Fryer, commenting on **Whiskers Bowles**. He writes: 'Bowles became "bowels". The Latin for "bowels" is *viscera*. Pronouncing the "v" in Latin as "w" we get *wiscera*, whence the easy transfer to "whiskers".' One can compare the French headmaster who became **The Doe** (*La Biche*). Trying to maintain his dignity as he crossed the playground he stuck his chest out and looked rather haughty. A pupil remarked quietly that he was 'as proud as Artaban', a normal French simile that refers to a character in a play. **Artaban** became his nickname, but was soon changed to the more agreeable sounding **Artabiche**. This was finally shortened to **Biche**.

If anything like these complications led to the formation of medieval bynames, the philologists clearly have an impossible task before them where the elucidation of some surnames is concerned. Some of the bynames, one would think, must have been inspired in some way by whatever personal name an individual already had. Nicknames of this type are certainly very frequent. Mr. **Fryer**, for instance, remarks that he himself became **Tuck**, which one might call an *associated transfer*. A colleague whose surname is **Snow** is known as **Fairy** because of the soap powder *Fairy Snow*. Dr. T. Keough has also told me of a friend in his Canadian home-town who was **Twenty Below** because his name was **Ozero**. His sister was called **Scratch Below** for a slightly different reason.

Old **Boots** of Ripon, who could hold a coin between his nose and chin, had an occupational nickname. He cleaned customers' shoes at an inn. Miss Ann Bailey was known as **Angel** by the legal profession because of her long-fought claim to the Great Angel Estates. **Nice New** was a street character in Reading (Berks) in the early nineteenth century. He took his name from a street cry.

Link nicknames are even more common. Those based on first names we usually refer to as 'diminutives' or 'pet names', but **Maggie** from **Margaret** is just as much a nickname as **The Barrow Boy** from **Nabarro**. A newspaper correspondent, commenting on the nicknames of her class-mates, reveals that her own is **Ballbag**, based on her surname **Ball**. I am sometimes obliged to answer to **Dunkers**, and my nine-year-old son tells me he is **Dunks** to his friends.

Miss Ball goes on to say that her girl-friends have such nicknames as **Bun**, **Bondy**, **Snuff**, **Crunk**, **Melon**, **Twiggy** and **Spindle**, while the boys in the class are known by such names as **Primrose**, **Flapper**, **Squelch**, **Haggis**, **Leggy**, **Reverend**, **Fizz** and **Ribs**, all of which reveal a cheerful friendliness. Some of these are clearly descriptive, others might be further examples of surname links. With names like **Crunk** one suspects a verbal incident, perhaps a slip of the tongue one day when another word was intended.

Incident nicknames

Verbal incidents are well represented in nicknames, in the adult world as well as at school level. **Azzerwuz**, **Juicy**, **Banjo** and **Rabbit** have come into being in this way, from the favourite expressions 'As I was saying' and 'D'you see?'; because of a constantly repeated remark about being 'highly strung', and because of a teacher's remark about a certain family breeding 'like rabbits'. A comment by the head of a typing-pool: 'Let's have no bloomers today, girls', immediately earned her the nickname **Naughty-Naughty**, while a favourite remark, 'Leave it to me', was the reason for **The Pawnbroker**.

G. B. Stern, in her book *A Name To Conjure With*, tells of the house-party she attended at which all the guests adopted nicknames for the week-end. H. G. Wells was already **Jaguar**, but Miss Stern was unnamed. She remarked that she would like to be something between a tigress and a sphinx, whereupon he dubbed her **Tynx**.

A few pages later Miss Stern describes an incident name of another kind, perhaps what one might call an 'internal incident'. Her eight-year-old friend, Naomi,

> 'swallowed a penny and was seriously ill and away from school for several months. When she returned . . . she was greeted callously and a little cruelly by Upper and Lower School with "Hello, **Moneybox**!", while reeling from our own wit, we would beg her to cough up a penny to buy a bun, and keep the halfpenny change.'

Children *would* reel with their own wit, of course. They love playing with words and names and are delighted with names like **Woolly Wog**, **Ruby Nose** and **Lumber Bonce** for their sound alone. Where meanings are concerned, they have little time for euphemism, preferring to be simple and direct. Those who are named usually take no offence. Another of my own nicknames, **Pug**, was hardly complimentary, but I distinctly recall sharing the joke when it was proposed. There is a degree of pleasure gained *in being named* which offsets the thought of insult, and if one accepts the nickname it tends to lose its force in any case.

Descriptive nicknames

In a classroom situation, one or two of the brighter children will probably be throwing suggestions for nicknames into the continuous flow of group conversation. There will be instant acceptance, or counter-suggestion, or rejection. If the whole class is present and can see the steps that have led to the name, it will have point to the whole group. A larger community, such as a village, may have to use simpler names, based on characteristics that will be obvious to all. Many of these will be visual names, for just as locative names began by being a person's address, so these names are often verbal portraits. A good summary of their origins was given in 1682 by Sir Henry Piers, writing about the Irish:

> 'They take much liberty, and seem to do it with delight, in giving of nicknames; and if a man have any imperfection or evil habit, he shall be sure to hear of it in the nickname. Thus if he be blind, lame, squint-eyed, gray-eyed, be a stammerer in speech, be left-handed, to be sure he shall have one of these added to his name, so also from the colour of his hair, as black, red, yellow, brown, etc., and from his age, as young, old, or from what he addicts himself to, or much delights in, as in draining, building, fencing or the like; so that no man whatever can escape a nickname, who lives amongst them.'

Traditional nicknames

Nicknames *ought* to be tailor-made and meaningful, but there are some which are hand-me-downs, others which come as almost meaningless accessories with one's surname. The former arise partly because there are a number of human features which are always commented on, and a limited number of ways in which the allusions can be made. Baldness, for example, begins by attracting a name like **Baldy** or **Patch**, or is immediately contradicted with a name like **Curly**. Metaphorical descriptions then begin to apply, such as **Dutchy** (because of the appearance of some Dutch cheeses) and **Skating Rink**, shortened to **Skates**. There is a tendency to pass on such names, particularly in the Services, to each new generation of bald-headed men. There is still room for wit, of course, and not every bald-headed man needs to be dubbed with a cliché. A former teacher of mine was, I hope, grateful for his own **Cue-Ball**, bestowed by some unknown wag.

A list of nicknames used by school-children, collected by Iona and Peter Opie and published in *The Lore and Language of Schoolchildren*, shows how these avid nicknamers deal with a number of features. A fat person may be **Balloon**, **Barrel**, **Barrel-Belly**, **Billy Bunter**, **Buster**, **Chubby**, **Chunky**, **Diddle-Diddle Dumpling**, **Falstaff**, **Fat Belly**, **Fatty Harbuckle**, **Football**, **Guts**, **Piggy**, **Podge**, **Porky**, **Steam-Roller**, **Tank**, **Tubby** or **Two Ton Tessy** among others. But wide as this selection may appear to be, there is a great deal of duplication, for probably every class in every school has at least one person whose obesity calls for comment. The Opies make the interesting point that when children use names like Fatty Harbuckle (as they spell it) they are usually unaware that they are commemorating a real person, Roscoe **Arbuckle**, a star of the silent screen until his career ended in a scandal. It is unlikely, too, that many of them have actually read the Bunter stories or know of the original Two-Ton Tessie. Such evidence clearly shows the traditional nature of these nicknames.

WHEN IS THE BALLOON GOING UP ?

Clan nicknames

But though traditional and formalised, such names are at least still meaningful, telling other people something about the person named. Another class of personal nicknames, which have sometimes been described as 'inseparables', have almost no meaning at all. They are treated as if they were clan nicknames, applicable to anyone bearing a certain surname. The system leads to men called **Martin** automatically being nicknamed **Pincher** when they join the Royal Navy. Originally the nickname applied to Admiral Sir William F. Martin, a disciplinarian who had ratings put under arrest ('pinched') for the smallest offence. His

Clan Nicknames

Some examples of nicknames that have become associated with particular surnames.

Aggie *Weston*, naval, because of Miss Agnes Weston, who spent her life helping seamen.

Bang-Bang *Cannon*.

Bill *Sykes* or *Sikes*, because of the Dickensian character in *Oliver Twist*.

Birdy for *Sparrow*, *Wren*, etc.

Blacky *White*.

Blanco *White*, from the trade name of a whitener.

Bodger *Lees*.

Bogey *Harris*.

Bottomless *Pitt*, used by those who know that William Pitt was so called.

Bricks(an) *Morter*.

Bronco *Rider*.

Buck Taylor, from a member of Buffalo Bill's team.

Bungy *Cooper* or *Cowper*, naval, because of the bunghole in a cask.

Bunny *Warren*.

Bushey *Fox*.

Butch(er) *Lamb*.

Captain *Kettle* or *Kidd*.

Chalky *White*.

Chippa *Wood*.

Chunka *Wood*.

Daisy *Bell*, from the music-hall song.

Dandy *Evans*, naval.

Dick(y) *Richards*, or *Bird*.

Ding-Dong *Bell*.

Dixie *Dean*, from the name of a famous footballer.

Dodger *Long*.

Dolly *Gray* or *Grey*, from the music-hall song.

Doughy *Baker*.

Drawers *Chester*.

Duck(y) or **Ducks** *Drake*.

Dusty *Miller*, or *Rhodes* (roads).

Dutchy *Holland*.

Fanny *Adams*, from the name of a murder victim originally.

Fishy *Pike*, *Chubb*, etc.

Foxy *Reynolds*, because of Reynard.

Gillie *Potter*, after the famous broadcaster of that name.

Ginger *Beer*.

Gipsy *Lee* or *Leigh*, because of Gipsy Rose Lee.

Gunner *Moore* or *Muir*, from the name of a boxer.

Hackney *Downs* or *Marsh*, from the place names.

Happy *Day*.

Hooky *Walker*, because of a man known to seamen who had a large nose.

Hopper *Long*.

Iron *Duke*, because of Wellington's nickname.

Jelly *Pearson*.

Jimmy *Riddell*, from Cockney rhyming slang.

Johnny *Walker*, because of the whisky.

Jumper *Cross*.

Knobby *Coles*.

Lefty *Wright*.

Mark(s) *Spencer*, because of the high-street shops.

Muddy *Waters*, or *Walters*.

Ned *Kelly*.

Needle *Cotton*.

Nellie *Wallace*, because of a music-hall star.

Nick *Carter*, for a fictional detective.

Nigger *Brown*.

Nobby *Clark*, said to be because clerks had to look as if they were 'nobs' or gentlemen in spite of being poorly paid.

Nocky *Knight*.

Norman *Conquest*.

Nosey *Parker*.

Nosmo *King*, from 'No Smoking' signs.

Nutty *Cox*.

Pedlar *Palmer*, the name of a boxer.

Peeler *Murphy*, probably from 'peel a spud'.

Peggy *Legg*, from Peg-Leg.

Penny *Singleton*, from the name of a film star.

Piggy *May*.

Pills *Beecham*, from the trade name.

Pony *Moore*, from the name of a minstrel.

Poppy *Tupper*.

Powder *Horne*, from a character in a strip cartoon.

Quid *Pound*.

Rabbit *Hutch*, *Hutchins* or *Hutchinson*.

Rajah *Brooks*, a reference to the first white Rajah of Sarawak, Sir James Brooks.

Rattler *Morgan*.

Reelo *Cotton*.

Rusty *Steele*.

Sandy *Brown*.

Schnozzle *Durrant*, because of *Schnozzle Durante*

Sharky *Ward*, possibly from a pirate so named.

Shiner *Bright*, thence to *Wright* and *White*. Also *Black* because a 'black-eye' is

Ned Kelly, responsible for a clan nickname.

a 'shiner'. Also *Bryant* because of 'shine a light' being associated with Bryant and May on match-boxes.

Shoey *Smith*.

Shorty *Long* or *Little*.

Shover *Smith*.

Slide *Overett*.

Slider *Cross*.

Slinger *Wood(s)*.

Smitty *Smith*.

Smokey *Holmes*, perhaps a reference to Sherlock Holmes's famous pipe.

Smudger *Smith*.

Smutty *Black*.

Snip *Taylor*. Also *Parsons*, from parsnip.

Snowball, -drop, -flake, *Snow*
Snowy *Baker*, referring to white flour.

Soapy *Hudson*, *Pears*, *Watson*, from names associated commercially with soap.

Spider *Webb*.

Spike *Sullivan*, possibly because itinerant potato-pickers gave the name Sullivan when working on the 'spike'. Or from a prize-fighter.

Splinter *Wood*.

Spokey *Wheeler*.

Spongey *Baker*.

Spud *Murphy*, both 'spud' and 'murphy' being slang terms for a potato.

Steve *Donoghue* or *Donovan*, originally from the name of a jockey.

Swank *Russell*.

Sticker *Leach*.

Stitch *Taylor*.

Stormy *Gale*.

Sugar *Cain* or *Kane*.

Timber *Wood(s)*.

Tod *Hunter*, 'tod' being a fox.

Tom *King*, originally from a highwayman's name.

Topper *Brown*.

Topsy *Turner*, a play on 'topsyturvey'.

Tottie *Bell*.

Tubby *Martin*.

Tug *Wilson*.

Wheeler *Johnson*.

Wiggy *Bennett*.

Wilkie *Collins*, from the name of the novelist.

Youngy *Moore*, a joke based on *Old Moore's Almanack*.

name is still so well known in naval circles that associated transfer of his nickname follows.

A modern person so nicknamed reveals by it that he has probably been in the Navy, but nothing more personal is commented on. It is presumably the desire to emphasise this connection with a particular body of men that causes such nicknames to be given, but all spontaneity has been lost. There is not the range of names still available, for instance, at school where associated transfer is simply one method of nicknaming which *may* be used.

Criminal nicknames

Tradition dictates the use of clan nicknames, but a more practical reason for the use of nicknames is to conceal one's identity, especially from officials such as the police. It is very noticeable that criminals, both great and small, are very fond of nicknames. Their great ambition seems to be

to achieve the fame, or notoriety as we would call it, of such figures as **Scarface Al Capone** or **Jack the Ripper**. The public accepts the right of criminals to have nicknames, and is quick to bestow one on someone whose identity is unknown. A **Charlie Chopper** was terrorising New York in the early 1970s, the name apparently having been coined by local children. Most people remember **The Boston Strangler**, who will probably go down in criminal history under that nickname rather than under his real name, Albert De Salvo.

An early example of a criminal nickname, the highwayman **Mull'd Sack**, who probably had a liking for a drink of that name.

Elsdon C. Smith reports that the FBI has a Nickname File containing at least 150,000 entries as part of its background material, and presumably police forces everywhere are obliged to make similar collections. The New York file contains examples like **Gold Tooth Frenchy**, **Clothesline Slim**, **Wild Cat Alma** and **Iron Foot Florence**. **Fire Alarm Brown** was so named from his habit of raising a fire alarm, then picking pockets among the crowd that gathered. **Step Ladder Lewis** would pretend to be a painter and enter houses through upper windows.

Names like Wild Cat Alma for the women bring to mind the nicknames used by their sisters in what have been called 'houses of horizontal refreshment'. Bill Carmichael has listed many of them in his *Incredible Collectors*, and they are best left to speak for themselves: **The Roaring Gimlet**, **Sweet Fanny**, **Glass-Eyed Nellie**, **Tin Pot Annie**, **Rotary Rosie**, **The Galloping Cow**, **Smooth Bore**, **Madam Moustache**, **Madam Butterfly**. This last name was given a totally new meaning, of course, by Puccini but it was a genuine non-Japanese nickname for a prostitute before he made use of it.

Political nicknames

At such a level nicknames are simply amusing, but one should not forget that they can have more serious significance. Nicknames can help make public figures seem friendly and accessible however remote they remain in reality. **Dizzy** and **Old Hickory** performed this function for Benjamin Disraeli and Andrew Jackson. Gladstone, Disraeli's rival, was never given an affectionate nickname, which reflects his different kind of reputation. Some modern politicians consciously try to become known by a nickname in order to make an emotional appeal to the public.

Just what can happen to a politician's name is exemplified by Sir Robert Peel, British Home Secretary in the early nineteenth century. He acquired several nicknames, including the inevitable **Orange Peel** when he displayed anti-Catholic tendencies. He later became **The Runaway Spartan** when he changed his mind and worked in favour of the Irish Emancipation Bill. His surname was also adapted to **Peeler** and applied as a generic nickname for a policeman when he founded the Metropolitan Police in 1829. An alternative form, **Bobby**, was derived from his first name. This has lasted longer and has gone on to become a word.

Nicknames are important to the man in the street, not just to politicians. Psychological studies appear to show that people who are known by nicknames which they acknowledge are better adjusted socially than those who are known only by their correct names, or by nicknames which no one would dare say to their face. These are interesting indications, but not enough work has yet been done in this area. We need a major study of nicknames and their influence coupled with a study of first and surname influences, particularly among school-children.

More work needs to be done by researchers with other interests as well. When we remember that bynames are a kind of nickname, and that surnames are all derived from bynames, we can well understand Ernest Weekley's comment that 'every family name is etymologically a nickname'. In spite of this Weekley himself appears to have made no serious attempt to collect the nicknames of his time together with evidence about how the names had come into being. In his many books on names he stays well within his chosen philological area, rarely venturing past the Middle Ages. Other writers of equal eminence on surnames have dutifully nodded in the direction of modern nicknames, but once again none of them has made anything like a real attempt to get to grips with what is, in effect, the only living personal name system. There is an obvious need for a full-scale linguistic inquiry into personal nicknames and nicknaming today. The conclusions that would emerge from a thorough study could not fail to help the philologist in the interpretation of his data.

Previous works on nicknames

Julian Franklyn's *Dictionary of Nicknames* (1962) contains about 1,500 entries, but the examples are all of the institutional type. They apply to anyone who has a certain surname or first name, fits a descriptive category or fills a particular role. We learn that **Trugs**, for instance, is a nickname given to a lazy man and that it is 'Scottish dialect'; that **Enzedder** is an Australian way of referring to a New Zealander, and so on. These are fossilised nicknames, generic names that border on being common names.

Within this rather restricted area Franklyn's work is valuable for reference purposes, an advance in many ways on studies such as Latham's *Dictionary of Names, Nicknames and Surnames* and Albert Frey's *Sobriquets and Nicknames*. Both of these do actually contain truly individual nicknames—those borne by major historical figures—but there are not enough of them. Latham also goes beyond personal nicknames to take in some of those attached to towns, states, battles, institutions, newspapers and anything else. But both writers restrict themselves to names that occur in polite literature and are careful not to descend to the level of everyday speech.

It is precisely that, of course, that is needed. It may only be of anecdotal interest to know that a nurse was nicknamed **Tonsils** because several doctors wanted to take her out, or that a young man was called **Yankee** because he doodled all day, but enough examples like this gathered together would soon reveal patterns of name formation, related to statistics, for worthwhile statements to be made about certain linguistic habits. The vast majority of names, obviously, would not be amusing puns, but they would have their own interest. Whoever does eventually take on the task will not find it a dull one. Nicknames comment, and always have done, on every conceivable aspect of human behaviour.

Obsolete nicknames

One must not be misled by the relatively simple types of nickname that developed into our surnames. Our ancestors did not name everyone by the colour of his hair, his job, his father's name or where he lived. These are, it is true, the types of name that have mainly survived, but a great many others that are now obsolete are recorded in medieval Subsidy Rolls, Tax Returns and the like. The following examples were all solemnly written down, in their Middle English form, in documents of this kind in order to identify individuals. They allow us to gain some idea of the names that must have been in colloquial use: William **Breakwomb**, William **Catchmaid**, Simon **Cutpurse**, Hugo **Lickbread**, Leofric **Lickdish**, Geoffrey **Lickfinger**, Robert **Eatwell**, John **Skipup**, John **Spillwater**, Emma **Spoilale**, Muchman **Wetbed**, John **Leavetoday**, Serle **Gotochurch**, Adam **Hangdog**, Adam **Fairarmfull**, Elias **Overandover**, Robert **Moonlight**, Arnold **Pokestrong**. Dozens more like this, including many that are rather too obscene to reproduce here, occur in the documents. Fuller lists of them are cited by Dr. Reaney in his *Origin of English Surnames* and Professor Weekley in his *Surnames*.

Mention of Latham's *Dictionary* a moment ago serves to remind us that nicknames are not restricted to people. They can replace any proper names, ranging from those of football teams such as **Arsenal (The Gunners)**, to regiments—**The 11th Hussars (The Cherry-pickers** or **Cherubims)**; newspapers—**The Times (The Thunderer)**; cities—**Portsmouth (Pompey)**; States—**Pennsylvania (The Keystone**

A **Beefeater** and a **Cherry-picker**. 'Beefeater' was once a rather contemptuous term for any servant who looked well-fed, but it is now considered to be the exclusive nickname of a Yeoman of the Guard or Warder at the Tower of London. The 'Cherry-pickers' were probably nicknamed for their cherry-coloured breeches.

State); shops—**Marks and Spencer (Marks and Sparks**); periods of time—**The Silly Season**; musical works—**Haydn's Symphony No. 96 (The Miracle)**; railways—**Somerset and Dorset (Slow and Dirty)**, and many others.

Where there is not an obvious linguistic connection between name and nickname, there is usually an anecdote to be told. 'The Thunderer' was originally the personal nickname of Edward Sterling, a contributor to *The Times*, but was extended to the newspaper itself. 'The Miracle' was named at the first performance of the symphony, when the audience miraculously escaped injury from a falling chandelier. Nicknames of all kinds do as they claim, in other words—they eke out real names, augmenting them with wit, biographical detail or anecdote. They are a fascinating study, jewels in the great treasury of names, and we should be grateful for them.

Chapter 11
A Local Habitation and a Name

So far in this book we have talked mainly about the names of people—the names they inherit, are given or adopt. Men have obviously named one another from time immemorial. After themselves they named their gods, then they named the places in which they lived and the rivers, hills and natural features around them.

The earliest place names

The English-speaking countries in the modern world contain layers of place names which stretch back century by century into the remote past. The oldest names are those given by the earliest inhabitants of each country and which have managed to survive in one form or another. In Britain some names are thought to be pre-Celtic, which would take them back to before 500 BC. The name of the River **Wey**, for example, cannot be explained by Old English or Celtic scholars, and they assume it to be older than names in either of these languages. Other words were added much later to give place names such as **Weybridge** and **Weymouth**.

In America it is impossible to date accurately the Indian names that were taken over by settlers, but these are certainly the earliest names there. With nothing known at the time of Indian languages or customs, it was inevitable that such names should change their sound and form considerably. **Chicago** may well have been the Algonquian word 'stinking' originally, but if so one cannot be sure whether the reference was to wild onions, stagnant water or skunks.

Australia has its ancient names such as **Murrumbidgee** and **Woomera**, and here again there are often difficulties of interpretation. While these two names are normally translated as 'big water' and 'throwing stick'—or 'boomerang', as we have adapted it—**Paramatta** might have meant anything from 'the dark forest' to 'the head of the river' or 'the place where eels lie down' when it was first given. The Aborigines had a great many languages which they did not write down, and even intelligent guesses are difficult to make in such circumstances.

In New Zealand the Maori names are relatively numerous and quite well preserved. As the New Zealand writer Mrs. C. M. Matthews points out, in her *Place Names of the English-Speaking World*, there is only one

Maori language. Then Captain Cook took with him from Tahiti a boy called Tupia, who discovered that the Maoris could understand his own Polynesian words. Cook was able to talk to the natives through Tupia and record their place names, while later missionaries learned Maori and interpreted them well. Sometimes the words seem simple, but the original meaning was a metaphorical one. **Rangi** means 'sky', and by extension 'light' or 'day'. **Rangitoto** is therefore 'day of blood', not 'sky of blood', and is a reference to the wounding there of a folk-hero. The name is typical in its recording of a historical incident, a favourite Maori practice and one which leads to some very lengthy combinations. **Taumata** is the shortened form in daily use of a name which stretches to eighty-five letters and means 'the place where Tamatea, the man with the big knee who slid, climbed and swallowed mountains, known as Traveller, played on his flute to his loved one'.

Maori names were more fortunate than native names elsewhere. European settlers from the sixteenth century on had a strong tendency to rename their colonies in Africa, North America and elsewhere by transferring familiar names to them or describing them as they themselves saw them. A respect for the original names only arose in the later nineteenth century, and they began to appear on maps as well as being heard in native speech. The new attitude affected the Victorian explorers of Central Africa, who mostly made an effort to record the names they found rather than impose new ones. Even then, patriotism revealed itself in **Lake Victoria** and the like.

In general we must remember that countries are usually settled or taken over by highly practical men rather than scholars. They are concerned with convenience and their own pride when they name places, and are not inclined to stand back and take an enlightened historical view. The Romans and Normans look like exceptions to this rule, for they made very few changes to the place names they found in Britain, but both groups lived as a separate, ruling class and had a rather different attitude from the normal settler.

Difficulties of place name studies

One way for us to examine place names is to take them layer by layer according to age, but it is best to stay within definite geographical boundaries when doing this. Names which may have come into being at roughly the same time, but in different parts of the world, are likely to have very little in common. The beliefs and attitudes of the namers are more important than the time of naming, and these—perhaps more so in the distant past than now—varied considerably from tribe to tribe, nation to nation. Since it is usually easier to assign a place name to its language, and therefore to the people who gave the name, rather than to an exact period, we will do well to follow familiar paths through the place name jungle.

The jungle, as it may justly be called, is primarily a linguistic one. In Britain the number of languages concerned is relatively small, with Celtic—or Primitive Welsh, Gaelic, Old English, Old Norse, Latin and

Norman French being the more important. In America there are the many Indian tribal languages, which began to receive serious attention only in recent times. As one travels round the world, African, Polynesian and Aboriginal languages make their appearance. With each language one has to do also with the culture that lies behind it.

This linguistic jungle, however, has had its Spekes and Livingstones. England has been especially fortunate, for a determined army of scholars, mostly gathered together in The English Place Name Society, has been hacking away at the undergrowth for over fifty years. Names like Stenton, Mawer, Gover and Ekwall are mostly unknown to the general public, but these are a few of the men who first penetrated into really difficult areas. Other men and women now use the methods they established to explore new areas and refine our knowledge of the others, but the quantity and quality of work done by the pioneers was quite outstanding. In America George R. Stewart has also made a particularly noteworthy contribution to place name studies, though as a social historian rather than a philologist.

Paths, then, have been established and made familiar. A fuller list of the scholars who have helped lay them appears in the Bibliography of this book, but some may be overlooked. Scholars know that it is the fate of road-builders to make travel easy for others and be forgotten themselves.

Celtic place names

Let us start out, then, along the first main path. It is as well to begin with British place names because, as with surnames, so many of them were later transferred to other countries. The first layer of names that have a known meaning are those left by the Celts, who came to Britain from central Europe from about 500 BC onwards. **London** is one of their many place names that remains in use today, but opinions differ as to its exact meaning. It is likely to have been 'the settlement of **Londinos**', a man (or god) whose name in turn meant 'the bold one'. **Carlisle** is another Celtic name, its modern form having been influenced by French-speaking clerks who adapted what they heard to fit their own spelling system. What they heard was **Cair Luel**, with *cair* being an earlier version of the Welsh *caer*, 'fort'. The Venerable Bede noted in the eighth century that Luel was how the Latin name **Luguvallium** was then being pronounced. The Latin version of the name indicates what the Romans had heard the natives saying centuries before, an original name which may have meant 'strong in Lugus', Lugus being a popular god. The links in this complex chain, from Carlisle back to Luguvallium, happen to exist in this case, but with many names there is no such help available.

Carmarthen contains the word 'fort' twice, for besides beginning with *caer* it ends with what was once *din*, which had the same meaning. The name was originally the 'fort near the sea', represented by the Romans as **Mari Dunum**. The Welsh made it **Myrddin**. Just as we might now talk of Carmarthen Castle, unaware that Carmarthen already twice refers to a castle, so by the eighth century it was forgotten that Myrddin contained the word. *Caer* was added, and **Caer Myrddin** was interpreted four centuries later by Geoffrey of Monmouth as 'the castle of Myrddin'. The

Merlin painting the young knight's shield. He owes his existence in the Arthurian legend to a misinterpretation of the place name **Carmarthen**.

non-existent Myrddin became *Merlinus* in Latin and has been part of the Arthurian legend ever since.

Similar mistakes made by our ancestors are often useful to us. They show that the Anglo-Saxons who invaded Britain from the fifth century onwards took over many Celtic names *as names*, without understanding their meaning. Professor Cameron, in his *English Place Names*, cites **Penhill** as an example of the Old English *hyll* having been added to Old Welsh *penn*, both words meaning 'hill'. In Lancashire Penhill developed into **Pendle** and was subsequently expanded to **Pendle Hill**, or 'hill-hill-hill'. Other evidence, however, suggests that the meaning of some Celtic names *was* understood by the newcomers, for they correctly adapted them into their own language in a plural form.

The Anglo-Saxons did not immediately occupy the whole of England, and a study of place names enables their progress across the country from the east to the west to be traced. They appear to have killed or driven away most of the people in the eastern area, for very few of the original Celtic names remain. As they slowly pushed west, leaving behind settlers, they took over or adapted more and more names. The adaptations often appear as *hybrids* of the Penhill type, with elements of more than one language joined together. The density of Celtic names or elements increases all the time until one comes to Wales and Cornwall, where we have as much proof as we want that the Britons continued to live their own lives and speak their own language.

The Angles pushed north into Caledonia, but this area was later over-run by migrants from Ireland, called 'Scots'. The Scots gave their name to Scotland, and eventually displaced or absorbed the mysterious Picts, who lived in the Highlands. Gaelic, Old English and Pictish names are found in Scotland today, together with Scandinavian and Norman names that were introduced later. It is hardly surprising that many names remain unexplained. **Edinburgh**, for example, has a second element meaning 'fortress', but 'Eidyn', which is the first element, cannot be interpreted. All that can be said with any certainty is that Edinburgh does *not* mean 'Edwin's fortress' as is popularly supposed. The evidence for the refutation is best set out in *The Names of Towns and Cities in Britain*, by Nicolaisen, Gelling and Richards.

Ireland's place names derive mainly from Gaelic, but their forms have been much distorted by non-Gaelic-speaking officials. P. W. Joyce says in his *Irish Names of Places* that it was necessary to ask local people how they pronounced the names before the origins became at all clear. **Dublin** is well known to be *dubh linne*, an exact translation of which appears in the English name **Blackpool**. **Belfast** takes its name from its proximity to a natural sandbank formed near the mouth of a river by the opposing currents and able to be used as a *farset*, or 'ford'.

As it happens, these two names are characteristic of the majority of both Irish and Scottish place names in that they describe natural features. The Welsh and Cornish also preferred to describe rather than link their own names to their place names. Local saints and legendary heroes are mentioned in Celtic place names, however, as one might expect among peoples who have always loved to recite traditional tales to one another.

To return to England, one of the place name facts that most people know is that 'caster', 'chester' or 'cester' in a name indicates Roman connections. This is true, but it was not the Romans themselves who named places in this way. For them *castra* was a military camp, but they did not bother to add this word to the names of the camps. It was the Anglo-Saxons who did so, having taken the word into Old English as *ceaster*.

The Romans had actually withdrawn from England before the Anglo-Saxons invaded, but wherever the newcomers went they would have found the very distinctive signs of Roman occupation. One must assume that the Celts had taken *castra* into their language and were able to pass it on to the Anglo-Saxons. The latter made full use of it, sometimes attaching it to a Celtic name, as in **Gloucester**, where the first element meant 'bright'; sometimes adding another of their own words, as in **Chesterfield**, with 'field' originally meaning 'open land'. The Romans had frequently referred to camps by the names of nearby rivers, and this led to place names like **Doncaster**, **Lancaster** and **Exeter**, from the rivers **Don**, **Lune** and **Exe**. By no means every Roman settlement, however, had a *ceaster* added to it, and some names that were given it lost it again quickly. London was referred to as **Lundenceaster**, for instance, but this was clearly felt to be too unwieldy.

The Romans themselves had attempted to call London **Augusta**, but like most of their attempts at bestowing place names in Britain, this failed. To all intents and purposes, the Romans left behind them in Britain no place names of their own invention. What they did during their long stay of over three centuries was to record in Latin the Celtic names they heard, but it was not these written forms that were passed on to the Anglo-Saxons. The Celtic names the latter took over—mostly the names of larger settlements and rivers—would have been passed to them by word of mouth. Many others had to be given, and this the Anglo-Saxons proceeded to do.

Anglo-Saxon clan names

The earliest Anglo-Saxon names reflect the fact that they were moving across new territory. What was important to them at the time was their own identity as a group, which was the one thing that remained constant. They travelled as bands, each with a leader whose name they took. If the leader was Reada, then they were *Readingas*, his followers and dependants. Eventually, when they decided to settle, that place would be known as 'the Readingas' place', **Reading** as it is today. Some names of this kind also add a '-ham' or '-ton' to indicate a settlement.

Not every English place name that contains 'ing' can automatically be given this kind of meaning. The suffix '-ing' can also mean 'place' or 'river', and sometimes it refers to an Old Norse *eng*, 'meadow'. A '-ridding' is a 'clearing', a '-ling' often a 'bank' or 'ridge'. A place name student must have evidence that the '-ing' was once a plural before he can say that it refers to a clan name. In a few cases this plural has survived, as in **Hastings** and **Cannings**.

The clan names were in use at the end of the fifth century. Although at that time they described people and not places they changed their nature completely long before the byname period. Once they had permanently settled the small groups who had borne these names gradually joined together and formed larger kingdoms. The later place names of the Anglo-Saxons were obviously true place names from the beginning, but the existence of these early transferred names is a great help to historians. Plotting them on a map helps to show not only where the Anglo-Saxons went but when they went there.

The clan names (sometimes called '-ing names' or 'folk names') often contain the personal name of the clan leader, but it is not only these names, transferred to places, that contain personal names. Thousands more link the name of an individual farmer or landowner with his property. These are not the great names of history, but the names of ordinary people. As we saw when we looked at the history of first names the typical Anglo-Saxon names—**Eanwulf**, **Helmheard**, **Cynewulf**, **Beornred** and the like—were later replaced by names of foreign origin, though many are known to us from coins and charters. Many others, however, live on only in place names such as **Hauxton**, **Hawkesbury** and **Hawksworth**, all of which mention a man called **Hafoc**.

There were other ways of describing in a place name the people who lived there without using a personal name. **Sussex** uses the tribal name, describing the 'South Saxons', and **Grantchester** the name of a river. The '-chester' here is a modern form of Old English *saete*, meaning 'dwellers', not the usual *-ceaster*, so the name meant 'dwellers on the River Granta'. The *-ingas* of the clan names can also occur attached to a generally descriptive word instead of a personal name. **Epping** was once the 'people of the upland', not the 'followers of Yppe'. **Norfolk** and **Suffolk** are other obvious descriptive names of people, dividing them into northern and southern groups.

Other Anglo-Saxon place names

The majority of other place names given by the Anglo-Saxons are descriptive of some aspect of the places themselves. If the latter were inhabited, elements like '-ham' ('homestead'), '-ton' ('farmstead'), '-worth' ('enclosure') and '-wick' ('building') were added in their Old English form to words which described natural features, neighbouring buildings, crops, animals, rivers, etc. Places which were originally uninhabited became known by whatever feature distinguished them most easily. Once again certain elements are common in such names. They were originally words which meant grove and wood, river and ford, glade and thicket, hill and valley. A list of these common place name elements is given on pages 136 and 137.

The Anglo-Saxons appear to have done little conscious naming of the places in which they came to live. Most of the names clearly began as phrases in normal speech and gradually became fossilised. In the place names that arose during the Anglo-Saxon period there is therefore a true picture of England as it was, filled in with many fine details. Apart from the country itself, many names tell us about the people, their beliefs and customs. The Anglo-Saxons came to Britain as pagans, for instance, but were slowly converted to Christianity. We know this from other sources, but the change can be seen in the place names. Some early names contain references to heathen temples, as in **Harrow-on-the-Hill** and **Weedon**, or are theonymic links, as in **Tuesley** and **Wednesbury**. The latter names naturally remind us of the day names **Tuesday** and **Wednesday** in which the names of the gods **Tiw** and **Woden** again appear. Pagan customs such as sacrificing animals and burying the dead alongside their weapons and domestic items are probably hinted at in names like **Gateshead**, 'goat's head' and **Hounslow**, 'Hund's burial mound'.

Christian place names often mention a monastery or church, as in **Warminster** and **Cheriton**, 'minster on the River Were' and 'village with a church'. Saints' names also occur: **Felixstowe**, **Bridstow**, St. Felix and St. Bridget being linked with '-stow', which often meant 'holy place'. 'Holy' itself, Old English *hālig*, is seen in **Halliwell** and the like, while many other names refer to priests, canons, abbots, nuns, monks and bishops.

Lay society is also reflected in many place names. **Kingston**, **Queenborough**, **Aldermanbury** are self-explanatory, but modern Englishmen no longer refer to 'churls' in the sense of 'free peasants'. **Charlton** and **Chorlton** refer to farms held by such men. 'Knights' are still with us, but this word has been considerably upgraded. The Anglo-Saxons used it to refer to a youth, and **Knightsbridge** was therefore a bridge where young men met.

All this is very proper, but the Anglo-Saxons had their thieves and other criminals whom they dealt with in no uncertain manner. **Shackerley** was

a 'robbers' wood', **Warnborough**, 'felon stream', a stream where they
were drowned. The gallows are referred to in many local names, often the
names of the fields where the executions took place. **Dethick** is thought to
derive from a name given to a particular tree, 'the death oak', where no
doubt Anglo-Saxon justice was frequently carried out.

The name of a small London stream, **Tyburn**, came to have an ominous meaning for many because of the gallows erected near it.

Place name Elements

A selection of elements that occur in place names throughout Britain is given below. The elements were originally words in Celtic (Old Welsh), Gaelic, Old English and Old Norse. In their passage through the centuries they have undergone many changes, and what was once the same word may exist in many modern forms. It is never possible to explain the original meaning of a British place name on the basis of its modern form alone. Only by examining the earliest forms known to be recorded can a philologist give a judgment as to the intended meaning; even then he must always consider topographical information about the natural features as well as linguistic facts.

In the list an element that normally occurs as a prefix is shown thus: *Aber-*; *Ac-*; *Aird-*, etc. An element that is normally a suffix is shown thus: *-beck*; *-borne*; *-by*, etc. Elements that can occur as names in themselves, or as prefixes or suffixes, are shown thus: *Barrow*; *Firth*; *Haigh*, etc.

Aber- 'river mouth'.
Ac- 'oak'.
Aird- 'height'.
Ard- 'height'.
Auch(in)- 'field'.
Avon- 'water, river'.
Bally- 'farm, village'.
Bar- 'barley'.
Barrow 'hill, tumulus, grove'.
-beck 'stream'.
Ber- 'barley'.
-ber 'grove'.
-berry 'burial mound'.
Bold- 'building'.
-borne 'stream'.
-borough 'fortified place'; 'burial mound'.
-bourne 'stream'.
Bryn- 'hill'.
Bur- 'fortified place'.
Burn- 'stream'.
-burgh 'fortified place'.
-bury 'fortified place'.
-by 'farm, village'.
Cam- 'crooked'.
Car- 'fortified place'.

Carl- 'churl'.
Carn- 'heap of stones'.
-caster 'Roman settlement'.
Charl- 'churl'.
Chat- 'wood'.
Chep- 'market'.
chester 'Roman settlement'.
Chip- 'market'.
Coat- 'cottage'.
-combe 'deep valley'.
Comp- 'deep valley'.
-cot(e) 'cottage'.
Crick- 'small hill'.
Dal- 'dale'; 'meadow by a stream'.
Darwen- 'oak tree'.
Dean- 'valley'.
Den- 'valley'; 'fortress'.
Din- 'fortress'.
-don 'hill'.
Down- 'hill'.
Drogh- 'bridge'.
Drum 'ridge'.
Dub- 'black'.
Dun- 'hill'; 'fortified place'.
Ea- 'water, river'; 'island'.

Eglo- 'church'.
Ey- 'island'.
-ey 'water, river'; 'island'.
-fell 'hill'.
Firth 'fiord'.
-ford 'ford'; 'fiord'.
Gal 'stranger'.
Garth 'enclosure'.
-gethly 'wood'.
-gill 'narrow ravine'.
Glais- 'stream'.
Glas- 'stream'; 'greeny blue'.
Graf- 'grove'.
-grave 'grove'.
-greave 'grove'.
-guard 'enclosure'.
Hag- 'hedge, enclosure'.
Haigh 'hedge, enclosure'.
Hal(e) 'corner'.
-hall 'corner'; 'hall'.
Ham 'homestead'; 'water-meadow'.
-haugh 'hedge, enclosure'.
Hayle- 'salt water'.
Hel- 'salt water'.
-hithe 'landing-place'.

Holme 'small island'.
Holt 'thicket'.
Hoo 'high land'.
Hop- 'valley'.
Hough 'high land'.
How(e) 'mound, hill'.
Hurst 'wooded hill'.
Hythe 'landing-place'.
Inch 'island'.
Innis 'island'.
Inver- 'river mouth'.
Kil- 'monastic cell, church'.
Killi- 'wood'.
Knock- 'small hill'.
Kyle 'strait'.
Lan- 'enclosure, church'.
-law 'mound, hill'.
Lee 'glade'.
Leigh 'glade'.
Lin 'lake, pool'.
Lis- 'court, hall'.
-low 'mound, hill'.
Lyn(n)- 'lake, pool'.
Magher- 'coastal plain'.
Mar- 'lake'.
Mal- 'hill'.
-mel 'sandbank'.
Mel- 'hill'.

Mer 'lake'.
-mere 'lake'.
Mine- 'mountain'.
Mon- 'mountain'.
Mor- 'sea'.
Moy- 'coastal plain'.
Mynd 'mountain'.
-ness 'cape'.
-ock 'oak'.
Oke- 'oak'.
Or- 'bank'.
Pen- 'head'.
Pol- 'pool'.
Rath- 'fort, court'.
-rith 'ford'.
Ros(s) 'moorland'.
-rose 'moorland'.
Ru- 'slope'.
-ryn 'cape'.
-scar 'rock, reef'.
Sel- 'sallow (a tree)'.
-set 'hill pasture'.
Shaw 'small wood'.
Sher- 'bright'.
Shir- 'bright'.
Sil- 'sallow (a tree)'.
Skerry 'rock, reef'.
Slieve 'range of hills'.

Stain- 'stone'.
Stan- 'stone'.
-stead 'place'.
-sted 'place'.
-ster 'place'.
Stock 'holy meeting-place'; 'tree-stump'.
Stoke 'holy meeting-place'.
Stow(e) 'place'.
Strat- 'Roman road'.
Strath- 'a wide valley'.
Stret- 'Roman road'.
Thorp(e) 'farm, village'.
Thwaite 'glade, clearing'.
-tire 'land'.
-ton 'farm, village'.
Tre- 'farm, village'.
-try 'shore, sands'.
Ty- 'house'.
Tyr- 'land'.
Usk 'water'.
Wal- 'foreigner, Briton'.
Wen- 'white'.
-wich 'dwelling, farm'.
Wick 'dwelling, farm'; 'sea inlet'.
Win- 'white'.
Worth(y) 'enclosure, farm'.
Wyke 'dwelling, farm'.

Scandinavian names

The Anglo-Saxons settled and named their places, and the time of their coming receded into the past. In the ninth century it was the turn of new invaders, the Vikings, to establish a permanent foothold in Britain. By 886 King Alfred had signed a treaty with Guthrum, the Danish leader, and the Danelaw came into being. The newcomers responded exactly as the Anglo-Saxons had done before them to the place names they found— accepted them as they found them, adapted their pronunciation to suit their own language (usually called 'Old Norse'), added words of their own to existing names, thus creating new hybrids, or gave entirely new names. Naturally their own personal names, and those of their gods, were also linked to their place names, which are especially concentrated in Yorkshire and Lincolnshire.

Old Norse and Old English had far more in common with each other than with Celtic or Gaelic, but there were differences of vocabulary and usage. The distinctive word of the Danes was *by*, used instead of Old English *tun*. They also made frequent use of *thorp*, whereas the Anglo-Saxons were not fond of their equivalent *throp*, both of which meant an 'outlying farm'. Typical pronunciation preferences are reflected in **Keswick**, the Scandinavian way of saying **Chiswick** 'cheese farm'; **Skipton** and **Shipton**, 'sheep farm'. Once again, the plotting of Scandinavian place names on a map of Britain provides evidence of where they settled and in what numbers.

Norman influence

Invasion and settlement did not end with the Vikings, but place name scholars tend to talk of the Norman influence on English place names rather than French names. The Normans came to England 200 years after the Vikings, and by then place names were thick on the ground and well established. Not many Normans came and they did not settle in the same way as the Vikings and Anglo-Saxons. They became rulers, not farmers, and were concerned with the building of castles rather than cottages.

When they did give names they were frequently subjective descriptions rather than the down-to-earth factual descriptions of the past. **Bewley** is another form of **Beaulieu**, 'beautiful place'. **Merdegrave**, an Anglo-Saxon name probably referring to 'martens', they hastily changed to **Belgrave**, an interesting early example of whitewashing a name (*merde* in French meaning 'faeces'). Rather similar was their change of **Fulepet**, 'foul pit', to **Beaumont**, 'beautiful hill'.

The ordinary Englishman, as the Normans must have quickly realised, could not cope with French names, which had sounds and spellings totally strange to him. But the same was true of the Norman clerks who tried to write down English names. They wrote what they heard, but in their own spelling system. When English sounds did not exist in French they wrote the nearest thing. Often they turned the '-chester' ending into '-sester', spelling it '-cester', as in **Gloucester**, **Cirencester**.

Another change was with names beginning with 'th', which became 't'.

Turton was originally 'Thuri's farm', and changed its form partly because of the Normans' inability to cope with the name's pronunciation.

There eventually came a time when the spelling of place names was fixed, but this did not stop changes in pronunciation. In every area there are place-name shibboleths, waiting to catch out the stranger. The latter will try to pronounce the name as it is spelt, but the locals may have a different version altogether. It is that local version which is the 'correct' one, representing the natural development of the language.

There have been many other changes to place names in Britain since the Middle Ages, apart from changes in pronunciation. Names have been changed by folk-etymology, the process that turns the unfamiliar into the familiar. **Chartreuse**, for instance, was turned into **Charterhouse**, which seemed more meaningful to Englishmen. Names have been shortened over the centuries, but they have also been lengthened. **Ditton**, 'a farm by a dyke or ditch', split into **Thames Ditton** and **Long Ditton**, two more precise locations. They might have become North and South, Great and Little (*Magna* and *Parva*), High and Low. They could have taken the names of different landowners, as has frequently happened in English place names. Instead one took a simple adjective, the other became linked to one of the world's most famous river names.

The general process of adding a second name in order to locate a place more precisely naturally reminds us of bynames being added to personal names. Natural duplication and transfer have led to many names being repeated within the same country or elsewhere, so that we sometimes add the county or state name in order to avoid confusion. When discussing European names Americans often mention the country, though for some reason it never fails to amuse the British to hear someone speak of 'London, England' or 'Paris, France'.

The origin of **Thames**, incidentally, which was mentioned a moment ago, is not known. It is possibly a simple description, 'dark river', parallel to a tributary of the Ganges, **Tamasa**. The older river names are mostly of this type, many of them simply meaning 'water' or 'river', with no qualification of any kind. **Avon**, **Dore**, **Dover**, **Lent**, **Esk**, **Axe**, **Exe**, **Don**, **Ouse**, **Arrow** and others all have such an origin. I find it easy to understand this. Like everyone else who lives near a river I go down 'to the river' for a walk without ever specifying it more exactly. When Thames *is* used for any reason, the 'h' is not pronounced of course. The letter was artificially inserted centuries ago, as a 'b' was in words like 'doubt' and 'debt', but has never been pronounced.

The study of river names is a special aspect of place name studies. Eilert Ekwall spent several years looking for early forms of the names in unpublished medieval documents and travelled round England looking at the rivers themselves. The results of his researches are to be found in his *English River Names*, but this is primarily a book by a philologist for other philologists.

Field names

Among the many other specialised aspects of place name studies may be mentioned that of field names. Town-dwellers rarely hear these names,

County Names

Present and former county names of the United Kingdom.

Aberdeenshire 'mouth of the Don' (formerly Devona, 'goddess').

Anglesey 'Angles' island'.

Angus (belonging to) 'Aeneas', brother of Kenneth II.

Antrim 'Aentrebh', name of a monastery in the fifth century.

Argyll 'boundary of the Gaels'.

Armagh (Queen) 'Macha's height'.

Ayrshire from the Ayr, 'running water'.

Banffshire 'young pig' (possibly alternative name for the Deveron). Or 'Banba/Banbha', a poetic name for Ireland used as a district name in Scotland. Animal names for rivers do occur, but the young pig reference might also be to totemism.

Bedfordshire 'Bieda's ford'.

Berkshire 'hilly'.

Berwickshire 'barley farm'.

Breconshire 'Brychan's territory'.

Buckinghamshire 'land belonging to Bucca's clan'.

Bute 'beacon' or 'hut, bothy'.

Caernarvonshire 'the fort in Arfon, opposite Mona (Anglesey)'.

Caithness 'ness of the Cataibh'.

Cambridgeshire 'bridge on the Granta'. (Grantabridge became Crantbridge, Cantbridge, Canbridge, Cambridge.)

Cardiganshire 'land of Ceredig'.

Carmarthenshire 'fort near the sea'.

Cheshire 'Roman camp'.

Clackmannanshire 'stone of Manau'.

Cornwall 'the Welsh (foreigners) in the land of the Cornovii tribe'.

Cumberland 'land of the Cumbrians (Britons)'.

Denbighshire 'little fort'.

Derbyshire 'village or farm near a deer park'.

Devon 'territory of the Dumnonii'.

Dorset 'dwellers in the Roman town of Durnovaria ('fist play'—with reference to a nearby amphitheatre).

Down 'fort'.

Dumfriesshire 'fort of the copses'.

Dunbarton 'fortress of the Britons'.

Durham 'island with a hill'.

East Lothian from a personal name.

Essex 'East Saxons'.

Fermanagh 'Monach's men'.

Fife presumably from a personal name.

Flintshire 'the flinty (rocky) place'.

Glamorgan 'Morgan's territory'.

Gloucestershire 'Roman town of Glevum (bright)'.

Hampshire 'estate on a promontory'.

Isle of Wight possibly 'that which juts from the sea; an island'.

Herefordshire 'army ford'.

Hertfordshire 'hart ford', i.e. crossing-place for stags.

Huntingdon and Peterborough 'huntsman's hill' and 'St. Peter's town'.

Inverness-shire 'mouth of the Ness'.

Kent 'coastal area'.

Kincardineshire 'at the head of a wood'.

Kinross-shire 'head of the promontory'.

Kircudbrightshire 'St. Cuthbert's Church'.

Lanarkshire 'glade'.

Lancashire 'Roman fort on the Lune'.

Leicestershire 'Roman town of the Ligore tribe'.

Lincolnshire 'Roman settlement (*colonia*) by the lake'.

London, Greater based on 'Londinos', a personal name.

Londonderry 'London (because of a charter granted to the Livery Companies of the City of London) + oak wood'.

Merionethshire based on personal name 'Marion'.

Middlesex 'Middle Saxons'.

Midlothian probably based on a personal name.

Monmouthshire 'mouth of the Mynwy'.

Montgomeryshire after a castle built by Roger de Montgomery, a Norman.

Moray 'territory by the sea'.

Nairnshire 'the river'.

Norfolk 'northern people'.

Northamptonshire 'north settlement'.

Northumberland 'land north of the Humber'.

Nottinghamshire 'settlement of Snot's clan'.

Orkney 'whale islands'.

Oxfordshire 'oxen ford'.

Peebleshire 'shiels, huts'.

Pembrokeshire 'end land'.

Perthshire 'copse'.

Radnorshire possibly based on 'red' (referring to colour of land?).

Renfrewshire 'flowing brook'.

Ross and Cromarty 'moor' and 'crooked bay'.

Roxburghshire 'Hroc's fortress'.

Rutland 'Rota's land'.

Selkirkshire 'hall church'.

Shetland based on a personal name.

Shropshire 'fortified place of Scrobb's clan', or 'in the scrub land'.

Somerset 'dwellers at the summer village'.

Staffordshire 'ford by a landing-place'.

Stirlingshire no satisfactory explanation can be proposed.

Suffolk 'southern people'.

Surrey 'southern district'.

Sussex 'land of the southern Saxons'.

Sutherland 'the southern land'.

Tyrone 'Owen's territory'.

Warwickshire 'dwellings by the weir'.

West Lothian as *Midlothian*.

Westmorland 'land of the people west of the (Yorkshire) moors'.

Wigtownshire 'dwelling-place'.

Wiltshire 'village on the Wylye'.

Worcestershire 'Roman settlement formerly inhabited by the Weogora tribe'.

Yorkshire 'estate of Eburos'. *Riding* is 'thridding', a 'third'.

The re-organisation of local government in England and Wales has recently led to the adoption of the following 'new' county names. Most of the names are, in fact, restorations of ancient names or transferred river names.

Avon from the river name.

Cleveland 'the hilly district'.

Clwyd from the river name.

Cumbria the name of an ancient tribe.

Dyfed name of an ancient province.

Gwent name of an ancient province.

Gwynedd name of an ancient province.

Humberside based on a river name.

Manchester, Greater 'the Roman town *Mamucium*'. *Mamucium* is of uncertain meaning.

Merseyside based on a river name.

Midlands, West descriptive.

Powys name of an ancient province.

Salop from *Salopesberia*, a Norman-French version of *Scrobesbyrig*, or *Shrewsbury*.

Tyne and Wear from two river names.

and are perhaps unaware that they exist, but countless thousands of them are there. They were applied first to open stretches of country cleared of trees, for this was the earliest meaning of 'field'. Later they identified the furlongs of open fields and finally they were applied to the enclosed fields we think of today.

Just as street names usually contain a word that means some kind of street, so field names usually contain a substitute for 'field', such as 'bottom', 'erg', 'jack', 'slang'. The first of these is used for land in a valley, the second for pasture used only in summer. 'Jack' refers to common land while a 'slang' describes the narrowness of the field.

Accompanying the wide variety of 'field' words are descriptions of the land's size and shape, its distance or direction from the village, its soil or crop, its plants or animals, its buildings or natural features. The names of the owners are often linked to them, and there are transferred names such as **Bohemia** and **Zululand** as light-hearted references to remote fields. A humorous reaction to unproductive land leads to names like **Bare Arse**, **Muchado**, **Pinchgut**, **Cain's Ground** and the like. Names given after the eighteenth century may be arbitrary conversions, reflecting the whim of the namer but saying nothing about the fields themselves.

One interesting aspect of field names is that there is scope for the amateur researcher. In many areas the names have not been collected yet, and a real contribution to a worthwhile study can be made. The names often fall within the bounds of local history rather than philology, though the interpretation of older names needs the help of an expert. Field names often repay in themselves the time that has been spent searching for them. I am rather fond, personally, of some Scottish names —**Knockmarumple**, **Glutty** and **Gruggle O' the Wud**, but English field names offer similar pleasures. Many examples are to be found in John Field's *English Field Names*, details of which are given in the Bibliography. Those wishing to collect field names are invited to contact The Names Society for further information.

The amateur can often interpret field names, but it must be said once again that the interpretation of place names must on the whole be left to the specialist. This has not prevented a great many mythological explanations being offered by sages of the past. H. G. Stokes quoted a favourite place name legend in his *English Place Names* concerning the village of **Kirkby Overblow**, where the second half of the name actually refers to early smelters. The locals tell the tale of a lovelorn maiden flinging herself from a nearby cliff in despair, but floating harmlessly down when her petticoats and skirts acted as a parachute. It is surprising that the legend does not extend to the invention of the parachute itself.

Pleasures of place names

Legends of this kind are one of the pleasures of place names if one is not too deadly serious about the whole subject. Another pleasure is to be found in many of the names themselves. Many people collect interesting place names that have a happy combination of sounds and hinted meanings. Stokes let his imagination run riot with **Bursteye** ('What an address for a film studio!') and delighted in names like **Bouncehorn**, **Rhude**, **Furtherfits**, **Badnocks**, **Shambelly**, **Undy**, **Snoring**, **No-bottle**, **Nicknocks**, **High Harpers**. A. A. Willis, another ardent collector, listed such names as **Shavington-cum-Gresty**, **Stank End**, **Dottery**, **Snoreham in Ruins**, **Maggots End**, **Great Fryup** and **Finish**. Surely we all recall, when we speak these names aloud, the time when language was new to us, when every word acquired was a linguistic toy waiting to be played with? The speaking aloud is important, for as our eyes run over the printed page we do not always translate into sound.

Poets may respond to place names in a different way:

> Our maps are music and our northern titles
> Like wind among the grass and heather, grieve.

Ivor Brown begins his poem 'The Moorland Map' with those fine words. John Betjeman has played poetically with Dorset place names, and many other poets have sensed the poetry inherent in ancient names.

We are not all place name specialists, humorists or poets, but there is something in certain place names for us all. There are names which have for us that private meaning that we spoke of at the beginning of this book, a thousand and one personal associations. Some names spoken aloud will be like pebbles thrown into a pool of memory, recalling our childhood or other periods of our lives. One must never forget this quality of names, which may make them hardly meaningful to some people but very meaningful indeed to others.

When the Great Age of Discovery began in the sixteenth century, British place names already had these intense personal meanings for the explorers and colonists. It is hardly surprising that they frequently transferred those names to the new lands. Even without being attached to new places, many of the names would have spread round the world, for they had now become the names of the emigrants themselves. On the *Mayflower*, for example, were men named **Allerton**, **Billington**, **Bradford**, **Britteridge**, **Chilton**, **Crackston**, **Eaton**, **Holebeck**, **Howland**, **Leister**, **Rigdale**, **Standish**, **Tilley**, **Warren** and **Winslow**, all of which remain to this day in one form or another as English place names. There too among the names on the land are **Cromwell** and **Raleigh**, **Lincoln** and **Washington**. Our place names may have had humble beginnings, but they have sometimes become the proudest names of all.

Chapter 12
Names Take Their Places

The place names of the English-speaking countries other than Britain reflect the histories of those countries as clearly as British place names tell the story of the Celts, Gaels, Romans, Anglo-Saxons, Vikings and Normans. A historical approach to them has accordingly been made by writers such as George Stewart and Mrs. C. M. Matthews, both of whom bring a literary elegance to name studies that is very refreshing. Details of their books, together with others on which this chapter is based, are given in the Bibliography.

My own approach will not be primarily historical, for when the Age of Discovery began in the fifteenth century it seems to me that we entered a new era of place naming that was quite unlike anything that had happened previously. Broadly speaking, place names that came into existence before the tenth century evolved naturally in the midst of descriptive speech. Place name transfers did not occur, and those place names that contained personal names were accidentally evolved links. People wanted to distinguish between one habitation and another and one natural way for them to do it was to link them to their owners' names. 'Ecga's homestead', say, and 'Ceabba's homestead' gradually became the accepted labels for those two places, surviving even after **Ecga** and **Ceabba** were forgotten. **Egham** and **Chobham** had taken the first step to becoming real place names. At no time had Ecga and Ceabba done the naming—it was their neighbours who made use of their names.

Signs of conscious naming appeared with the Normans, when the names they gave to their castles indicated an interest in the names themselves. **Beaurepaire**, later **Belper**, meant 'beautiful retreat', and was clearly never intended to be descriptive in a functional way. British place names would have changed in kind as well as language had the Normans done far more naming, but Britain had most of the names it needed by the time they came. There was, therefore, a gap of several centuries before the naming of places began again in earnest on the other side of the ocean, and this time the name giving was normally deliberate. Often the same names as those that had arisen in Britain were given to new places, but those names had changed in kind. Their origins had usually been forgotten, but they had acquired new 'meanings'.

Transfer of place names

It is easy to see why the principle of name transfer was taken for granted by the Europeans when they went to the New World. (We must obviously say Europeans rather than British, for many of the place names now in the English-speaking world were given by Spanish, Portuguese, French and Dutch explorers and settlers.) These men all had far more place names as part of their total vocabulary than had been the case with their ancestors. They knew their own countries more thoroughly, and knew more about one another's countries.

Secondly, they had all become used to name transfer in other nomenclatures. The development of first names and surnames had been roughly parallel throughout Europe, and both systems established a stock of names which was re-used as required. Finally, and perhaps most importantly, many place names had become usable almost as words because of their meanings. **Plymouth**, for example, must have meant almost the same as 'home' to a seventeenth-century Englishman when he was far from home himself. A settlement of that name could bring security and familiarity to a strange land. The name might no longer be relevant to the new place that bore it, in that it was not 'the mouth of the River **Plym**', but it was very meaningful to the namers.

There seem to be no signs of this kind of place name transfer in the earlier naming period, though another kind of transfer had its faint beginnings with the Anglo-Saxons and Vikings. We have seen how they occasionally linked the names of their gods to places, as in **Grimsdyke** and **Grimsbury** (**Grim** being an alternative form of **Woden**). This linking *between nomenclatures* obviously increased as time passed and affected name transfers. By the sixteenth century the present-day situation, whereby names can be transferred with almost total freedom from one naming system to another, had been established. The great explorers of the period lived with a constant reminder of this fact, for the very ships in which they sailed often had transferred names.

Columbus and Columbia

Columbus made early use of the name of a flagship, the **Marie Galante**, by transferring it to an island which has kept the name to this day. He may have been the first to take a name from a ship and root it firmly on the land, but he was certainly not the last. Captain Cook, for example, named a strait and a river after his ship, the **Endeavour**. When America had at last discovered Columbus (as Professor Stewart brilliantly puts it) another ship was sailing round the American coast with Robert Gray as its master. This ship's name commemorated Columbus himself in the form **Columbia**, and when Gray found a new river, he transferred his ship's name to it.

Columbia almost became the name of the United States of America. Poets of the eighteenth century referred to the new country by this name, but the statesmen failed to ratify the choice. The opportunity was missed, for others were quick to seize on a name which was historically apt and

The Names of the American States

Alabama Indian tribal name originally, influenced by Spaniards.

Alaska 'mainland' (Aleutian).

Arizona 'place of the small spring' (Papago).

Arkansas Indian tribal name, pronounced *Arkansaw*. The 's' was added erroneously by the French to make a plural.

California an invented literary name for an imaginary island, said to have been transferred by Cortés.

Carolina, **North** and **South** Successively after Charles IX of France, Charles I and Charles II of England. (Latin form of Charles.)

Colorado Spanish 'reddish'; describing water of the river.

Connecticut Algonquian, 'long river'. The second 'c', like the 'h' in Thames, was inserted artificially but has never been pronounced.

Dakota, **North** and **South** Indian tribal name, branch of the Sioux.

Delaware after Thomas West, Lord de la Warr (1577–1618).

Florida Spanish 'flowered, flowery', but also suggesting Easter, when the name was given.

Georgia after George II.

Hawaii 'place of the gods', with particular reference to the volcanoes.

Idaho an Apache name of uncertain meaning.

Illinois Algonquian tribal name, 'men, warriors'.

Indiana Latinised name in honour of the Indian tribes.

Iowa an Indian tribal name of uncertain origin.

Kansas based on name of an Indian tribe.

Kentucky Iroquois, 'meadow land'.

Louisiana after Louis XIV of France.

Maine 'mainland' altered later by French to conform with name of a French province.

Maryland after Henrietta Maria, wife of Charles I.

Massachusetts Algonquian, 'at the big hills'.

Michigan Algonquian, 'big lake', or 'forest clearing'.

Minnesota Sioux, 'cloudy water'.

Mississippi Algonquian, 'big river'.

Missouri from an Algonquian name for the river, possibly 'muddy'.

Montana Spanish, 'mountainous'.

Nebraska Sioux, 'flat water', the River Platte.

Nevada Spanish, 'snowed upon, snowy', i.e. the Sierra Nevada Mountains.

New Hampshire named by a settler (John Mason) who came from Hampshire.

New Jersey named by Sir George Carteret, who came from Jersey.

New Mexico named in the hope that the territory would become as rich as Mexico.

New York after the Duke of York, brother of Charles II.

Ohio Iroquoian, 'beautiful river'.

Oklahoma Choctaw, 'red people'.

Oregon possibly a name that arose from a misreading of river name Wisconsin, spelt 'Ouaricon-sint' on an eighteenth-century map, with last four letters on next line.

Pennsylvania after William Penn + vaguely Latin word meaning 'woodland'.

Rhode Island by comparison with Greek island Rhodes, Dutch interpreting name as 'red', referring to colour of earth.

Tennessee from a Cherokee river name.

Texas possibly the name of an Indian tribe, or an incident name arising from misunderstanding of a greeting meaning 'good friend'.

Utah Indian tribal name.

Vermont based on French words for 'green mountain'.

Virginia and **West Virginia** after Elizabeth I, the Virgin Queen.

Washington after George Washington, first President of the USA.

Wisconsin Algonquian river name, 'long river'.

Wyoming Algonquian 'broad plains'.

pleasant in sound. It was given to a city and to the **District of Columbia** as well as the river. **British Columbia** and **Colombo** came into being subsequently, as did towns called **Columbus**, **Columbiana** and **Columbiaville**.

Long before all this Columbus was revealing his own deeply religious convictions by naming islands after churches, which had already been named after saints. **Santa Maria La Antigua De Sevilla** was one such name, though it was later shortened to **Antigua**, 'ancient'. This was as far from Columbus's original intention as **Rum Cay**, which he had named **Santa Maria De La Conception**. British seamen were responsible for the renaming, which incorporates a local word meaning 'sandy island'. They also changed **St. Christopher**, which he named in honour of his patron saint, into its diminutive form, **St. Kitt's**.

Royalty in place names

Columbus dutifully tried to bestow some names in honour of his royal patrons, but names must live in the mouths of men in order to survive, not just on charts and maps. Most of these early royal names disappeared, but during the seventeenth century new ones appeared in profusion, especially when **New England** was founded. Prince Charles, for instance, was invited by John Smith to strike out native names that had temporarily been inserted on the map and give more suitable names. The young Prince responded to the invitation with pleasure. **Cape Elizabeth**, **Cape Anna** and **Cape James** were immediately named after his sister, mother and father. Cape James did not survive, for local people had already been speaking of it as **Cape Cod** for a long time, and the fish were still there to make the name a suitable one.

New England in the seventeenth century, after Prince Charles had added some place names to Captain John Smith's map.

Charles named the **Charles River** after himself and was later to honour himself yet again, in Latin, with **Carolina**. His wife's name was linked to **Maryland**. A glance at the map will show many other royal names that have been transferred or linked to places. **Georgetown**, **Georgetown**, **Williamsburg**, **Annapolis**, **Frederick County**, **Fredericksburg**, **Augusta**, **Orangeburg**, **Cumberland** and **New York** represent a small selection. The last of these was after the Duke of York, later James II. **Victoria** naturally appeared everywhere during the nineteenth century. French royalty was similarly commemorated in names like **Louisiana**, and at least one American town called **Isabella** was named after the Spanish queen of that name.

Many of these royal place names owe their existence to unctuous courtiers, but with some there may have been a more noble motivation. A royal personal name could take on a meaning as a national symbol, becoming almost a synonym of the country's own name. This might have led, in the case of some of the American names, to their being changed when anti-English feeling was running high, but their original meanings obviously faded away quickly. They became meaningful in a new way as place names, and were convenient and pleasant sounding.

Royalty established a naming fashion that was to be extensively imitated. Kings and queens might give their names to large areas of land, but there were a million smaller places to be named. The early explorers naturally put their own names on the maps, though many of them were extremely modest about it. **Cook**, **Tasman**, **Vancouver**, **Cabot**, **Cartier**, **Drake**, **Flinders** and the like are all attached to places which show where they travelled, but since all of them needed a great number of names to identify the places they came across, they made use of all the names they knew. They had a golden opportunity to please other people, such as their superior officers, shipmates, friends and relations, at no cost to themselves, and it was natural for them to do so.

Sometimes the people whose names found a permanent place on the maps had a real connection with the places they named. Captain Cook buried a seaman named **Sutherland** and gave the name to that area. It lives on as a suburb of Sydney. **Sydney** itself, however, was named after Lord Sydney, an English statesman. The city has made his name known throughout the world, but he himself was never to set eyes on Australia.

Names of people great and small have been transferred or linked to place names since the sixteenth century. In more recent times men have gone a long way from the relative dignity of royal first names or noble surnames. **Snicktaw**, in California, reverses the name of a local journalist; **Squeaky Creek** in Colorado incorporates the nickname of an earlier settler; **Ekalaka** in Montana comes from the name of the Sioux wife of a settler. Such names somehow seem to be quite at home in states that are rather more poetically named themselves.

But in spite of all the names of people in place names, still more are simple transfers from other places. **Plymouth** was mentioned earlier, a name that can be found today in twenty-five American states. Contrary to popular belief, the Pilgrim Fathers did not actually name their new settlement: it had already been done for them by Charles Stuart. When he ran out of family names that could be used for place names on John Smith's map, he inserted the names of some English towns. The *Mayflower* was thus able to sail from Plymouth to Plymouth. Later settlers arrived at the same port, then went inland to found new towns which needed naming. It was natural for many of them to turn to the name of the last town they had seen in the homeland and the first in the new.

The duplication of so many British names in America, Canada, Australia, New Zealand and other countries has an odd result for present-day travellers. They are likely to find clusters of familiar place names strangely rearranged as if by a giant earthquake. The pronunciation of the same names can also differ from country to country. In Britain an old name will usually have an unstressed ending, so that **Chatham** becomes 'Chat-em'. Elsewhere it is likely to be pronounced as spelt, with the '-ham' given its full value.

Other names transferred to places

It should be stressed that there are many possible sources of transfer for place names. Saints' names were often bestowed because a place was first seen on their feast-days. **Garryowen** in Montana was named for the regimental tune of the 7th Cavalry; the Bible has supplied names like **Shiloh** and **Bethesda**; **Buccaneer Bay** in Canada was named after a race-horse; poetry led to **Hiawatha** and **Avoca**; **Kodak** was borrowed from the trade name for places in Kentucky and Tennessee. The endlessness of the possibilities is perhaps best exemplified by **Truth or Consequences** in New Mexico. The name was transferred in 1950 from a radio programme as a result of certain inducements to the citizens, who voted on the matter.

While few transferred or linked place names come into being because of such specific advantages, most of them at least do so for positive reasons. It is hard to imagine a hated name being bestowed on a place, but this happened in Canada. The towns of **Luther** and **Melancthon** were named by a Roman Catholic surveyor because 'as it was the meanest tract of land he had ever surveyed he would name the country after the meanest men he ever heard of'.

Charles II also had vindictive intentions when he insisted on William Penn's name being linked to the suggested **Sylvania**. He knew perfectly well that **Pennsylvania** would greatly distress the modest Quaker, making him seem proud before his followers. Penn made desperate attempts to get the name changed, but perhaps it is as well that he did not succeed. Time has made the name a fine memorial, with the original unpleasant motive forgotten.

William Penn, whose name was maliciously included in **Pennsylvania** by Charles II.

Mention of Penn brings number names to mind (for reasons which will become clear when we deal with street names). There is a group of such place names, and they show that such names can be as evocative as any other names. **Seventy-Six**, for instance, is a place in Kentucky which reminds everyone of the year of Independence. **Fortynine Creek** links the place with 1849, when wagon-trains poured through it. **Forty Fort** is a reminder of the number of settlers who built the stockade. In West Virginia the name **Hundred** arose because Henry Church and his wife both lived to be over 105 years old. **One Hundred and Two River**, in Missouri, translates the French name **Cent Deux**, but this probably represented a mis-heard Indian word that meant 'upland forest'.

Another group of North American place names are not quite what they seem to be. **Battiest**, **Loving**, **Kilts**, **Breedlove**, **Schoolcraft** and **Buncombe** are all perfectly straightforward transferred surnames from early settlers and the like, whatever else they might suggest. Similarly, **Otter Point** in British Columbia contains the surname 'Otter' rather than a direct reference to the animal. When a very unusual surname becomes a place name, however, later residents may adapt it in an effort to make sense of it. **Swearing Creek** in North Carolina is from the Swearington family, while **Due West** in a neighbouring State shows what can happen to a name like **De Witt**.

Folk-etymology can accidentally conceal a transferred name, but there can also be deliberate concealment at the time of naming. **Subligna** in Georgia is an attempt to translate the surname 'Underwood' into Latin, while **Irvona** in Pennsylvania vaguely Latinizes the name 'Irvin'. A place **Neola** in West Virginia owes its name to **Olean** in New York, but the namer preferred to mix up the letters. Back-spellings are even commoner in the USA than anagrams, **Remlap** and **Remlig** being examples from Alabama and Texas.

Link place names

Place names which are blends of other names are links rather than transfers, but once again they usually conceal their origins. Parts of names may be used, or parts of names coupled with other elements. The results look like **Clemretta**, **Texhoma**, **Ethanac**, **Fluvanna**, **Cresbard** and **Ninaview**. The various paths leading to such names include putting together parts of two cow names, Clementine and Henrietta, for a place in Canada; blending the state names Texas and Oklahoma because a town borders on both; using parts of Ethan A. Chase, the name of an early landowner; putting part of the Latin *fluvius*, 'river', next to Anna (a similar name being **Rivanna**); joining parts of two surnames, Cressey and Baird; adding a common element to the name Nina.

Blends are meaningful names at the outset, as are all other links and transfers. They differ from the earlier British names, however, in being meaningful to the namers rather than to what is being named. Once they come into existence, whatever the reasons for their 'origins', the usual process of acquiring 'meanings' begins. The meaning of a place name can be fairly generally shared, and it is only in this way, perhaps, that place names which began as blends vary from names formed in exactly the same way and used as modern English house names. House names are usually in restricted use and do not take on a public meaning.

We shall be looking at house names shortly; meanwhile it is as well to remember that the idea of blending name elements is far from new. It was regularly done in order to create new personal names by the early Germanic tribes. What seems to distinguish modern blends from the old is the simultaneous transfer from one name system to another. Our ancestors did not blend personal name elements to arrive at place names, only to form new personal names.

Incident place names

Another way of arriving at names that was known to our remote ancestors was description or conversion arising out of an incident. In the place names of the English-speaking world there are many that recall incidents connected with the places concerned. One of the best known is **Cannibal Plateau** in Colorado, where a certain Alfred Packer kept alive through the winter by eating the five companions he had killed. Other place names refer to a **Murder**, **Suicide**, **Earthquake** or **Battle**. An island called **Naked** supposedly received its name from a crazed Indian woman who was found wandering there, but the name may originally have referred to the lack of vegetation. One of the problems with names of this type is sorting out the genuine explanations from the later myths.

The first fleet entering **Botany Bay** on 18th January, 1788.

The names just mentioned were almost certainly given by early settlers, who were a hardy breed. Their rawness is aptly reflected in many other names they gave, which are among the most genuine on the map. Genteel residents who come later, however, are apt to change such names. Both Cook and Flinders, when they were sailing round the coast of Australia, were much influenced by incidents when they were giving names. Cook, for example, changed his mind about **Stingray Harbour**, a name he had just decided on, when the botanists who were sailing with him, including the famous Joseph Banks, came back to the ship in high excitement. They had found a great number of previously unknown plants. Cook thought of Botanists' Bay, and finally decided on **Botany Bay**. Banks himself was remembered by **Cape Banks**, and he was later to give his name to the genus of flowers that so excited him.

Flinders named **Cape Catastrophe** and **Memory Cove** after the loss of a boat and its crew. A meeting with a French ship, which might have led to a battle, caused him to name **Encounter Bay**. One entry in his log reads: '**Anxious Bay**, from the night we passed in it.' Incident names are all of this type, in fact—sudden glimpses into the diaries of the namers. They are the least formal of place names, recalling the intimacy of some nicknames. They are the names on the map which stir even the dullest imagination with their suggestion of real-life drama.

Invented place names are unlikely to have such an effect. **Tono**, in Washington, was first connected with a railway, but no one can be sure what was in the namer's mind when he gave the name. One suggestion is that it is taken from 'ton of coal'. If so, it is not a particularly attractive part-conversion. **Sob Lake** in Canada has done rather better, especially when one thinks that it began as the phrase 'son of a bitch', used to describe a trapper who had a cabin there.

Another kind of converted place name is far less arbitrary, for it represents a deliberate attempt to supply a name of good omen. **Accord**, **Concord**, **Optima**, **Utopia** and **Paradise** are all found in several English-speaking countries. Oklahoma has a place name **Fame** which was intended to bring just that. Florida has a **Niceville**. This seemingly French blend is all American, for 'ville' was extremely popular as a place name element in America from the end of the eighteenth century. Even the German immigrants who lived in Pennsylvania liked it, and were not averse to creating place names such as **Kleinville** and **Schwenk-ville**. The suffix '-ville' is the truly American equivalent of '-ton', a distinctive element in settlement names. As for being French, it is said that there are more places in America which end in '-ville' than there are in France.

Indian place names

Each of the English-speaking countries has its own special kind of place names which help to add interest to a world gazetteer. The other typical American names are naturally those taken over from the Indians, though they may have changed their form somewhat. **Suckabone**, for example, represents an Algonquian *suc-e-bouk*, which meant a place in which either potatoes or ground-nuts grew. **Minnehaha** is a Siouan name, 'waterfalls', and in this case it is the meaning rather than the form of the name which has been changed in the popular imagination. The '-haha' was assumed to mean 'laughing' for obvious but unfounded reasons, and Longfellow took it over as 'laughing waters'.

Other tribal languages that have led to American names include Choctaw—**Seyoyah Creek**; Potawatomi—**Shabbona**; Ojibway—**Sha-Bosh-Kung Bay**; Aleut—**Einahnuhto Hills**; Muskogean—**Egoniaga**; Athapascan—**Mentasta**; Iroquoian—**Sacandaga**. The variety of

A Selection of World Place Names Explained

Amsterdam (Netherlands) 'dam on the River Amstel'.

Athens (Greece) after Athene 'queen of heaven', patron goddess.

Baghdad (Iraq) 'God's gift'.

Bermudas (Atlantic islands) after Juan Bermudez, the discoverer.

Belgrade (Yugoslavia) 'white city'.

Bombay (India) earlier Bombain, after Mumbain = goddess Mumbadevi.

Bonn (West Germany) 'town'.

Brisbane (Australia) after Sir Thomas Brisbane, the founder.

Brussels (Belgium) 'buildings on a marsh'.

Buenos Aires (Argentina) 'good winds', part of a title for Our Lady.

Cairo (Egypt) 'victorious', part of full Arabic name 'Mars the victorious', Mars being visible when city was founded.

Chattanooga (USA) 'rock rising to a point'.

Cologne (West Germany) Roman 'colony' of Claudia Agrippina.

Copenhagen (Denmark) 'merchants' harbour'.

Denver (USA) after General James Denver, former Governor.

Des Moines (USA) 'of the monks', probably by folk-etymology from an original Indian name.

Dover (England) 'waters'.

Dresden (East Germany) 'forest-dwellers'.

Edmonton (Canada) transferred from Edmonton, London = 'Eadhelm's estate'.

El Paso (USA) 'crossing, ford'.

Glasgow (Scotland) 'green hollow'.

Helsinki (Finland) 'Helsingi' was the name of the tribe living here.

Istanbul (Turkey) possibly Turkish corruption of *Constantinople* = 'Constantine's city'.

Jamaica (Caribbean island) 'island of springs'.

Liverpool (England) 'pool with clotted water'.

Los Angeles (USA) 'the angels', part of a title for Our Lady.

Madrid (Spain) 'timber'.

Manitoba (Canada) 'great spirit' or 'prairie lake'.

Marseilles (France) for the Massili tribe.

Melbourne (Australia) for Lord Melbourne, British Prime Minister.

Memphis (USA) transferred from ancient Egyptian city.

Miami (USA) 'peninsula-dwellers'.

Minneapolis (USA) a blend of 'Minne-' from *Minnesota* + Greek *polis*, 'city'.

Moscow (USSR) from River Moskva.

Munich (West Germany) 'monk', because city founded on site of monastery.

Naples (Italy) 'new town'.

Ontario (Canada) 'beautiful (lake)'.

Oslo (Norway) 'mouth of River Lo' or 'forest clearing'.

Ottawa (Canada) 'big river' or 'traders'.

Peking (China) 'northern capital'.

Pittsburgh (USA) for William Pitt, the English statesman.

Quebec (Canada) 'place where the river narrows'.

Rome (Italy) from River Ruma.

Seville (Spain) 'lower land'.

Shanghai (China) 'on the sea'.

Sheffield (England) 'open land by the River Sheaf'.

Tokyo (Japan) 'eastern capital'.

Trinidad (West Indies) 'Trinity'.

Vienna (Austria) from River Vienna.

Wellington (New Zealand) after the Duke of Wellington.

Winnipeg (Canada) 'muddy water'.

Yukon (Canada) from River Yukon' 'big river'.

languages and corruption of the names often makes their interpretation difficult or impossible, but most Indian place names appear to be topographical descriptions or incident conversions.

Canada also has its Indian names, such as the rivers **Illecillewaet**, which apparently means 'swift water', and **Incomappleux**, 'fish'. Its French names are both important and distinctive. **Montreal** captures 'royal mountain' in an early form of French, the mountain being the extinct volcano on whose slopes the city stands. **Frontenac** is a form of **Frontignac**, a place in France which gave its name to the Duke of Frontenac, Governor of New France for twenty-seven years. It is said that he asked to be sent to North America in order to escape his shrewish wife.

American Indian place names are scattered throughout North America. The Indians themselves have interesting names. Shown here are **Calf Child, Herbert Lawrence, Medicine Owl, Charlie Rye Eater**.

Australia's Aboriginal place names are a fine heritage, and the national accent also seems to come through in names like **Bargo Brush, Bong Bong, Blue's Point, Broken Hill, Cobbity, Diggers' Rest, Gippsland, Kissing Point, The Paroo, Pretty Sally's, Violet Town** and **Yackandandah**. New Zealand is rightfully proud of its Maori names, many of which can be accurately translated. **Waimakiriri** is beautiful either in that form or as 'snow-cold water'. **Taupo Nui A Tia**, 'the big cloak of Tia', names the country's largest lake by poetic metaphor.

Wherever one looks, the place names of a country manage to individualise it in spite of the vast number of duplicated British names. South Africa has its Dutch names mixed in with the English, Rhodesia its native names. Countless languages have contributed to the great reservoir of names, from the Polynesian **Hawaii**, 'place of the gods', to English, German and French, as in **Applebachsville**. New names continue to appear, some disappear, others are consciously changed.

The changes may be regrettable from an onlooker's point of view, but they are understandable. **Skull Creek** in Colorado is now **Blue Mountain**, for instance. The former name conjures up a vivid picture of early reality, the present one suggests a reproduction painting for a popular market, but this is no criticism of the people who made the change. Just as we admitted the need to change some surnames because of the image they create, so we must admit that some place names, in the ordinary run of daily life, give a false impression of a place and its in-habitants. It is the inhabitants who matter. The name of the place in which they live is, in a sense, their collective name, and they have a right to adjust it.

Some name changes manage to satisfy everyday interests and those of the scholar at the same time. These are the old names that are restored after being out of use for a long time. **San Salvador** is a name of this kind, for though it was one of the first names given by Columbus when he arrived in the West Indies (it means 'holy saviour') the name did not survive. It was restored fifty years ago after careful research had established which island had been so named. Other changes satisfy everyone by being pleasant jokes. Local residents can enjoy the collective impression they give of being wits. The best example is the community in West Virginia that made a **Mountain** out of a **Mole Hill**.

We shall be looking in a later chapter at the further possibilities offered by place names for light-hearted games. We have already seen how some place names can take on very special meanings and pass into the ordinary language. For the moment we must remember that 'places' are often towns and cities which have a complex internal structure of neighbourhoods and streets. Naturally, all these have names, and it is to these names within place names that we will now turn.

Chapter 13
Neighbourly Names

The name of the street in which we live can take on a deep personal significance. It can evoke an area that we know in detail and a small community of people whom we know well. Another street name that we have known in the past might instantly recall our childhood and a thousand small incidents, reminding us of friends and neighbours and the passing years.

Street names can have this private meaning, but they are also felt to have a more public meaning. As with place names, street names reflect on the people who live in the streets concerned, particularly on their social status. Few people, therefore, care to live in **Thieves Lane**, say, or **Cowdung Street**, though such names almost certainly indicate that the street has been there since the Middle Ages. For that matter, few class-conscious Englishmen, it seems, care to live in a street that is actually called a street.

'Street'

This curious fact has impressed itself on estate-developers all over the country. As an official explained to *The Daily Telegraph* in 1971:

> 'Streets have gone out of fashion and no one wants to live in one. When people think of a street they imagine something like the **Coronation Street** image of old terraced back-to-backs. You can call them roads, avenues, lanes, groves, drives, closes, places—anything but streets.'

It was about this time that a builder was complaining of customers who were cancelling orders for new houses. They had learned that the street in which they stood was going to be referred to as a 'street' in its name.

As it happens, there are plenty of euphemisms available nowadays. They have a certain interest in themselves, and I have listed them as street name elements on page 158. But this sensitivity to the generic word in a street name is a sure indication that residents will look very closely indeed at the element attached to it to see whether that reflects on their status. The result is a steady flow of applications to local councils asking to change existing names to something that 'sounds better'.

Sometimes the local authority itself quietly 'loses' certain names in the cause of respectability.

What sort of name disappears? A few that have disappeared from London, include **Foul Lane**, **Stinking Lane**, **Hog Lane**, **Bladder Street**, **Grub Street** and **Pudding Lane**. Of these, 'foul' and 'stinking' were accurate descriptions no doubt in medieval times, while hogs and bladders would have been sold in the streets concerned. 'Puddings' were the entrails of animals which were carried along Pudding Lane to be dumped in the Thames. Grub Street probably included the name of an early resident, though a reference to caterpillars or worms is just possible. The street may have been infested with them.

Grub Street is now **Milton Street**, which shows an especially interesting change. The original name had come to be associated with low-quality writing because of the hack-writers who lived there in the seventeenth century. In the nineteenth century the residents deliberately decided to use the name of the poet in an attempt to raise the street's status.

The loss of Foul Lane and the like for general purposes is inevitable, though such names are carefully examined by the historian. Like obsolete surnames and place names they can help to paint an accurate picture of medieval life. Non-historians are quite happy for the names to be in records of the past, but they do not want to see them displayed on the street corner. They are also not fond of names like **Foundry Street**, which blatantly implies that manual work goes on in the district.

A similar kind of reaction to street names is discernible in the United States. Estate agents know that a suburban house will be easier to sell if the street name contains an element suggestive of rural peace, such as 'Hayloft' or 'Corncrib'. Streets laid out in strict geometric patterns are no longer popular, nor are the efficient number names that went with them. **Seventh Avenue** may be easier to find than **Rosemont Drive**, but there is actually prestige to be gained these days in being difficult to find.

Number names for streets

Such names, however, are thoroughly established both in the USA and Canada. They owe their existence, primarily, to William Penn, who was far from being the non-literary person such names might suggest. He was a classical scholar who coined a Greek name for the city he founded in 1682 — **Philadelphia**, 'brotherly love'. Had he wanted to he could certainly have suggested similar names for the streets.

When Penn came to Philadelphia many houses had already been built. People were referring to the existing streets by the name of the most important person living there. But Penn was founding a Quaker colony, and the last thing he could allow was a street name system that raised some people above others. Like all Quakers he objected strongly to any social custom that emphasised different ranks of people. He had deeply offended his father, for instance, by refusing to take off his hat in his presence.

A Street By Any Other Name

Many of the following words occur in street names as substitutes for the word 'street' itself. In some cases the original meanings of the words have been considerably stretched, but others are genuine synonyms.

Acre
Alley
Approach
Arcade also used of an avenue of trees forming an arch.
Avenue
Backs behind buildings.
Bank a raised shelf or ridge of land.
Bottom land in a valley.
Boulevard
Broadway
Bullring
Butts usually transferred from a field name where it referred to land at the boundary of the field, or land covered with tree-stumps.
By-Pass
Carfax from Latin *quadri-furcus*, 'four-forked', used where four or more roads meet.
Causeway raised way across a marsh or a paved way.
Chase originally unenclosed land reserved for hunting.
Circle
Circus where there is a circular ring of houses.
Close an entry or passage.
Commons common land.
Coombe a small valley.
Coppice plantation of young trees.
Copse=coppice.
Corner
Cottages
Court
Cranny a narrow opening.
Crescent
Croft an enclosed field.
Cross for a cross-roads.
Cut where an excavation has been made to allow road to pass.

Cutting=cut.
Dale a valley.
Dene (also *Dean*) a wooded valley.
Drang (dialectal) an alley.
Drift a track.
Drive
Droke (dialectal) a narrow passage.
Drove a road along which cattle was driven.
Embankment
End
Esplanade=promenade.
Expressway (USA)
Extension (USA)
Fair on former fair-ground.
Farrow a path.
Fennell (dialectal) an alley.
Field
Fold
Freeway
Front
Gardens
Garth (dialectal) an enclosure.
Gate Old Norse *gata*, 'road'.
Ginnel (dialectal) narrow passage.
Glebe land assigned to a clergyman.
Glen
Green
Ground
Grove
Gully
Hangings a steep slope on a hill.
Hard a sloping roadway or jetty.
Hatch fenced land.
Hey fenced land.
Highway
Hill
Houses
Jigger (dialectal) an alley.
Jitty (dialectal) an alley.

Lane
Lawn='laund', a stretch of untilled ground.
Lea untilled land.
Line (USA)
Loke (dialectal) an alley.
Mall where pall mall, a game with mallet and ball, was played.
Market
Mead=meadow
Mews stables.
Midway (USA)
Motorway
Mount
Narrows
Ope an opening.
Orchard
Oval
Pantiles properly roofing-tiles but sometimes used to describe paving-tiles.
Parade
Park
Parkway
Passage
Path
Pavement a roadway in USA.
Pickle a small enclosure.
Pightle=pickle.
Place
Plain
Plaisance (USA) a pleasure-ground.
Plaza (USA) Spanish, 'market-place'.
Poultry a poultry market.
Promenade
Prospect a place affording a view.
Quadrant a square.
Quay
Range
Retreat a secluded place.
Ride
Riding

Ring
Rise
Road
Row
Scarp the steep face of a hill.
Side
Skyway (USA)
Slope
Slype a covered way, especially one leading from the cloisters of a cathedral.
Sneck (dialectal) a narrow passage.
Sneckett = sneck
Snicket = sneck
Square
Steps
Sweep
Terrace
Thoroughfare 'thorough' is an old form of 'through'.
Throughway
Tollway (USA)
Turnpike a toll-gate.
Twitchel (dialectal) a narrow passage.
Twitchet = twitchel.
Twitten = twitchel.
Twitting = twitchel.
Tyning land enclosed with a fence.
Usage a public right of way.
Vale
Viaduct
View
Villas
Walk
Wall a footpath next to a wall.
Way
Wharf
Wood
Wynd (dialectal) a narrow street.
Yard

The Quakers referred even to Sunday as **First Day**, thus removing the pagan reference, and this may have inspired Penn to use a similar system to identify the streets of his city. These were not the haphazard sprawl of a typical English town, but were laid out at right angles to one another at regular intervals. Penn began at the eastern boundary with **First Street** and continued with his simple sequential names from there. For the streets which crossed from north to south he decided on verbal names, but once again he was careful to avoid links with people. He turned to nature and 'the things that spontaneously grow in the country'. **Chestnut Street**, **Walnut Street**, **Spruce Street**, **Pine Street** and the like were created. For a road that faced the river Penn wrote of **Front Street**, and he allowed the use of such names as **Market Street**.

Whether there was a general appreciation of the high principles which had led to the Philadelphian street name system, or whether the practicality of at least having a system of some kind made its appeal, we shall never know, but other towns quickly followed suit. Not only were the number names transferred elsewhere—often the tree names were borrowed too, regardless of whether the trees concerned grew in the area. Yet with all its apparent simplicity, the number name system posed problems for the towns that adopted it in Ohio, Kentucky, Louisiana, Virginia, Tennessee and elsewhere. Where was First Street to be, for example, and would it remain First Street?

St. Joseph had a **First Street**, **Second Street** and **Third Street** at one time, but the land caved into the river and left **Fourth Street** to begin the sequence. A more frequent occurrence was for towns to develop later beyond the original boundary, causing no problems at the open end of the number sequence but considerable problems at the beginning. Number names were always interpreted as being sequential in space, not time, and an **Eighty-seventh Street** could not be placed out of order on the basis that it merely recorded that eighty-six streets had been built previously. The usual solution was for suburban streets to take on verbal names and remain outside the general system.

When Washington was laid out at the beginning of the nineteenth century the street names included the usual number names in one direction. Letter names were introduced, however, for the streets that crossed them, and important streets, called 'avenues' for the first time, were linked to the names of states. **A Street**, **B Street** and the like did not appeal to other city-planners, but some copied the idea of using the names of the states. What really caught on everywhere was the use of 'avenue', though even this may have been influenced as much by New York as Washington. A few years later, when New York was extended, the ultimate in street name systems was devised. The **First Street**, **Second Street**, etc., from Philadelphia were there, but crossing them were **First Avenue**, **Second Avenue** and so on. A few streets that lay outside the grid became **Avenue A**, **Avenue B**, **C** and **D**. There were also occasional survivals of established street names, such as the Dutch **De Bouwerij**, 'the farm', in its anglicised form **The Bowery**, and **Breede Wegh**, which easily became **Broadway**. These were mostly streets which ran diagonally and thus cut across the basic grid pattern.

The streets of **Washington**.

New York's system would no doubt have been widely followed, but it came late in the day. One other city that influenced American street names because it gave an example from an early date was Boston. Here one cannot talk of a system unless one calls it the English non-system. All streets were named, either by description as in **Commercial Street**, by conversion, as in **Congress Street**, after national and local figures, or from the places the streets led to. Other towns followed Boston's example, or the English example as it may have been in many cases, if local usage established street names before the City Fathers turned their minds to the matter. Occasionally there must have been a deliberate rejection of number names, the reason for their use not being known or respected. There must also have been occasions when the people who were in a position to influence street names already had their own family names linked to them. In such cases they would obviously have been tempted to allow them to remain undisturbed.

Medieval street names

Britain had no William Penn who could start a national street name fashion with a single flash of original thinking, and there were not, of course, cities to be founded in the same way. Towns and cities had been growing naturally for centuries, and the streets within them acquired the same kind of naturally descriptive names as the places themselves had done. The principal street in medieval times was the **High Street** in Southern England, **High Gate** in the North. 'Street' had been borrowed from Latin in Anglo-Saxon times to describe the Roman roads, which were far superior to anything previously known in Britain. The Northern 'gate' was not the kind of gate one opens and shuts but the Old Norse *gata*, 'street'. The ordinary 'gate' also occurred in medieval street names to indicate the entrance to a walled town or the presence of a water-gate.

The name 'High Street' was taken at first to the New World, but 'high' tended to be interpreted as 'elevated' rather than 'important'. In most cases **Main Street** came to replace it. 'Main' is also used in Britain, but usually in connection with a road rather than a street. The original distinction between a 'road', which was an unmade way along which horses were *ridden*, and a paved 'street' lasted until at least the end of the Middle Ages. 'A main road' tends to be a descriptive phrase rather than a name.

Early English street names commented on their relative positions, as in **North Street**, etc., **Upper Street** and **Nether** ('lower') **Street**; on their surfaces, as in **Chiswell** ('pebble') **Street** and perhaps **Featherbed Lane**, a reference to soft mud. **Summer Road** in Thames Ditton would have been **Summer Lane** or **Summer Street** in medieval times, but the meaning would have been the same—a road which was unusable in winter. Other old names were of the type **Bollo Lane**, where a 'bull hollow' is referred to, and **Woodgate**, a road along which wood was transported. Commodities sold in the streets often gave those streets their names, the usual items being salt, pepper, milk, fish and bread.

There were formerly several **Love Lanes** in London, and as in any city these also referred to something being sold rather than a romantic lovers'

A Selection of London Street Names

Adelphi Terrace from the group of buildings *The Adelphi* (Greek *adelphoi*, 'brothers') designed by the Adam brothers.

Aldwych possibly 'old wick' or settlement.

Baker Street after William Baker, once controller of the Marylebone estate. Sherlock Holmes lived at 221B according to Conan Doyle.

Barbican a word brought back from the Crusades. An outer defensive wall and watch-tower.

Bayswater Road Bayard's (or Baynard's) watering-place.

Belsize Square from the manor of *Belassis*, 'beautifully situated'.

Berkeley Square where the nightingale sang. Baron Berkeley had a house there.

Bevis Marks earlier *Beris Marks*. Land within the marks 'boundaries' of the Abbots of Bury.

Birdcage Walk where Charles II kept birdcages.

Blackfriars Road for the Dominicans who settled there.

Bow Street the famous police court is in this street shaped like a bow.

Cannon Street formerly the street where the candle-makers lived.

Carmelite Street the friars of Our Lady of Mount Carmel, or 'Whitefriars' lived there.

Carnaby Street famous in the 1960s as a fashion centre. From Carnaby in Yorkshire(?).

Charing Cross Road 'Charing' refers to a *turning* of the Thames; the cross commemorated Queen Eleanor, whose funeral procession passed this way.

Clerkenwell Road a well where parish clerks gathered annually.

Cockspur Street in the days of cockfighting the cocks wore spurs, which were sold in this street.

Cornhill a hill where corn was grown.

Dean Street for the Dean of the Royal Chapel.

Downing Street the official residence of the Prime Minister. Sir George Downing, an unpopular diplomat, was an early leaseholder.

Farringdon Street from the surname of an early Sheriff of London.

Gower Street for the first Earl Gower.

Gracechurch Street the church was St. Benet's; 'grace' was formerly *grass*, perhaps with reference to a turf roof, or to a fodder market.

Gray's Inn Road The inn was a hostel for law students owned by the Grey family.

Great Windmill Street a windmill was there in the seventeenth century.

Grosvenor Square otherwise *Little America* because of the Embassy, etc., was owned by the Grosvenor family.

Hanover Square honoured George I, son of the Elector of Hanover.

Harley Street famous as a gathering-place for the élite of the medical profession, is on an estate owned by the Harley family.

Haymarket was a hay market.

High Holborn from the *bourne* ('stream') in the *hollow*.

Kingsway for Edward VII.

Leadenhall Street for a hall that had a leaden roof.

Liverpool Street in honour of Lord Liverpool.

Marylebone High Road the church St. Mary Bourne, the 'bourne' being the Tyburn stream. Later thought to be *Mary la Bonne*.

Middlesex Street the official name that is rightfully ignored by every Londoner, who knows that petticoat-makers who worked here in the seventeenth century caused the street to become *Petticoat Lane*.

Moorgate a gate led to the *moor*, 'marshy wasteland', outside the north wall of the City.

Old Bailey often used as a synonym for the Central Criminal Court which is situated there. The *bailey* was once a mud rampart just outside the city wall.

Old Bond Street after Sir Thomas Bond, who owned the land.

Oxford Street formerly *Tyburn Way*, leads to Oxford but was named after Edward Harley, second Earl of Oxford, the landowner.

Park Lane runs beside *Hyde Park*, once a 'hide' or measure of land.

Pentonville Road was owned by Henry Penton.

Petticoat Lane see *Middlesex Street*.

Piccadilly see page 166.

Portland Street the Dukes of Portland owned land here.

Portobello Road to commemorate the capture of Porto Bello in the Gulf of Mexico, 1739.

Praed Street after the banker William Praed.

Procter Street after a former inhabitant, Bryan Procter, solicitor and poet.

Regent Street after the Prince Regent, later George IV, and meant to link Carlton House and Regent's Park.

Rosebery Avenue the fifth Lord Rosebery was the first Chairman of the London County Council, and this street was named after him.

Russell Square owned by the Russell family, Dukes of Bedford.

St. Giles High Street a leper colony was established here in medieval times, the hospital and church being dedicated to St. Giles.

St. James Street from a hospital dedicated to St. James.

Shaftesbury Avenue in honour of the seventh Earl of Shaftesbury who did much philanthropic work for the people who formerly lived in this area.

Sloane Square after Sir Hans Sloane, a distinguished physician whose library formed the nucleus of the British Library.

Soho Square *So-ho* was a hunting cry like 'tally-ho'. There may have been an inn in this area which took the cry as an incident name.

Southampton Row the owner was Thomas Wriothesley, Earl of Southampton.

Theobalds Road led in the direction of Theobalds, in Hertfordshire, where Lord Burghley had his home and lavishly entertained Elizabeth I and James I.

The Strand was formerly the 'strand', or shore of the Thames.

Threadneedle Street from a sign of a house or inn with three needles on it, perhaps the arms of the Needlemakers' Company. But one writer mentions the folk-dance *Threadneedle*, where dancers form arches for one another.

Tottenham Court Road the court of 'Totta's ham' or village.

Wardour Street now mainly linked with the film industry. Sir Edward Wardour was former owner.

Watergate a rather insignificant London street bears this highly significant name. There was once a gate giving access to the Thames.

Whitefriars Street see *Carmelite Street*.

Whitehall Cardinal Wolsey owned the palace of this name, which passed to Henry VIII.

Wigmore Street one of the Harley family, the landowners, was Baron Harley of Wigmore, in Herefordshire.

walk. In his *London Lanes* Alan Stapleton suggests humorously that **Huggin Lane**, which was near a Love Lane, might be connected with it and not derive its name from an early resident called Huggin or from the sale of hogs. In several towns there is a **Grope** or **Grape Lane**, which really is a synonym for Love Lane. One writer has explained the name as 'a dark, narrow alley through which one groped one's way', but the full medieval forms of the name make it quite clear that another meaning was intended.

Other common street names in medieval times mentioned where the streets led, including either a place name or a generic term such as 'ferry' or 'castle'. **Gallows Street** survives in some places as a reminder of the grim realities of earlier times, but **Dead Lane**, which has usually been 'lost' as a street name, was a simple reference to a cemetery. The residents of a street were often described in its name, as with **Lombard Street** and **Walker Lane**, the latter being where the walkers, who processed cloth, lived and worked.

These medieval street names throughout Britain have obviously received attention from historical students of place names. They often supply much incidental information about medieval urban life. But relatively few of the names survive in living use. They were bestowed casually by people who always called a spade a spade, and they were doomed when the guardians of public morality began to appoint themselves in the nineteenth century.

While this early layer of street names has come in for a general scrutiny, the more usual approach to street names has been on a geographical basis. The street names of particular areas have been investigated, and the results often published as street name dictionaries. It will be worth looking in some detail at examples of these dictionaries, beginning with major cities and going on to smaller localities. It is in the smaller towns and districts that a great deal could still be done by enterprising local historians or teachers who want their students to do project work. The educational aspects of such work are especially interesting and I shall comment on them later.

London street names

The street names of London, like those of several other European capital cities, have received a great deal of attention. By 'London' the City of London is primarily meant, but several dictionaries have included some of the main suburbs. All writers on the subject begin with a reading of Stow's *Survey of London*, which was first published in 1598. Stow himself knew sixteenth-century London well, and he was also a student of early records. This showed him that many street names had already changed their form. **Belliter Lane**, for instance, had earlier been **Belzettars Lane**, which indicated more clearly its connection with the bell-makers. There was a large group of such men, for the bells in the many London churches were much used. The lane still exists as **Billiter Street**.

Stow was not a student of names as such, and neither was Henry Harben, whose *Dictionary of London* was published in 1918. The dictionary

was the result of work carried out over thirty years, and is another
standard work to which writers on London street names are obliged to
turn. The first actual street name dictionary for London, however,
appears to have been *London Street Names*, by F. H. Habben. This was
published in 1896, so that it had to rely mainly on Stow. In his intro-
ductory remarks Habben remarks sensibly that names cannot usually be
dismissed 'with a curt etymological sentence and nothing more'. He talks
of the 'facts or circumstances round about the name' which need to be
given, and he gives them himself.

Nothing is known of Habben, but his frequent quotations of Chaucer,
Milton, Longfellow and other poets, and his willingness to guess at an
Old Norse personal name origin for names like **Snow Hill** makes one
think that the 'B.A.' mentioned on the title-page was probably a degree
in English. In the case of Snow Hill he rightly directs his readers to
Dickens's graphic description of it in *Nicholas Nickleby*, a novel in which
Dickens displays to the full his wide interest in names of all kinds.

One famous London street owes its
name to the game of **Pall-Mall**
(or **Pell-Mell**) which became popular for a time in the seventeenth
century.

Louis Zettersten's *City Street Names* was published in 1917, but the
author does not seem to have been aware of Habben's *Dictionary*. Zettersten was a Swedish businessman who worked in London, and once again
he was obliged to accept the explanations of Stow and one or two others
as facts. His great strength, however, was to produce an attractive little
dictionary that could easily be read by a layman, and there seem to be
very few instances where he would seriously mislead his readers. In his
article on **Fleet Street**, for instance, he says that the name derives from a
bridge over the River Fleet rather than the river itself, a comment based
on a thirteenth-century reference to *vicus de Fletebrigge*. As it happens, later
writers have unearthed a still earlier reference which would make the

explanation 'street leading to the Fleet River', but this is hair-splitting. When a real problem occurs, as it definitely does with the **Snow Hill** (earlier **Snore Hill**) already mentioned, Zettersten makes it clear that there is a problem and that suggestions as to the original meaning can only be tentatively made.

In many ways Zettersten's little book is more satisfying than that of his compatriot, Eilert Ekwall, who published *Street Names of the City of London* in 1954. Ekwall is a pure philologist of the highest quality writing for other specialists, and for him a street name's origin is all that matters. Subsequent associations of a street, which may have given it a meaning that is recognised throughout the world, are totally ignored. He does not mention journalism, for example, when he deals with Fleet Street. He says quite clearly that he is interested only in names 'which go back to medieval times', and could have added that his interest even in those names is highly restricted.

The point perhaps needs stressing for Ekwall, as the heavyweight scholar, has tended to overshadow Zettersten, the intelligent amateur, and others like him. The amateurs respond instinctively to street names and see them as meaningful wholes rather than linguistic specimens under a microscope. I believe very firmly that the 'amateur' approach is the right one, the linguistic facts forming only a part of the whole story.

In between Zettersten and Ekwall several other studies of London street names appeared. These were mostly imitative of the earlier works, but in 1935 E. Stewart Fay published *Why Piccadilly?* in which he abandoned the dictionary style in favour of a discursive work. He begins by writing of **Piccadilly** for three pages, attributing it to the 'pickadills', or ruffed lace collars, made by the tailor Robert Baker in the seventeenth century. Baker made enough money from these highly fashionable articles to buy a house, which others quickly named **Pickadilly Hall**. The name eventually spread to the area, and has survived several official attempts at various times to change it.

Stewart Fay states his view of street names immediately after the Piccadilly explanation. For him the names lead directly to human anecdotes, the

> 'hundreds of such stories hid behind the often prosaic names of London streets, squares and localities. To search these out is to lay bare a cross-section of the pageant of London from the earliest times down to the living present . . . **Spring Gardens** will inform us of a royal practical joke. **Hatton Gardens** conceals a scandal concerning the frailty of Elizabeth . . .'.

He gives further examples designed to whet the appetite, and it is difficult not to read on. The 'royal joke' he refers to was a sundial which stood in **Spring Gardens**. It had a concealed spring tap nearby on which people stepped when they went to look at the dial. A jet of water would then spurt out and soak them. In spite of this, Spring Gardens is far more likely to have got its name because of the 'spring' of young trees formerly planted there, but who would sacrifice the anecdote? The **Hatton Gardens** story is made into a playlet by Stewart Fay and is rather overwritten, but the essential facts about Elizabeth I and her 'dancing Chancellor' are given. Sir Christopher Hatton danced his way into the Queen's favour, then persuaded her to let him take over most of the Bishop of Ely's house and gardens. Hatton gave his name to the gardens, and later—in rebus form—to a nearby public house, the **Hat and Tun**.

The style of *Why Piccadilly?* is often successful and is a good example of an imaginative writer's approach to names. Although no philologist the author is generally able to sort out fact and fiction in the works he has consulted. On **Snow Hill**, which is always something of a test case, he mentions the story of stage-coach passengers snoring by the time they arrived at the Saracen's Head public house only in order to dismiss it. For a man who was clearly deeply fascinated by names, he also has many sensible things to say about American number names for streets. After praising the functional advantages of the New York system he goes on to say that number names can take on a meaning and value like any other names. Names do not have, he reminds us, 'an inherent stamp of quality; their reputation is derived solely from the nature of their associations'. He gives the example of **Mayfair**, which was notorious at the beginning of the eighteenth century because of the riotous celebrations which took place at the beginning of May each year but which later changed its meaning completely.

Stewart Fay's discursive method was partly emulated in 1952 by Hector Bolitho and Derek Peel in *Without The City Wall*. Their sub-title refers to 'an adventure in London street names, north of the river', and their aim is to take the reader on a series of excursions—which are mapped out—explaining the names encountered. It is an interesting idea, and shows yet another approach to street names. These authors too make it clear that they are not scholars, but they have gone to respectable sources of information and then applied their own common sense. Wherever possible they checked 'facts' in their own way, so when told that **Chiswell Street** took its name from Old English *ceosel*, 'gravel', they telephoned the Borough Engineer to ask about the geological strata in that area. He confirmed that there were large deposits of flint and gravel there.

A philologist would say that such a check was unnecessary in the case of such a well-attested word, but the attitude displayed is a healthy one. Their whole approach, in fact, firmly relates the names to the streets themselves. The same can be said of Alan Stapleton's two books, *London's Alleys, Byways and Courts* and *London Lanes*. The first of these appeared in 1924, the second in 1930, and they take up a comment by Dr. Johnson that 'if you wish to have a just notion of the magnitude of this city, you must not be satisfied with seeing its great streets and squares, but must survey its innumerable little lanes and courts'.

Stapleton surveys them thoroughly, 'robbing', as he remarks, 'everyone who has written a book on London' for his text but making an outstanding contribution of his own in the form of sketches. As with the other discursive works, explanations of the names are woven into an intricate pattern of anecdote and narration.

And still books on London street names appear. A London taxi-driver,

Al Smith, brought out his *Dictionary of City of London Street Names* in 1970. It is a personal selection of historical material gathered from standard sources. Gillian Bebbington's *London Street Names* appeared in 1972. It covers a wider area than previous dictionaries and makes a further useful contribution by displaying the family trees of important landowners. This enables one to see at a glance how the names of their relations and estates, or their own titles, were used for blocks of street names. For general reference purposes it is probably the best dictionary of its kind.

London's street names, then, have received much attention, though they still lag a long way behind those of Paris in this respect. What is interesting is to see how different people have dealt with the street names of the same place. All must turn to the philologist for specialist advice in the case of the early names, but it is open to anyone from that point to clothe each name, to show how the events of centuries have given meanings to names which were not inherent in them. There are stories to street names, and they need to be well told.

Johannesburg street names

An interesting contrast to London street names is provided by those of Johannesburg. They have been carefully studied by Anna H. Smith, whose monumental *Johannesburg Street Names* was published in 1971. At that time the city was still only eighty-five years old, and it might be thought that in such a case there are no difficulties for the researcher. These names were given, however, by a large number of early land-owners and surveyors, who usually kept no records of why the names had been chosen. Naming was not taken very seriously, and sometimes the draughtsmen preparing maps were left to select names. They usually made them as short as possible for their own convenience.

Miss Smith omits number names from her dictionary as being self-explanatory, but mentions in her Introduction that there are 'forty or so **First Avenues**, **Lanes**, **Roads** or **Streets** in Johannesburg'. This reflects, presumably, the parallel development of different areas by early pioneers. There was certainly no attempt made to evolve an over-all street name system, though the City Council now tries to exercise control.

As with most towns in Britain, a wide variety of people are commemorated in Johannesburg street names. There they include entertainers, admirals, artists, authors, sportsmen, prominent city residents—including landowners, musicians, kings and queens, scientists and inventors, prominent persons in South African history, surveyors and government officials. Street names that link with first names—usually those of women —were often meant to honour the relations of the namers. Place names are usually meant to be reminders of the pioneers' home-towns. One pioneer, at least, must have come from very close to where this book is being written, for he named an **Esher Street** and **Surbiton**, **Kingston**, **Hampton**, **Molesey** and **Ditton Avenues**, all of which places are within a mile or two of my house.

Other names linked to the street names include those of battles, churches, companies, farms, hotels, mines, mountains, mythological figures, rivers, saints and ships. Transferred names from ships show particularly well the dangers that lie in wait for a researcher less thorough than Miss Smith. **London Street**, **Suffolk Road**, **Dunrobin Street**, **Ivanhoe Street**, **Mars Street** and **Zebra Street** are names that one would naturally be inclined to explain as being other than ship names, which they happen to be. It is never possible to take a name purely at its face value. Even **Winning Way** turns out to be named after a Mr. Winning.

South African wildlife is well represented in Johannesburg street names, and there are descriptive names ranging from **Greenhill Road** to **Parkview**. Major events inspired such names as **Jubilee Road**; minor incidents names like **Error Street**, which records a survey error. Several Greek letter names occur because surveyors sometimes identified land that was not yet named in that way, only to have their temporary identifications become **Delta Place**, **Epsilon Place** and the like. Blended names such as **Julbert Road**, from Julius and Robert, and **Hannaben Street**, from Hanna and Benjamin, are found, together with back-spellings such as **Ubla Lane**, from a company called the 'Albu Group'. Since there are also invented names such as **Windeena Avenue** all the normal categories of a nomenclature seem to be present.

What Miss Smith's dictionary does to perfection is to illustrate in great detail the problems faced by a researcher into modern as opposed to ancient street names. People with personal knowledge had to be contacted, newspapers and documents scanned, official records searched. The result is a book that gives us great insight into the minds of our fellow men, into what they thought important or trivial as they set about making history in their own way. Johannesburg is more fortunate than most modern cities in having such a record, which will be particularly appreciated by future generations.

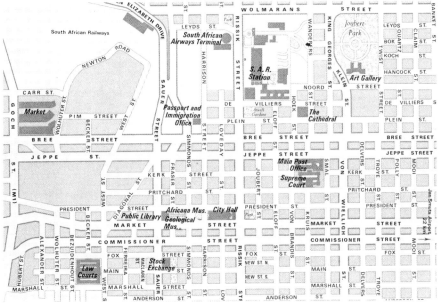

The streets of **Johannesburg**.

Other street name dictionaries

In a more modest way, there is great scope for local historians and others to compile street name dictionaries in their own areas. An excellent method is to make use of the local newspaper, publishing a series of articles street by street giving the facts so far known. Earlier forms of older names are vital, and with more modern names it is essential to know when the names were given. Local residents will usually respond by giving further information which can be included when the material is published later in more permanent form.

The earliest example I have seen of such articles, leading to a discursive work in this case rather than a dictionary, is *Greenock Street Names*, by Gardner Blair. This was published by the *Greenock Herald* itself in 1907. A more recent example is *Warrington and the Mid-Mersey Valley* by G. A. Carter. Several newspapers are currently publishing articles about local street names, both in Britain and elsewhere. The *Winnipeg Tribune*, for example, has a long-running series written by Vince Leah. It is quite clear that readers of the *Tribune* enjoy having their memories stimulated by such articles.

Local historians working independently have produced very satisfying street name dictionaries for places like Lewes, Bristol, Watford, Stevenage, Acton (Middlesex) and Shrewsbury (see the Bibliography). Articles on the street names of other areas have appeared from time to time in specialised magazines, and in many public libraries there exists a collection of catalogue cards on which street name information is given. Naturally there are many more places where the basic research still needs to be done.

Street name projects

Many projects can be based on names (including first names, surnames and place names) which have the highest possible educational value, but it is difficult to imagine a project more satisfying than one based on local street names. It can be adapted to different age-groups, so that very young children will be content to discover the first layer of facts about each name —which queen was referred to in **Queens Road**, what the tree mentioned in **Beech Avenue** actually looks like, and so on. The teacher will have to give this basic information to young children, who can then illustrate and decorate a little guide to local street names.

As the age of the children increases, so they will be capable of finding out for themselves why streets bear certain names. Each name can then become a springboard for further project work. The most prosaic of names, such as **Station Road**, can be turned into a marvellous investigation of the railways, and the changes they brought to society when they were first introduced. An obscure name can at least demonstrate the thrill of research, 'detective work' as it can be called. As for poetic names—well, I happen to live in the street with the most poetic name in England, **Aragon Avenue**. It has point because Catherine of Aragon once lived half a mile away in Hampton Court Palace and probably rode across the land where the street now stands. But the name recalls more than that unhappy lady. There is the kingdom from which she took her name, with its 'torrent at the door', as Hilaire Belloc calls its river in his poem 'Tarantella'. What a wealth of history there. One can even link the name to the distinguished French poet and novelist, Louis Aragon, for his surname shows that his ancestors came from that part of Spain.

A hint of what can be done educationally using street names as a base has been given in the Usherwoods' *Street Names* (History from Familiar Things), published by Ginn. But what *could* be done by senior students in teacher-training colleges, colleges of further education and the like is far more than has been suggested. These larger institutions have the facilities now to publish limited editions of specialised works. Properly researched street name dictionaries would make ideal publications. They could be modest or ambitious according to the funds available, and each one would help with the eventual compilation of county street name dictionaries.

Teachers, lecturers and others who are interested in preparing such local dictionaries should consult the further information section of this book. There are people with experience who are willing to help. Meanwhile, problems of time and space force us to move on. Street names were our names within places: we now go on to look at names within streets. But I leave street names reluctantly. Someone said to me once how dull they were, which is strange. I have never found a dull one yet.

Chapter 14
Signing a Name

Britain has some seventy thousand or so 'pubs'. The earlier terms 'inn' and 'tavern' appear to have referred originally to different kinds of pub. The inn was obliged to remain open at all hours in order to receive guests. Taverns were for casual refreshment and were obliged to close at a certain hour. But the two terms became confused at an early date, and few modern writers on the subject use them consistently with their original meanings. Both have in any case been replaced by 'pub' in normal speech, so we will refer to pubs and their names throughout this chapter.

Pubs carry on a tradition of convivial hospitality which began to be established in the Middle Ages. Many writers have written eloquently about their charms, but we must concern ourselves here with their names. These are often distinctive and intriguing in themselves but they have, of course, another famous characteristic. Each name is usually accompanied by its visual representation, its sign. Pub names and signs together add to the interest of any journey through Britain, and this interest can only be deepened when one looks into the past to see how and why the names and signs arose.

The ale-stake

The classic writers on signboard lore, Larwood and Hotten, conclude that our medieval ancestors must have imitated the Romans when they began to make use of trade signs. The Romans certainly identified their various tradesmen by symbols. A tavern keeper would tie a bunch of evergreens to a pole, the 'ale-stake', and display it in the street. He was crudely honouring Bacchus, the god of wine, who was always shown with ivy and vine leaves. The **Bush** appeared in medieval England as a pub sign and is still to be found as such.

The Bush is technically a generic sign, rather like the three balls that symbolise any pawnbroker or the red and white striped pole that still sometimes announces the presence of a barber. In a street where each establishment carries on a different trade such signs are adequate, but the custom whereby particular trades were associated with special streets seems to have begun early. As soon as there were several butchers, bakers or whatever next door to one another in a medieval street it became necessary to distinguish them more individually. Today in such a situation we would do it very simply, by showing the different shop names. At a time when hardly anybody could read, shops needed names for spoken use but signs that could be used for visual identification.

It is important to realise that for several centuries city streets in Britain were filled with signs of all kinds, not just pub signs. All tradesmen needed them, and even private householders found them necessary. This was an age when there were no numbered houses, and one's address was a descriptive phrase that made use of any convenient landmark. Many people found it easier to display a personal sign outside their houses so that they could speak of living 'at the sign of the **Star**' or something similar. Some surnames derive from these sign names, which came into use at the end of the surname period.

Influence of emblems

But did the use of signs consciously imitate the Romans? They could just as easily have come upon the scene as a natural reflection of medieval life. People could not read or write but they could recognise simple pictures. One might say that they were trained to do so. One of the greatest educational influences of the era was the Church, which itself used a system of name signs.

Three saints with their emblems as portrayed at Chartres. St. **Philip** holds a long cross, as a reminder of his crucifixion. St. **Matthias** was beheaded, so his emblem is an axe. St. **Bartholomew** is said to have been flayed alive, so he holds a flaying knife.

These name signs are still to be seen in churches but few of us are now very adept at 'reading' them. The medieval church-goer, by contrast, would look at a stained-glass window which showed a woman holding a basket of fruit or flowers and know immediately that this was St. Dorothy. A nearby statue of a man holding a key or keys was St. Peter. The saints were known by their *emblems* which performed much the same function as name plates might have done. By the end of the fourteenth century many of these emblems had become standardised throughout western Europe.

Some of them were highly individual, others had more in common with the Bush in that they were symbolic in a general way. A book might be held not only by the Evangelists but by any saint who had a reputation for learning or devotion to the liturgy. A sword was a symbol of execution and a palm indicated martyrdom by other means. All of these and many more the ordinary person was able to interpret. He went to church often and was frequently told the stories behind the emblems. They came to form a simple kind of hieroglyphic language.

Today we think of pictures of any kind as adjuncts to words and names. If we see a pub with even the simplest of signs outside it, such as a **Red Lion** or **Plough**, we still expect to see the name written with it. A complex sign outside a private house, say, with a sheaf of rye to be seen and a hare near it, the sun shining in the background, would baffle us completely. Even if we knew that the people living there were called **Harrison** we would still not make the 'hare-rye-sun' connection. A few centuries ago we would have been far more practised in deciphering such 'silent names', as Camden calls them when he gives the Harrison example. We would have had to be, for the signs of the time did not bother to give the verbal forms of the names.

Mistaken interpretations

This is not to say that all men would immediately have seen the point of the Harrison rebus. There is ample evidence that many signs have been mis-interpreted in the past. The mistakes began with the saintly emblems, with new explanations for them being invented by fertile minds. St. Denis was usually shown holding his head in his hands, for example, as a reminder that he had been decapitated. A myth soon arose to the effect that he had walked from Montmartre to the place of his burial carrying his head.

Out in the street the signs were often poorly painted, and artists might not manage to convey the impression they wished. A sign which was meant to announce the **Coach and Horses** pub might become the **Coach and Dogs** by a brutal piece of art criticism. A **Black Swan** could likewise become the **Muddy** or **Mucky Duck**. The **Heedless Virgin**, corrupted by folk-etymology to **Headless Virgin** and shown on a sign as a decapitated saint, could accidentally or deliberately be interpreted as the **Silent Woman**, implying an 'at last!'.

Misinterpretation of this kind sometimes led to establishments being known simultaneously by more than one name. The **Rose**, in Bristol, was also known to local people as the **Cauliflower**. The **Swan and Lyre** could be referred to as the **Goose and Gridiron**. When the alternative

name became widely known it was sometimes thought desirable to keep
it and create a new sign that intentionally matched it.

Influence of heraldry

Another kind of name sign that came into being for practical reasons
during the Middle Ages was the coat of arms. Men went into battle heavily
armed and were difficult to recognise. It became the custom for them to
adorn their shields and to decorate their helmets with distinctive crests.
As an idea this was not new, for the Greeks and Romans had fought behind
shields painted with animals and the like, but these do not seem to have
become conventional symbols, always associated with one family. Coats
of arms accompanied the development of surnames in Britain, becoming
hereditary in the same way.

It would have been logical for coats of arms to take over the designs used
on seals, which were used to authenticate documents in Britain from the
eleventh century onwards, but the opposite seems to have happened. The
seals were again name signs, the upper-class equivalent of the X that was
used as the mark of more humble men who could not write. At first they
were freely chosen signs used by individuals, but they later reproduced
the coats of arms. As F. J. Grant says in *The Manual of Heraldry*: 'but for the
fact that few persons were able to write and had to authenticate all deeds
and transactions they entered on with their seals, we should not now have
these records of the early armorial designs'.

General illiteracy, then, led to names being represented pictorially at
all levels of medieval society. Sign names were to remain in practical use
for several centuries. They are now little more than decorative fossils,
whether coats of arms or pub signs, but they attract in both forms enthusiastic modern students. It is the pub signs with which we are now
concerned but that does not mean that we can immediately put heraldry
to one side. A large number of pub signs, and therefore pub names, derive
from coats of arms. The **Red Lion** and **White Hart** are probably the best
known of these, the first referring to the coat of John of Gaunt, the second
to that of Richard II. The word 'arms' itself was later to become so
strongly associated with pub names that it became almost a synonym for
'inn', 'tavern' or 'pub'. Modern names such as the **Junction Arms**,
Bricklayers' Arms, **Platelayers' Arms** and **Welldiggers' Arms**
show the trend.

Sign names

There is a marked difference between most of the pub names that came
into existence before the late eighteenth century and those that have
appeared since then. The earlier names may well have been the names of
the signs themselves. When the Knights Templars established a hostel for
pilgrims and others and identified it by a sign that showed an angel, it is
unlikely that they thought in terms of 'naming' what was in effect a primitive pub. They would have wanted an appropriate sign to indicate that the
hostel was under divine protection and which was easily recognisable as a

A Selection of Pub Names Past and Present

Many names have more than one possible origin and these are indicated. For heraldic names the immediate source rather than the ultimate origin is given.

Adam and Eve popular figures in medieval pageants; arms of Fruiterers' Company.

Air Balloon often commemorates first ascent at Versailles in 1783 with animals as passengers.

Alice Hawthorn a famous racehorse.

Alma for the Battle of Alma, 1854, in the Crimea. A river name.

Anchor an easily illustrated sign; often a retired seaman as landlord.

Axe and Compass arms of Carpenters' Company.

Bag O'Nails reputedly a corruption of *Bacchanals*, a festival in honour of Bacchus.

Bear where bear-baiting took place; occurs in many coats of arms.

Beehive a convenient 'object sign'. One pub so named had a living sign, occupied by a swarm of bees.

Bell used by bell-ringers or bell-makers; near a bell-tower.

Bible and Crown a common toast of the Cavaliers.

Bird in Hand a joking reference to the proverb, especially if a *Bush* was near by; a falcon on a gauntlet common in heraldry.

Bleeding Heart a reference to the Virgin Mary; arms of the Douglas family.

Blue Boar arms of Richard, Duke of York. Corrupted to *Blue Pig* in one instance.

Blue Boys Bridewell boys—orphans and foundlings—dressed in blue; scholars of Christ's Hospital; postilions of George IV (whose coach stopped at an inn of this name).

Blue Vinny a Dorset Cheese.

Brockley Jack a notorious highwayman.

Bull often because bull-baiting took place before it was forbidden in 1835.

Bull and Mouth commemorates Henry VIII's victory at Boulogne Mouth, or is a corruption of '*bowl and mouth*'.

Canopus after a flying-boat.

Cardinal's Error referring to Wolsey's suppression of Tonbridge Priory.

Case is Altered local anecdotes account for different instances, e.g. a pub replaces something less desirable; departure of a military camp causes loss of trade; new landlord cancels outstanding debts. Ingenious but highly unlikely explanations include a corruption of *Casey's Altar* or *Casa de Saltar* ('house of dancing').

Castle and Ball perhaps a corruption of *Castle and Bull* in arms of Marlborough family.

Cat and Fiddle usually a joking reference to the nursery rhyme. Corruptions of *La Chatte Fidèle* ('the faithful cat') ; *Caton le Fidèle* (the governor of Calais) and *Catherine la Fidèle* (Catherine of Aragon) have also been suggested.

Cat I' Th' Window a Catherine Wheel window; from a stuffed cat placed in the window.

Charles XII a racehorse.

Chequers formerly emblem of money-changers; indication that draughts or chess could be played; common element in coats of arms; from a simple decorated post used as sign.

Church Inn near a church, though Defoe described one inn of this name as the Devil's Chapel, with a larger congregation than the church itself.

Clickers for the shoemakers.

Clipper's Arms referring both to a ship and sheep-clippers.

Coach and Eight in one instance the reference is to rowing.

Cock and Bottle the 'cock' being a spigot, indicating that draught and bottled beer was sold.

Comet a stage-coach name.

Compleat Angler for the book by Izaak Walton, 1653.

Cow and Snuffers occurs in an early play as a satirical example of a pub name and perhaps taken from there. Another source says it was the result of a bet to find an incongruous name.

Cromwell's Head an oblique reference to the Restoration.

Crooked Billet a shepherd's crook; a weapon; a yoke; bishop's crosier; part of tankard; arms of Neville family.

Cross Foxes arms of Williams-Wynn family.

Crown formerly Crown property; showing allegiance to king.

Cutty Sark the short shirt worn by men and women in the Border Country; name of ship.

Curiosity for its collection of curiosities.

Daniel Lambert a man who died in 1809 weighing fifty-two stone.

Dirty Dick Nathaniel Bentley was so called in the eighteenth century. He lived as a hermit after his bride-to-be died on wedding-day.

Discovery after Captain Scott's ship.

Doff Cockers an invitation to locals to take off their leather gaiters.

Dog and Duck spaniels were set to chase ducks on nearby ponds.

Dolphin and Crown arms of French Dauphin.

Duke of York after the battleship in one instance.

Eagle and Child arms of Earls of Derby.

Eagle and Lion arms of Queen Mary.

Eclipse usually transferred from the race-horse rather than an actual event.

Elephant and Castle for the Cutlers' Company; often said to be corruption of *Infanta de Castille*.

Falcon a frequent element in coats of arms; formerly a popular bookseller's sign.

Falstaff after Shakespeare's much-loved rogue.

Fifteen Balls Cornish coat of arms.

Fighting Cocks for a 'sport' abolished in Great Britain in 1849.

First and Last usually refers to location of pub at edge of town or village.

Fish and Ring a reference to St. Kentigern's having his ring returned to him by a fish when he dropped it into a stream.

Five Alls usually a king, parson, lawyer and soldier who say they rule, pray, plead and fight for all, plus a taxpayer who pays for all, or a devil who takes all, etc.

Fleece for those in woollen industry.

Flower Pot usually a simple object sign led to name; some claim it is Gabriel's emblem.

Flying Bull after *Fly and Bull*, two stage-coach names.

Flying Dutchman usually after the racehorse of this name.

Flying Horse Pegasus; from roundabout on nearby fairground.

Fox and Grapes Aesop's fable; two signs combined.

Frighted Horse formerly *Freighted Horse*, a pack-horse.

Gate near a church gate, toll-gate, prison gate or gate-keeper's lodge.

George and Dragon to proclaim English patriotism.

Goat in Boots as a caricature of a Welshman; sometimes explained as corruption of Dutch *Goden Boode*, a reference to Mercury.

Goat and Compasses arms of Wine Coopers' Company; a legend that it is a corruption of 'God encompasseth us' is widely believed.

Green Man for foresters and woodmen; for Robin Hood; for May King, Jack-in-the-green.

Greyhound usually a stage-coach name.

Gunners nickname of Arsenal Football Club.

Hammers nickname of West Ham United Football Club.

Hat and Feathers early seventeenth century reference to fashion in plumed hats.

Hole in the Wall local anecdotes account for the name, e.g. a debtor's prison that became a pub had a hole through which food was passed; pub is reached by passing under viaduct arch that looks like a hole in the wall.

Honest Lawyer a joke name, usually showing a headless lawyer unable to speak.

Intrepid Fox after Charles Fox, not the animal.

Iron Devil plausibly a corruption of *hirondelle* ('swallow') on arms of Arundel family.

Jacob's Well a biblical joke, for 'whosoever drinketh of this water shall thirst again'.

Key for locksmiths; Jane Keye kept an inn of this name in the seventeenth century.

Labour in Vain originally religious, for Psalm 127 says: 'Except the Lord build the house, they labour in vain that build it.'

Lamb and Flag formerly a religious reference to the Holy Lamb with nimbus and banner; arms of Merchant Taylors.

Lamb and Lark proverbially one should 'go to bed with the lamb and rise with the lark'.

Leather Bottle formerly much used by shepherds.

Lion and Antelope arms of Henry V.

Lion and Bull arms of Edward V.

Lion and Unicorn arms of James I.

Little John variant of *Robin Hood*, itself often used as a pub name.

Little Wonder a racehorse.

Live and Let Live usually a comment by a landlord on competition which he considers unfair.

Mad Cat probably from a badly painted heraldic fox.

Mall Tavern from the game of pall mall (or pell mell), played with a mallet and ball.

Man with a Load of Mischief a famous sign reputedly by Hogarth shows him with a woman, a monkey and a magpie among other things.

Master Robert a steeplechaser.

Mermaid a popular sign, easy to illustrate.

Moon and Sun a rebus for the Monson family.

Mother Redcap a legendary woman who lived to be 120 'by drinking good ale'.

Nag's Head one sign shows a woman's head; usually a horse.

Naked Man formerly a tailor's sign; sometimes meant to be Adam; in one case said to be for a tree struck by lightning that resembled a man.

New Inn usually of great age.

Noah's Ark formerly sign of dealer in animals.

No. Ten and other examples such as *No. Five, No. Seven* refer to houses that had only number names when granted a licence.

Oliver Twist one pub of this name is in *Oliver Road*, which has a bend or twist in it.

Ordinary Fellow in honour of King George V, who once described himself in this way.

Pewter Platter for Pewterers' Company; to show that food is obtainable.

Pig and Whistle almost certainly a corruption, but origin not clear. A 'peg' was a measure of drink, a 'piggin' a drinking-vessel. 'Wassail' in one of its several meanings may have been origin of 'whistle'.

Pin and Bowl where ninepins and bowls could be played.

Pride of the Valley a reference to Earl Lloyd George.

Printer's Devil frequented by printers' apprentices.

Ram arms of Cloth Workers.

Ram Jam a kind of drink; legend says landlady made to ram and jam holes in barrel with her thumbs by trickster who left without paying bill.

Rampant Cat a reference to a heraldic lion by irreverent locals.

Red Cat for a badly painted lion.

Ring o' Bells usually for hand-bell ringers.

Rising Sun heraldic reference to House of York.

Rose Revived reference to Restoration of Charles II; a *Rose* re-opened after closure.

Royal Mortar probably *Royal Martyr* originally.

Running Footman whose job was to run before a coach to clear the way.

Saracen's Head variant of *Turk's Head* when Crusades made the Turks common topic of conversation.

Sedan Chair introduced to England in 1623.

Seven Stars a reference to the Virgin Mary; the Plough constellation.

Ship an easy to illustrate sign, popular everywhere; in some instances meant to be *The Ark*.

Ship and Shovel used by coal-heavers who came from nearby ships and left their shovels at the door.

Silent Whistle a former *Railway Hotel* where branch line was closed.

Silver Bullet a locomotive name.

Sky Blue in honour of the local football club colour (Coventry).

Smoker a racehorse name.

Star referring to Star of Bethlehem or to the Virgin Mary; a simple visual symbol.

Stewpony corruption of *Estepona*, birthplace of landlord's wife.

Swan and Antelope arms of Henry IV.

Swan With Two Necks probably badly painted sign of two swans originally. Often explained as 'swan with two nicks' on bill to show that it belonged to Vintners, but this would have made a difficult-to-identify sign.

Tabard a sleeveless garment worn outdoors by monks, soldiers, etc.

Talbot breed of hunting-dog used in arms of Earl of Shrewsbury.

The Sparkfold name of a hunt.

Three Compasses arms of Carpenters and Masons; sometimes accompanied by advice 'to keep within compass'.

Three Tuns arms of Vintners, said to be an unlucky sign associated with tragedy.

Trip to Jerusalem an old name where 'trip' probably means 'troops of men'.

Tumble-Down Dick a reference to Richard Cromwell; to an eighteenth century dance; to Dick Turpin.

Two Angels arms of Richard II.

Unicorn formerly sign of goldsmith or apothecary.

Waltzing Weasel weasels actually 'waltz' round their victims.

Why Not a racehorse name.

World Upside Down popular when Australia was being discovered.

Yorker a cricketing reference to the type of delivery perfected by Spofforth, the bowler.

Some examples old and new of pub signs. The unnamed signs at the top are the **Bull and Mouth** and **Three Kings**. At the bottom left is the sign of the **Eagle and Child**.

generic symbol. The name **Angel** would only occur later, when people shortened the phrase 'at the sign of the Angel' or 'the Angel sign' to 'the Angel'.

Similarly, the signs that indicated loyalty to the throne were meant to do precisely that, but not necessarily to create such names as the **Crown**, **Sceptre**, **King's Arms** and **Queen's Arms**. Such signs were especially useful in being widely known. The names that derived from them could be classed as descriptive, but once again descriptive of the signs rather than the places.

Many heraldic signs were subjected to a kind of visual folk-etymology. What was perhaps meant to be interpreted as the **Warwick Arms** became the **Bear and Ragged Staff**. The **Prince of Wales** might emerge by a similar process as the **Feathers**. Such names seem to indicate that familiar as certain famous coats must have been in former times, ordinary men could not interpret them as easily as the saintly emblems. These names also show quite clearly that the signs came first, the names afterwards.

One class of pub names, however, which appeared early definitely began as names and were then deliberately converted into visual form. These were often surnames which ended in '-ton' and were easy to illustrate by means of the tun, the large cask in which beer was stored. A lute, thorn, ash tree and the like could be shown with it to pun on **Luton**, **Thornton**, **Ashton**, etc. The pub names would nevertheless emerge as the **Lute and Tun** type. The **Tun and Arrows**, for instance, was meant to be the **Bolt in Tun** for **Bolton**. The **Hand and Cock** was similarly the sign used by a publican called **Hancock**. In spite of the punning intention, these remain descriptive names.

Shop sign names

Names chosen in modern times differ from the original sign names in that the names almost always come first, the signs afterwards. A point was reached where the signs were in danger of being abandoned altogether, the names having taken complete precedence. Before this happened, however, the density of signs and names in large cities had become very great, and the signs constituted a public nuisance. They blotted out the daylight from the narrow streets, made a continual creaking noise by swinging back and forth, and occasionally caused accidents. There was a notorious incident in London in 1718 when a heavy signboard pulled down the wall to which it was attached, killing some passers-by.

The density of sign names had also caused them to change in kind. The early signs had always been familiar objects or symbols, but there was only a limited supply of these and they were quickly used up. Partly in an effort to avoid duplication, sign names were formed by deliberately combining elements, such as the **Whale and Crow**, the **Frying Pan and Drum**. Such names could also arise, however, when a publican or shop-keeper went to a new establishment. He would want to take his personal sign with him but retain the goodwill associated with the existing sign, so he would combine the two.

In a famous *Spectator* essay of 1710 Addison commented on street signs of his time and gave in passing another possible explanation of the combination names:

> 'Our streets are filled with **Blue Boars**, **Black Swans** and **Red Lions**, not to mention **Flying Pigs** and **Hogs in Armour**, with many creatures more extraordinary than any in the deserts of Africa. . . . I should forbid that creatures of jarring and incongruous natures should be joined together in the same sign; such as the **Bell and the Neat's Tongue**, the **Dog and the Gridiron**. The **Fox and the Goose** may be supposed to have met, but what has the **Fox and the Seven Stars** to do together? And when did **Lamb and Dolphin** ever meet except upon a signpost? I must, however, observe to you upon this subject that it is usual for a young tradesman at his first setting up to add to his own sign that of the master whom he served, as the husband after marriage gives a place to his mistress's arms in his own coat. . . .

Addison uses heraldic terms metaphorically, of course, but at the back of many shop and tavern-keepers' minds must have been the wish to become known by a sign that would act in the same way as a coat of arms.

Appropriate sign names

A century before Addison wrote his essay Thomas Heywood had light-heartedly commented on the way different pub signs attracted different kinds of customer. The gentry, he wrote, would go to the **King's Head**, the bankrupt to the **World's End**, the gardener to the **Rose**, the church-men to the **Mitre**, etc. An extended version of this appeared in the *Roxburgh Ballads*. It was said, for instance, that the drunkards by noon would go to the **Man in the Moon**, while

> The Weavers will dine at the **Shuttle**,
> The Glovers will unto the **Glove**,
> The Maidens all to the **Maidenhead**,
> And true lovers unto the **Dove**.

Addison turned the whole idea round and commented on the relationship between the namer and the sign name: 'I can give a shrewd guess at the humour of the inhabitant by the sign that hangs before his door. A surly, choleric fellow generally makes choice of a **Bear**, as men of milder dispositions frequently live at the **Lamb**.'

There is obviously a serious point underlying both of these approaches to sign names, or any names for that matter, but the majority of signs in Addison's time gave little indication that they had been carefully chosen. The sheer size of a sign became the most important factor in some cases, or the extravagance of its supporting ironwork. All the time they were becoming more purely decorative, since standards of literacy were rising and names could be interpreted in their linguistic form.

By the 1760s official action was taken against street signs. In many areas it was forbidden to have signs that projected into the streets. Number names of houses and shops were to become compulsory before long, again making the sign names superfluous. Inevitably they began to disappear from the streets, and might have done so totally but for their survival as pub signs, and in a different way as trade marks. Pub signs survived for several reasons. From the fifteenth century onwards publicans had been required to display signs by law, so that the tradition of signs and sign names was particularly strong in their trade. The shopkeepers had never been under such an obligation. There was also a difference for a long time between taverns in the cities and inns elsewhere. For the inns on the coaching roads a sign was not lost among a hundred others but was something of a landmark in itself. Even today signs are still more frequent in the country than in the towns. Finally, the withdrawal of street sign names by the shopkeepers gave a new kind of meaning to those that remained. The mere presence of a sign now had the same generic significance as the early ale-stake as well as a more individual meaning.

Types of pub names

All that has been said so far about the general background to pub signs has been necessary in order to explain pub names as they exist today. The nomenclature has unique characteristics which can only be explained by reference to a time when it was desired not so much to create a name as to allow a locative phrase, 'at the sign of . . .', to come into being. In modern times the usual processes that affect name systems have come into operation. Many names are transferred to new pubs because they are felt to be unambiguously pub names. Others are created to fit into the traditions established by the early names. The **Air Hostess** and the like are converted names, while the **Sherlock Holmes** and **Sir Walter Scott** are normal transfers. The pub signs give visual support to the names.

Other categories of names are also found. Names that described the pubs themselves rather than the signs naturally became more common when projecting signboards were banned, but a few had existed previously. Publicans sometimes looked at the characteristics of the buildings they occupied and described these in the name. The **White House**, **Red House**, **Blue House** and the like may have been deliberately arrived at by painting the buildings for the purpose, or they may simply have reflected what was there. This was almost certainly the case with names such as the **Green Lattice**, a lattice being fixed across a pub's open windows to give those inside the building some privacy. When the lattices gave way to the more usual windows the word was likely to be misunderstood. In at least one instance a **Green Lettuce** later came into being.

By metonymy objects directly associated with the pub could be used for its name. The **Brass Knocker** is one kind of example, while the food offered inside the pub accounts for names like **Round of Beef**, **Shoulder of Mutton**, **Boar's Head**, **Cheshire Cheese** and so on. Drink was obviously not forgotten and led to the **Jug and Glass**, **Foaming Tankard**, **Malt and Hops**, **Full Quart** and many more. The **Black Jack**, for instance, was a primitive kind of leather bottle, sometimes lined with metal. A fashionable drink of the past is remembered in the **Punch Bowl** and other names that mention 'punch', though the nearest pub of this name I can actually get to derives its name from The Devil's Punch Bowl, a metaphorically named hollow in the hills.

The inn-keepers

Even nearer, however, is one of my 'locals', the **Swan**. In the early nineteenth century it was kept by John Locke who had a wife 'absolutely incomparable in the preparation of stewed eels, and not to be despised in the art of cooking a good beef-steak or a mutton-chop'. So wrote William Hone in 1838, while a few years earlier Theodore Hook sat in a punt on the Thames and wrote a poem about the pub. He also mentioned the inn-keeper's wife, being struck by her 'bright blue eyes' as much as her cooking.

A pub's dependence on its landlord and landlady has long been recognised. In many areas it leads to the unofficial renaming of a pub by its publican's name. Edinburgh, for example, formerly had many establishments known by such names as **Lucky Middlemass's Tavern** and **Jenny Ha's Change House**. 'Lucky' was a pleasant way of addressing a woman, especially a grandmother, and it became the specific term for the keeper of an ale-house. Jenny Ha's was a reference to another 'lucky', Janet Hall.

It is largely due to the inn-keepers, one imagines, that the pub has survived as a national institution in Britain. They have helped to give familiar names like the **Rose and Crown**, the **Bell**, **George and Dragon**, **Wheatsheaf**, **Coach and Horses**, **Talbot** and **Ship** a very special meaning, an accumulated goodwill built up by centuries of relaxed social gatherings. There are not many names among the millions in existence to which such a remark could apply.

Other pub names

Mention of landlords and their ladies has taken us inside the pubs, and while we are there we can look at some of the names we find. Often, for instance, the individual rooms have names. The well-known **Shakespeare Hotel** in Stratford on Avon has rooms named after the plays. A member of The Names Society once told me that she was a little disconcerted, when staying there with her husband, to learn that they would spend the night in a room called **The Taming of the Shrew**. The **Mouth**, a pub mentioned by Taylor, the Water Poet, had rooms called the **Pomegranate**, the **Portcullis**, **Three Tuns**, **Cross Keys**, **Vine**, **King's Head**, **Crown**, **Dolphin** and **Bell**, all of which could occur as pub names in their own right.

Also within a pub are to be found the vast number of names for the various drinks. Gin, for instance, has also been known at various times as **Cuckold's Comfort**, **Ladies' Delight**, **Gripe Water**, **Eyewater**, **Blue Ruin**, **Mother's Ruin**, **Flash of Lightning**, **Lap**, **Last Shift** and **No Mistake**. These are only a few of its nicknames. Beer has also come in for unofficial renaming, ranging from **Jungle Juice** to **Belly**

A Cocktail By Any Other Name

It is possible that 'cocktail' began as the proper name of a particular mixed drink, then went on to become the general term. Whatever its origin, it remains a fanciful word for something that traditionally attracts fanciful names. The following are a small selection.

Amour
Angel's Kiss
Appendicitis
Atta Boy
Banco
Between the Sheets
Biter
Black Baby
Blonde
Blood Transfusion
Blue Monday
Boomerang
Brainstorm
Buster Brown
Cameron's Kick
Caresse
Cat's Eye
Champs-Elysée
Charleston
Clap of Thunder
Clover Club
Corpse Reviver
Cowboy
Damn the Weather
Depth Bomb
Devils
Earthquake
Eclipse
Elektra
Elixir
Eye-Opener
Fair and Warmer
Fascinator
Favourite
Five Fifteen
Flu
Forty-Seven
Four Flush
Fourth Degree
Frantic Atlantic
Full House
Gimlet
Gin N Sin
Glad Eye
Gloom Chaser
Gloom Raiser
Golden Glow

Good Night Ladies
Grand Slam
Great Secret
Green-Eyed
    Monster
Hanky-Panky
Hasty
Hell
Hesitation
Hole in One
Honeymoon
Hoopla
Hoots Mon
Hula Hula
Hundred Per Cent
Hurricane
Income Tax
Jabberwock
Jack in the Box
Jupiter
Kicker
Knickerbocker
Knock Out
Last Round
Leap Year
Leave it to Me
Lovers' Delight
Lucifer
Macaroni
Maiden's Blush
Maiden's Prayer
Manhattan
Marmalade
Merry Widow
Moonlight
Moonraker
Moonshine
Morning After
Mule
Mule's Hind Leg
Napoleon
New Arrival
New Life
Nineteenth Hole
Nine-Twenty
Oh Henry
One Exciting Night

Pansy
Paradise
Perfect
Ping-Pong
Poker
Pooh Bah
Poop Deck
Presto
Prohibition
Queen of Sheba
Reinvigorator
Resolute
Rolls Royce
Rusty Nail
S.O.S.
Screwdriver
Self-Starter
Sensation
Seventh Heaven
Sidecar
Six Cylinder
Slipstream
Snowball
Soul Kiss
Stinger
Strike's Off
Sweet Potato
Swizzles
Tempter
Third Degree
Third Rail
Thunder
T.N.T.
Torpedo
Tropical
Twelve-Mile Limit
Twelve Miles Out
Twentieth Century
Upstairs
Velocity
Ward Eight
Wedding Bells
Welcome Stranger
Whizz Bang
Whoopee
Widow's Kiss
Wow

Vengeance and **Dragon's Milk**. If one adds the nicknames of the inn-keepers, such as **Mother Louse** who kept an ale-house near Oxford in the eighteenth century, it is clear that one could fill a book very easily with pub names and those names that are connected with pubs.

Australian pub names

A list of popular and curious pub names, together with their explanations, is given on pages 176 to 178. They give a general idea of the types of names found in Britain today. But Britain is not alone in having pubs. They appeared in Australia at the end of the eighteenth century, for instance, and spread throughout that continent. In many places there pubs came before private houses, and in their relatively short history they have played a remarkable part in the country's social development. Pubs have served as churches, town halls, post offices, surgeries, and theatres. The first Australian zoo was at the **Sir Joseph Banks** in Botany Bay. The whole story is well told in Paul McGuire's *Inns of Australia*.

McGuire remarks specifically that 'most' Australian pub names 'were brought from Britain', but his book makes it quite clear that they quickly took on their own characteristics. One of the first pubs in New South Wales, for instance, was the **Three Jolly Settlers**. The **Bulletin** in Sydney was named after the Australian weekly newspaper as soon as it appeared, which may have been an innovation in pub-naming. There are pubs in Britain with names like **Express** and **Mail** but they were named after coaches.

One man who arrived in Australia in a ship called the **Buffalo** founded a pub called the **Buffalo's Head**. A model of the ship's figurehead was used as a sign. Pub signs therefore established themselves in Australia along with the names, but the many photographs in McGuire's book make it clear that not many pubs used them. They had none of the long history behind them to make them traditional, and they served little practical purpose. The fact that they were used at all merely reflected the vague feeling of British settlers that pubs should have a sign.

The Buffalo's Head mentioned above later became the **Black Bull** and acquired a double-sided signboard. A peaceful bull was shown on one side, a raging bull on the other. An inscription read:

> The bull is tame, so fear him not
> So long as you can pay your shot.
> When money's gone, and credit's bad,
> That's what makes the bull go mad.

Name, sign and inscription have unfortunately since been removed.

Australian **Halfway Houses** sprang up spontaneously (and optimistically in some cases) and cannot be said to be transfers from Britain. Another entirely Australian pub name, in origin at least, is the **Tiger** in Tantanoola. The tiger turned out to be a wolf, now stuffed and displayed in the bar. A man who traded on the 'tiger's' reputation for sheep-stealing in order to establish a private butchery in the bush was later sent to prison for six years. Two other pub names, **McDonald's** and the

Glenrowan, have now become totally Australian and Ned Kelly's.

Inside the pubs the food and drink appears to have taken on a national flavour as well. At **Scott's**, which was a club rather than a pub, one could eat Kangaroo Tail Soup, Curried Bandicoot, Parroqueet Patties and Aspic of Native Pigeon. In more ordinary establishments drinks—or 'throat-scrapers' and 'eye-openers'—with names like **Spider** (lemonade and brandy), **Maiden** (peppermint and cloves) and **Catherine Hayes** (claret, sugar and orange) were consumed. All in all it seems safe to say that Australian pubs, and the names that were attached to them in various ways, were well and truly Australian from the beginning.

Conclusions

Pub names have something for everybody. My own special interest lies in their complex relationship with the signs that accompany them. The only parallels that come to mind are certain American place names such as **Straddlebug Mountain** and **Ucross** which derive from brand marks on cattle. For others the appeal lies in the anecdotal explanations of many a curious name. And who could not be curious, for instance, about a name like the **Drunken Duck**? This pub in Westmorland is famous for the story of a former landlady who once found her ducks lying in the road. She thought they were dead and began to prepare them for dinner, but they turned out to be in a drunken stupor. Beer had drained into their feeding-ditch. The ducks were reprieved and allowed to sober up, and one hopes that they lived long and happily.

Chapter 15
Home-made Names

It has often been said that man has a 'need to name'. House names may sometimes owe their existence to this aspect of human nature, but they reflect also something that is less often mentioned—man's 'right to name'. An inventor who creates something new is thought to have the right to name it; a botanist has the right to name the new species he has identified. Whatever the legal technicalities, it is now usually looked upon as a mother's right to name the children. The situation where someone finds that he has this right to name does not often occur, and when it does it is not lightly thrown away. It is not surprising that many householders in Britain decide to use their prerogative and name their own houses.

Most houses, of course, already have a number name, and full use is often made of it. The previous owner of my own house had **Seven** made up in wrought iron and displayed it on the gate. I think it an excellent name and have given it even more prominence on the wall. Most sub-urban streets show similar examples of number names that have been put into verbal form and carved or painted on attractive boards. Higher number names can be dealt with in **One Three Six** style.

Touches of individuality are often added to number names by varying the spelling. **Numbawun**, **Nyneteign** and the like show a perfectly understandable determination to individualise common names. Synonyms of number names sometimes occur, as in **Gross House** and **Century House**, and they appear in translated form as **Douze** (12) or whatever. Associations of a number can lead to names like **Sunset Strip** for '77', and no doubt Bingo language has been called upon. An occasional name is added as a phrasal complement to the existing number name, the outstanding example being **Ornot** shown alongside '2B'.

Number names can be humanised, then, if this is felt to be necessary, but possibly the common objection to them is caused by the fact that they are imposed from outside by an anonymous authority. The house-owner feels that his right to name is being usurped. In some areas, especially those where all the houses are privately owned, the objection to imposed names may extend to the street names. Residents rightly feel that they, and not the local authority, have the right to choose the name. In other areas where there is a mixture of privately owned houses and council houses, house names may be used as an outward sign that the houses concerned *are* privately owned. As it happens, tenants of council houses could almost certainly bestow names on them if they wished. They would probably not be allowed to fix name-boards to the walls, but they could put them on posts in the garden. The only problems then would be the comments of the neighbours about snobbishness.

Snobbish names

The fairly widespread feeling that it is snobbish to name a house has partly come about because of inappropriate names that have been given. Flora Thompson smiles gently at **Balmoral** in Chestnut Avenue in her *Lark Rise to Candleford*, a book which itself led to **Lark Rise** becoming a popular house name. And to stay with literature—which is safer for the moment—one thinks naturally of **Dotheboys Hall**. Nicholas Nickleby (Knuckleboy as he was for Mrs. Squeers) was given a lesson about house names when he arrived in Yorkshire:

> 'Is it much farther to Dotheboys Hall, sir?' asked Nicholas.
> 'About three mile from here,' replied Squeers. 'But you needn't call it a Hall down here.'
> Nicholas coughed, as if he would like to know why.
> 'The fact is, it ain't a Hall,' observed Squeers drily.
> 'Oh, indeed!' said Nicholas, whom this piece of intelligence much astonished.
> 'No,' replied Squeers. 'We call it a Hall up in London, because it sounds better, but they don't know it by that name in these parts. A man may call his house an island if he likes; there's no Act of Parliament against that, I believe?'
> 'I believe not, sir,' replied Nicholas.

'Hall' carries a definite suggestion of historic grandeur, but the English language manages to make even 'house' snobbish if it becomes a house-name element. Just as the street I live in would be down-graded by being called **Aragon Street** rather than **Aragon Avenue**, so my house would be considerably over-graded if I called it **Aragon House**. 'Cottage' is still defined in the dictionary as 'a small or humble dwelling', but it probably has a positive cash value if it can be applied with reasonable appropriateness to a house.

The charge of snobbishness about house names is usually applied when a house also has a number name. If a house has no other kind of identification, the need for a name is accepted. Even then, villagers are likely to smile to themselves when a newcomer puts up a board with his own choice of name over the house he has just bought. If the house has been there for some time it will already have a name. This will remain in general use, or the name of the new owner may become attached to it. Local people will not easily allow a stranger to affect their linguistic habits.

A house which has no number name is normally in the country rather than the town, which gives it immediate status in the eyes of many town-dwellers. It is also often larger than the typical suburban 'semi'. Accusations of snobbishness aimed at someone who has added a name to his house are therefore accusations of misrepresentation. As with Squeers, it is felt, an attempt is being made to profit unfairly by favourable associations.

Defensive names

A defensive reaction to this situation can be seen in many house names which actually belittle the houses concerned. Favoured words like 'manor', 'grange' and 'cottage' are left aside and a house becomes **The Shack**, **The Igloo**, **The Hut**, **Little House**. **The Bothy** is less obvious, but its specific sense was once a one-roomed hut in which unmarried labourers lodged together. **The Hole** and **The Hovel** are hardly more complimentary, and the Australian **Wurley**, 'an Aboriginal's hut', is again modest to say the least.

A similar type of name refuses to comment on a pleasant view or something of the kind, emphasising instead the house's exposed position. **Windy Walls**, **Windswept**, **All Winds**, **High Winds**, **Wild Winds** and dozens of others have an admirable honesty about them that would have horrified Squeers. In Bermuda there is a **Rudewinds**. Bermuda, one should mention, has no number name system for its houses and is something of a happy hunting ground for house name enthusiasts. I have not had the pleasure of a personal visit, but the *Bermuda Telephone Directory* is one of my favourite books.

Other 'windy' house names include **Bicarbonate** and **Dambreezee**, the latter occuring in several spellings. There is no joking, however, with **Cold Blow**, **Gale Force**, **Western Gales**. It should not be forgotten that the winds themselves have names, **Zephyr** being the best known. This occurs as a house name but is complimentary, since the west wind is normally light and pleasant. **Mistral**, a cold north-west wind in France, has been borrowed as an English house name, and a correspondent who lives in Edinburgh tells me that his house name, **Snelsmore**, is a wind in that area.

Bleak House is hardly a complimentary name, though it has acquired a new meaning thanks to Dickens. He did not invent it, for old directories show that many such houses were in existence before he wrote his novel, but he choose the name with a sure touch. It is hard to imagine a starker name. It has the naturalness of country speech about it, though, not the appearance of consciously invented names. The latter can be seen in **Dryrotia**, **Dry-Az-Ell**, **Lean Tu** and **Isor** ('eye-sore') which relieve the negativeness with a touch of humour.

An anthropologist might want to link this deliberate denigration of a house with the custom in some tribes of naming a child negatively. The usual wish is to convince the gods that the child is worthless, for if the opposite impression is given the child might be snatched away from the parents in an early death. In British society the gods are the evil spirits of rumour and gossip who will drag down anyone who tries to stand higher than the rest. The house name is therefore made into an acknowledgment of lowliness, either of the house or its occupants. This may seem extraordinary, but the house names sometimes appear to support such an argument. **On the Rocks**, **Overdraft**, **Skynt**, **Stony Broke**, **Haz-a-**

Bill, **The Bank's**, **Little Beside** and many similar names show a healthy contempt for, but an awareness of, keeping up appearances. A pair of jerry-built houses proclaim **Ibindun** and **Sovi**. Other names publicly announce that inside the house there is **Chaos**, **Bedlam**, **Pandemonium**, **Panic**. More names which have a confessional quality include **Drifters' Lodge**, **Fools' Haven**, **Hardheads**, **Hustlers Haunt**, **Paupers' Perch**, **The Monsters** and **Ellinside**.

An alternative explanation for such names is that the householders are extroverts who are not so much naming a house as putting up a notice for the public to appreciate. A 'graffito instinct', as one might call it, is emerging. It is seen even more clearly in house names which have nothing to do with the house and very little to do with the householder, unless they can be said to reflect his philosophy of life. **Rejoice** and **Wiworry** say such house names, or as D. H. Lawrence discovered in Australia, **Wyework**. They may also throw out a greeting: **Ahoy**, **Cheers**, **Hey There**, **Yoo Hoo**. Next door to the last named, in Bermuda, is **Yoo Hoo Too**.

Houses with names like these need to be publicly situated, perhaps in a seaside town that attracts many visitors. They tend to be in such towns for another reason; the householders there are exposed to nomenclatures where frivolity is a tradition. The names of small boats and beach-huts are especially humorous. In quieter suburbs statement-type house names are neighbourly invitations, such as **Kumincyde**, **Popinagen**, **Popova** and **Havachat**, or they are quiet murmurs of satisfaction: **This'll Do**, **Thistledew**, **Sootsus**, **Dunbyus**, **Welerned**.

A small group of these names are rather aggressive. **Llamedos** on a house in Loughborough is not a Welsh name but a back-spelling. It was chosen, so I was told on the doorstep, because the family were feeling generally fed-up when they moved in. Mrs. E. Luhman has written to me in the past about the time she and her husband moved into a bungalow in Essex. A local busybody descended on them 'and after many questions as to who we were and where we previously lived, loftily enquired "What are you going to call this place?" My husband, who was by then exasperated, replied, "We were thinking of calling it **Oppit**." So Oppit it became.'

Other correspondents have written to me about **Fujia**, a reference to the householder's being all right regardless of Jack's condition, and a dual-purpose house name, **Wypyafeet**.

We were saying earlier that naming a house says in effect that the house is privately owned. Some people feel that the point needs emphasising: **Itzmyne**, **Myholme**, **Myowna Lodge**, **Ourome**, **Ourn**, **Jusferus**. Link names such as **Barholme**, where the family name is Bar, **Ednaville**, **Helenscot**, **Lynsdale**, **Silvanest**—for a De Silva family in Bermuda, serve a similar purpose. **Morgan's Cottage**, actually based on the wife's first name, caused her to be addressed as Mrs. Morgan by the neighbours, with a moment of embarrassment all round when she explained that she was Mrs. Dunstan.

These link names do not always emphasise ownership. They can become in-jokes for those who happen to know the owner's name. Thus, a **Bird**

This poster advertising a comedy by Peter Nichols gives a new meaning to **Chez Nous**, once the typical English house name.

Song in Middlesex picks up on the surname Bird, **Cornucopia** on Le Cornu (in Jersey), **Deer Leigh** on Deering, **Emblur** on Bulmer, **Little Parkin** on Parr, **Seltac** on Castle, **The Eddy** on Edwards, **The Huddle** on Huddy, **The Nuttery** on Nutt. **Little Manor** is a clever link with the surname Littman.

House-owners' names can also lead to house names without actually being linked to them. **Sixpenny House** was almost inevitable for the Tanner family in pre-decimal currency days, though the surname's origin was nothing to do with money. A Robin and Marion decided they had to live in **Sherwood**, and families with animal surnames, such as Fox and Lyon, are likely to live in **The Lair** or **The Den**.

Blends

It is in the house name system that blends come into their own. A blend is the special type of link name that is built up with parts of more than one name, especially the names of the family members. These names clearly have very great significance as a group to the family concerned, and it is natural that people should think of symbolically combining them to represent the family group.

A simple blend may 'marry' the first names of the husband and wife. Barry and Wendy form the name **Barwen**; Mary and Tony decide on **Marony**. Less often the two family names are blended to give names like **Shorrlin** from Shortland and Ling, **Kenbarry** from Kenyon and Barry. One trouble with blended names is that they often fail to conform to the normal rules of the language. It is quite obvious that **Lynmar** *is* a blend, from the daughters' names in this case. Similarly, **Margrek**, **Dorsyd**, **Lespau** and the like stick out like linguistic sore thumbs.

By contrast, blends can resemble words too closely and convey a meaning which is not intended. **Maveric**, for instance, and **Maudlyn** come far too close for comfort to 'maverick' and 'maudlin'. It is even possible for the namers to form a real word without knowing it. In *English House Names* I quoted the example of a Renee and Albert who called their house **Renal**, not realising that this means 'of the kidneys'.

Blended house names often confuse the passer-by, who is likely to be an amateur etymologist. Some householders have overheard remarkable explanations of the names they themselves formed, with people stating confidently that they have visited the places so named. Mrs. M. Evans also told me in a letter about the vicar's interpretation of **Maralan**, which derived from Margery and Alan. 'Ah! Latin *mare*, "sea", and Welsh *a-lan*, "high".' Mrs. Evans adds: 'As we were in the middle of a coal-field, with a grand view of coal-tips, I was speechless.'

A name blending more than two names may take only the initial letter of each. In **Kahne Lodge** the first word is for a Kathleen, Amber, Harry and Norman Ellis. An Australian **Kenjarra** is felt to honour John, Eric, Kenneth, Audrey, Joyce, Ross and Keith. One cannot help feeling that the most successful names of this type manage to build in more than one meaning. **Montrose** can thus be a transferred place name and a blend of Tom, Rose, Sheila and Tony at the same time.

It is not only family names that form the basis of blended names. **Tarrazona** is a reminder of two hotels where the householders spent their honeymoon; **Neldean** is from the song 'Nellie Dean' made famous by Gertie Gitana; **Lacoa** commemorates Los Angeles, City of Angels for someone who lived there for several years; **Hillside** includes elements from two previous house names; **Duke Leigh** is for H.M.S. *Duke of York* and a naval base. If the last example seems a very masculine one it is only fitting, for it seems to be the husband who more often than not names the house.

But why, one may ask, do some people instinctively turn to the idea of blending names while others would never dream of doing it? Whatever the conscious reason for choosing a name of this type there appear to be signs of name magic revealing themselves again. For me at least there is a parallel between blending names and the practice of mixing ingredients of special significance to arrive at a powerful potion. I do neither of these things personally, but the more I look at the naming practices of my fellow men, the more I detect these deep-rooted beliefs in name magic.

Transferred house names

Surveys I have made on large estates in the Midlands and South of England show that 32 per cent of suburban house names are transferred from other nomenclatures. The largest group consists of transferred place names, which are usually borrowed because of sentimental associations. The place mentioned may be a birthplace, where a couple met, became engaged, spent a holiday or honeymoon, or formerly lived. An Italian place name I once asked about was where the son of the family had been killed during the war. When you see tears in someone's eyes on an occasion like that you become aware of a name's private meaning in a way that no amount of abstract thinking could achieve.

Other reasons for place name transfer—leaving aside the large country-houses which are known by the name of the nearest village—include a liking for a song (**Sorrento**), a wish to honour a clan chief (**Rossdhu**), a combination of favourite hymn tune and holiday associations (**Melita**). Often it is only the namer who can explain the thought process that led to the transferred name, as with **Clairvaux** 'because it is associated with St. Bernard and our wedding day was his feast day'; **Pitcairn** because the couple met on a ship the day it arrived there; **Culloden** because the English wife and Scottish husband thought it appropriate to use the name of a battlefield where their nations once fought. I admit to having made completely wrong guesses about two other place names that have been used as house names—**Littleover** and **Knockmore**. Both turned out to have been chosen for the usual sentimental reasons, though I had thought the first a member of the 'money reference' group, the second a 'statement' name.

Transferred field names form another worthwhile group of house names. **Copstone**, **Pottersfield**, **Stone Brigg**, **The Gowter**, **The Yeld**, **Venborough**, **The Wainams** and **The Spawns** are some examples. It seems fitting that fields which are built on should at least leave their names in the area. Many live on by becoming street names; others have to wait for householders with a feeling for the past to rescue them from old documents. Street names themselves lead to house names, as do ship names, pub names, any names that exist. One couple met in a hospital ward, so the name of the ward became their house name. Famous race-horses such as **Arkle** and **Bandalore** have brought winnings to many and given house names to a few grateful backers. **Tia Maria** was suggested by a liqueur bottle, **Sunderland** not directly by the place but by the name of an aircraft flown during the war. Finally, some house names—but not as many as one might expect—are simply the family names of the people living there.

Descriptive house names

The householders who link and transfer names are probably sentimentalists; the down-to-earth prefer a no-nonsense, factual name. The house is on a hill, so let it be **Hilltop** or **Hillside**. It's a **Corner House**, has **Twin Chimneys**, **Blue Shutters** or is at the **Heathside**: the house names itself.

House names like these are obviously very sensible if they are given to houses which have no number names. They are the nearest verbal equivalent to number names—utility names. Activity names such as **The Vicarage** belong here, and little more need be said about them.

Other descriptions are by no means as functional. **Sunnyside** and **Dawnside** can hardly be put into the same category as **Barnside**. Nor are the metonymic descriptions which make use of flowers or trees that

A Selection of House Names

Alcrest from the phrase 'after labour comes rest'.

Allways husband used to close letters to his wife with this version of 'always'.

Almost There

Aroma opposite a brewery.

Arden a wartime sign 'Warden' lost its initial letter and was taken to a be a house name.

Aurora goddess of the dawn.

Bachelor's Adventure on a holiday cottage.

Bali Hai a house on a hill.

Banshee House a 'banshee' is a female elf thought to wail under the windows of a house when someone is about to die.

Bar None for a home in the style of a ranch house.

Barn Yesterday a converted barn.

Bassetts 'all-sorts' in family (four adopted children).

Bethany Biblical, 'house of poverty or affliction'.

Billion Bill and Marion.

Birdholme 'holme' means an islet, but is often used as a synonym of 'home' in house names.

Birdhurst 'hurst' can mean hillock or wood.

Bonanza Spanish 'prosperity'.

Boogaroph the opposite of *Kumincyde*.

Bruhaha French 'indistinct noise'.

Brytome 'bright home'.

Buffers on a converted railway carriage.

Ca d'oro name of a Venetian palace ('house of gold'). A sign on the gate of the suburban version says: 'Beware of the Doges'.

Cartref Welsh 'home'.

Chippings can refer to a kind of sparrow or squirrel.

Clover used metaphorically, 'to be in clover'.

Cobblers

Cobwebs 'currently owned by Woolwich Equitable

Building Society'.

Conkers for the horse-chestnuts that fall into the garden.

Copper Coin all that remained after paying for house.

Copper Leaves a retired policeman lives there.

Copper View opposite the police station.

Copsclose next door to a police station.

Cowries little shells found on near-by beach.

Crackers 'to have bought this house'.

Dalsida owner of a *Dal*matian, *Si*amese and Great *Da*ne.

Deroda a back-spelling.

Diddums Den

Dinnawurri another version of *Wyeworrie*.

Doo Town in Tasmania, where all the houses have names like **Yule Doo**, **Av Ta Doo**, **Zip Eddie Doo**, **Doodle Doo**, **Doo Us**, **How Doo You Doo**, **Didgeri Doo**.

Dulce Domum Latin 'home sweet home'.

Dunwistairs a bungalow.

Eleven Plus for the number name **11B**.

Elveston an anagram of 'lovenest'.

Emange M and G.

Emoclew a common back-spelling. Does one receive the reverse of welcome when calling there?

End in View at the end of a lane, inhabitants retired.

Eureka Greek 'I have found it'.

Fair Dinkum to show Australian connections.

Fir Teen the number name 13.

Foon Hai Chinese 'happiness', transferred from a Chow.

Forbidden Fruit on a holiday bungalow.

Fortitoo the number name 42.

Fost Un first house in Foston Avenue.

Four Walls Mr. and Mrs. Wall and their two children live there.

French Leave a holiday house.

Genista Mrs. Broom lives there.

Gnuwun 'new one'.

Gorldy Woods 'worldly goods'.

Halcyon Days 'calm days', a reference to a fabled bird.

Halfdan a Danish wife.

Hangover Hall in Temperance Road.

Happy Ours

Heimat a place name transferred by a trampoline enthusiast.

Hen House a reference to the number of daughters in family.

Highlight

High Loaning 'loaning' is a piece of uncultivated ground on which cows are milked, but the mortgage is also referred to.

Hindquarters for the Hind family.

Holmleigh usually a fancy spelling of 'homely'.

Hysteria next door to a house called *Wistaria*.

Itzit

Jacquaboo the daughter is Jacqueline, the son's nickname is Boo.

Jayceepayde

Justintime

Justinuff

Kayaness K and S live there.

Kef the enjoyment of idleness, a state of dreamy intoxication usually induced by drugs. An Arabic word.

Koldazel

Kon Tiki because they drifted there.

Kosinuk for 'cosy nook'.

Ladsani a father and two sons.

Lautrec because it has 'two loos'.

Little Boredom Mr. Bore lives there.

Loggerheads

Long Odds

Lucky Dip a holiday bungalow by the sea.

Mascot 'mother's cottage' but also 'anything which brings luck'.

Mews Cottage Whiskers is the name of the occupant.

Mini Bung

Moonshine house first seen in moonlight, and son interested in astronomy.

Morning Feeling Mr. Munday lives there.

Mutters the neighbours' reaction when they moved in.

Myob '*M*ind *y*our *o*wn *b*usiness.'

Offbeat a retired policeman lives there.

On the Rocks

Osterglay back-slang for Gloucester.

Owzat a cricketer who was stumped for a name.

Peelers a converted police station.

Pennings because of letters written to builders.

Poodleville for the dog.

Pretty Penny

Pro Tem Latin 'for the time', i.e. until a number name is allocated.

Ringside a retired boxer.

Robins Nest the Robinsons live there and hope not to fall out.

Roundabout Friday from the builder's favourite saying.

Round the Bend for a corner house.

Ruff Roof

Rumbling Winds

Seaview on a house in Clapham, London.

7777777 the number name of the house is 49.

Shieling a rough hut erected on pasture-land in Scotland, or the pasture-land itself.

Shilly Chalet

Sky Lark on a holiday cottage.

Spite Cottage because of a 'spite wall' built to spoil the neighbour's view.

Spooks across the road from a cemetery.

Stocking Cottage 'stocking land' has been cleared of stocks.

St Onrow a blend of John*ston* and *Row*berry.

Straw Hat a thatched cottage.

Stumbledon when houses were scarce.

Sunny Jim a pun on Sonny Jim, used to address any young boy whose name is not known.

Taintours on a Council estate.

Tamesis an older form of *Thames*.

Testoon a coin name used by a numismatist.

The Chimes the Bell family live there.

The Filling for a house sandwiched between others.

The Ginger House because of its orange-brown tiles.

The Jays sometimes refers to birds that visit the garden, more often to members of the family whose first names begin with 'J'. Also a metaphorical reference to people who chatter a great deal.

The Halfyard former field name, from a measure of land.

The Keep the Norman family live there.

The Hardies next door to *The Laurels*.

The Marbles in Elgin Road.

The Pride the Lyons live there.

The Rashers the Gammon family live there.

The Ripples it has a corrugated-iron roof.

The Speck one meaning of the word 'speck' is a small piece of ground.

The Stumps a dentist lives there.

39 Steps

Three-O for the number name 30.

Tiedam a back-spelling.

Tivuli a back-spelling.

Top Notch

Touche Bouais Jersey French 'touch wood' because number name is 13.

Touch Me Pipes from a Cornish miner's expression meaning 'to rest and have a smoke'.

Traynes near the railway.

Tre-Pol-Pen to show that the occupiers are Cornish.

Triangle House for the Corner family.

Troy Hector is the husband's name.

Tuksumduin

Tusikso the number name is 260.

Tu-Threes the number name is 33.

Twa Lums for the 'two chimneys'.

Tympcasa tympana (which the owner plays)+*casa*, 'house'.

Uno (United Nations Organization) husband and wife of two nationalities, children born in other countries.

Uprising Twenties the number name is 21.

Up Si Daisy

Valhalla in Teutonic mythology the hall where Odin held court.

Weemskat a dialectal form of 'we're broke'.

Well Away a holiday bungalow.

Whooff for the dog.

Widdershins also withershins, for a house facing in the opposite direction from those round it.

Wiktro '*w*ell *i*t *k*eeps *t*he *r*ain *o*ff'.

Wom dialectal for 'home'.

SJ 619714 the National Grid reference of the house.

happen to be growing in the garden as practical as the **Blue Gates** type of name. **Roseleigh** and **Oak House** show the most common elements of this kind of name. Animals and birds are often mentioned in house names, including **Dog Cottage**. This is one instance where the use of 'house' would have been humorous instead of snobbish.

Many names are actually of the **Woodside** type in that they describe the house's position in relation to something nearby, but the connecting element is omitted. **Rill Cottage** and **Bonny Brook** are examples of such names. The use of 'view' in a name implies nearness to whatever can be seen, but once again such names are not functionally descriptive. **Castle View** and the like are outward descriptions which by no means identify the houses concerned. Such names are really as vague as **Sunset View**.

Examples of environmental descriptions have already been given with the 'wind' names. 'Sunny' names are of the same kind, though clearly more positive in outlook. Names like **Sunshine** and **Sunnyhurst** may slip into the commendatory class, expressing what is hoped for rather than describing a real situation. They are commendatory in another sense when they are used for seaside boarding-houses along with such names as **Seascape** and **Seaview**.

We must consider as descriptive names those which describe the occupants of a house. The number of people in the family is often indicated as in **Izaners**, **Triodene**, **The Foursome**, **Fyve Fold**, **Us Lot**. The fact that the householder is retired is indicated in many names, especially the **Dunroamin** type, e.g. **Dunskruin** for a retired prison warder. Many converted names are also a direct reflection of the occupants' pastimes. **Extra Cover**, **Double Oxer** and **The Bunker** are probably as effective as any descriptions could be of someone's cricket, show-jumping and golf interests. Music-lovers are likely to choose names such as **Harmony** or transfer the names of composers or pieces of music to their homes. A love of literature leads to transfers from characters and titles of novels, but conversions such as **Brillig**, from the Lewis Carroll poem, also occur. One **House at Pooh Corner**, however, is because of a nearby sewage-farm.

Sometimes the house names which say most about the occupants are

not those which do so deliberately. Names like **Cosynest** and **Merriland**, **Sheerluck** and **Joys** are especially revealing of attitudes and philosophies, though names of all kinds do this to some extent. An astute door-to-door salesman, one would think, might be able to plan his opening remarks on the basis of the house name, which hints strongly at the character of the namer.

Apart from the category of name that is chosen, its form can reveal still more about the namer. Names in foreign languages are especially interesting in this respect. Why was **Chez Nous**, for instance, once *the* typical English house name, when many English people would have had no idea how to pronounce it and would not have been able to translate it? *Chez* represents an Old French *chiese*, Latin *casa*, originally a 'shepherd's hut'. *Chez nous* is a curious fossil in modern French, to be translated 'at our house', but it is even more curious that it should have appeared in countless English streets. It is now disappearing, though occasionally made a joke of in the form **Shay Noo**.

All the name was meant to do for the occupants of the house, we must assume, was to show knowledge of a foreign language. This would in turn hint at a good education and foreign travel. Knowledge of foreign languages and travelling abroad are no longer the status symbols they once were, though an amazing number of **Casa Nostras** have appeared since package tours began. It is probably names like these, almost pointless in themselves, which brought house names into general disrepute. Their meanings so clearly lie not in their translations but in their attempts at one-upmanship.

Names in Welsh, Gaelic, Manx, Cornish, Maori and Australian Aboriginal are obviously different in character. They show a national pride which is nothing to do with impressing the neighbours. Latin names are of several sub-categories, such as religious, botanical and learned. With these, and with Greek names, one is somehow far less suspicious of an urge to impress others. The names usually have some point to them and genuinely reflect the background or interests of the namers. Names in other languages—and The Names Society's files contain house names in at least forty-five languages—are often linguistic souvenirs after residence abroad or a sign that one of the occupants of the house is from the country concerned. Since they are so rarely understood by passers-by, they contrast strongly with the public-statement type of name we were looking at earlier.

Another form a name may take is a back-spelling. The motivation behind such names is difficult to understand but they undoubtedly please many people. Those who are reluctant to put their family names above the porch in its normal form are often quite happy to put it there spelt backwards. I suggest you try reversing your own name to get an idea of the dreadful results this usually achieves. **Gnilknud** is no worse than many which are to be found in suburban streets. The only common factor I have noticed with names of this kind when they have been explained to me is the tone of self-satisfaction used by the informants, but that is clearly a subjective impression. Everyone has his own way of grading names, and I just happen to dislike back-spellings.

As house names, however, they are part of the rich variety of names that are there for the consideration of a suburban stroller. They add the final personal touches to the historical anecdotes contained in place names, street names, pub names and the like. They have what one might call a language of their own which one must be prepared to study a little. It amply repays the effort.

Beach-hut, caravan and houseboat names

Those who do not live in suburban streets need not feel left out. A holiday stroll along the beach can often be enlivened by the names of those mini-houses, the beach-huts. Monstrous puns and jokes strike exactly the right note as the children play noisily in the background: **RR's by the Sea**, **Strip and Dip**, **The Winkle**, **Avarest**, **Taconap**, **Linga-Longa**, **Thut**, **Bikini Bay**, **Lang May Your Lum Reek**, **Brewden**, **Dormat**, **Bunk House** and **Hereur**. I once paid an out-of-season visit to a caravan site in order to collect similar names there. This led to my being arrested by a police dog (whose superb name turned out to be **Justice**), but I managed to note down such caravan names as **Brief Encounter**, **Cara Mia**, **Kip Inn**, **Pent House** (a marvellous comment on the confined space), **Tin Ribs** and **Leisure Daze**.

Houseboats provide a further field for investigation. Kelsie Harder has aroused my envy with a report of some name-collecting he did in the Valley of Kashmir, which has many houseboats bearing English names. Floating along on a lake in such a beautiful place must make one's investigations particularly pleasant. The names Professor Harder collected included many transferred girls' names, flower names and bird names. A **Cutty Sark** found a place near a **Miss England** on the lake in Kashmir just as it does on the cover of this book. **Highland Queen**, **H.M.S. Pinafore**, **Dream Boat** and **Buckingham Palace** hint at the wider range of names used.

The houseboats are often let to tourists, and carry announcements to that effect. When Mr. Khrushchev was in Srinagar a river-boat procession was arranged which passed by two such boats. They carried large signs which read: '**Miss America**: Running hot and cold: Ready for Possession' and '**Miss England**: Sanitary fitted: Ready For Occupation.' Mr. Khrushchev is said to have been highly amused.

Let Miss England bring us back to that country for a brief summary of its house names. They are thick on the ground in the South, but thin out as one travels northwards. There are more of them on the coast than inland. They are mainly transferred, linked or are descriptive, but they are also a fine repository of folk-humour. The humorous names are again found mainly in the South. Northern names are more dignified, as are Welsh and Cornish names.

As a naming system, house names have their own characteristics, which I hope have emerged in this chapter. They have a distinctive quality, a unique taste. Perhaps this is what we should expect. They are, after all, home-made names.

Chapter 16
Trading a Name

On several occasions in previous chapters the question of the 'image' created by a name has been mentioned. Personal names, place names and street names, as we have seen, have all been changed in order to create a different impression of the named entity. In our last chapter we had the example of **Dotheboys Hall** being used for business purposes more than as a house name. When we come to deal with trade names as a group, therefore, we are not moving into a totally new world.

Trade names share the basic characteristics of other nomenclatures and the same categories of names are found. The relative importance of those categories, however, is different. As with house names there are many blends, but invented names play a far greater role in the trade name system than in any other nomenclature we have yet examined.

Types of trade name

The reason for the importance of invented trade names will quickly emerge: first it is as well to distinguish between those trade names which were originally meant to identify one business enterprise rather than another, and those names which are designed to further business *in themselves*. **Guinness** is an example of the former, **Lux** of the latter. Guinness is a transferred surname, representing the Irish *Mag Aonghusa* or *Mag Aonghuis*, 'son of Angus'. **Angus** in turn is usually explained as 'one choice', with 'one' being used in the sense 'unique'. Having passed from family name to company name, Guinness was further transferred to the product, but there was never at any time an intention to make use of an intrinsic 'meaning' in the name in order to attract business.

Lux, however, was clearly a conscious attempt at bringing a name into being that would help to associate the product bearing it with certain desirable concepts, 'luxury' and 'luck'. These ideas are suggested without being stated, while the name itself retains a brevity and force useful for advertising purposes. When one notes, too, that its form almost certainly ensures that it will remain a name and not slip into the general vocabulary, it is seen to combine most of the features a trade name needs.

Lux represents a modern type of trade name which embodies current ideas about the use of language for persuasive purposes. Ideas as to what *is* persuasive have changed drastically in the last 150 years. In spite of the psychological insight that Dickens attributed to Squeers in his choice of Dotheboys Hall, the more usual thinking of the time (1839) is seen in an earlier chapter of *Nicholas Nickleby*. A Mr. Bonney is talking of a proposed new company, which will be known as **United Metropolitan Improved Hot Muffin and Crumpet Baking and Punctual Delivery Company**. 'Why,' says Mr. Bonney, 'the very name will get the shares up to a premium in ten days.'

Early trade names

Dickens makes fun of a tendency that was to continue for a very long time. Pomposity and prolixity were admired, as Dickens himself demonstrates on many occasions. The respectability of products was therefore thought to be assured if their names were based on Latin and Greek or made historical allusions. A soap powder being advertised in 1907, for instance, was **Phenozone**, which apparently relied on the public's understanding of the 'shining' allusion in the Greek prefix. Madame Downing of Charing Cross Road in London was offering a corset a few years earlier to male readers of the magazine *Society*. She called it **The Kitchener**. Lord Kitchener was still alive at the time and one wonders what he thought of this use of his name. To go with the corset gentlemen of the time were offered a hat known as the **Sans Souci**.

The last example shows how startlingly unsuitable a product name could be at this period. *Sans Souci* is certainly a famous name, and it is sometimes found today as a suburban house name. At least it has some point when it is so used. Frederick the Great gave this name to his palace at Potsdam, which made it well known to European high society. Voltaire, who often visited him there, had his doubts about the name, saying that in spite of its meaning ('without care') 'a certain renowned king was sometimes consumed by care when he was there'. Thackeray made a rather similar comment in his *Roundabout Papers*: '*Sans Souci* indeed! It is mighty well writing "*Sans Souci*" over the gate, but where is the gate through which Care has not slipped?'

It is difficult to see how such historical and literary associations, which would have been known to relatively few, could have been thought suitable for a hat. Perhaps the namer thought only of the literal meaning of the words, which he assumed the middle-class public would recognise or would never admit to not recognising. The hat seems to have been a soft one, so that it didn't matter if it became crumpled. It could be carried or worn 'without care'.

Such a thought process is likely to lead to a highly unsatisfactory trade name because it satisfies the namer rather than the people at whom the name ought to be directed. It was probably such names that Claude Hopkins had in mind when he wrote in 1923: 'The question of a name is of serious importance in laying the foundation of a new undertaking. Some names have become the chief factors of success. Some have lost for their originators four-fifths of the trade they developed.' Hopkins's comment needs a great deal of expansion. It applies in particular to converted and invented names, which must be chosen with minute care, but transferred surnames have certain points operating in their favour. In the case of a product a family name can carry with it an implicit guarantee. The name transfer suggests a complete identification of the producer with his product, and hints that a pride in the latter is linked with his fundamental self-respect. There is an uncompromising honesty in pinning one's own name to a business or product that will offset neutral qualities in the name itself. **Dunkling**, for instance, would hardly recommend itself as a linguistic unit to someone who was looking for a trade name, but a former namesake of mine who founded a jeweller's shop in Australia was right to use his name for trade purposes. By doing so he made a statement of good intent.

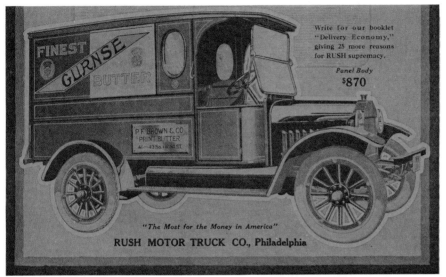

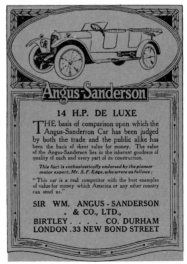

Some early motor names.

Surnames as trade names

The fact that **Dunkling** is established as a trade name, in one part of the English-speaking world at least, raises an interesting point. If I wanted to set up business as a jeweller in Australia I might not be allowed to use my rightful name for business purposes. I could be legally restrained from doing so if I implied by means of my name that I was connected with the established business. In Britain Messrs. Wright, Layman and Umney Ltd, for instance, obtained injunctions against a Mr. Wright which stopped the latter trading under a name containing Wright or Wright's. The company claimed that it had a wide reputation in certain goods under the name **Wright's**, and that Mr. Wright's similar goods would naturally be confused with theirs.

Surnames occur frequently as trade names, but the use of first names is less common. They are mostly seen as shop names, especially those of hairdressers, but they do not seem to be popular for products launched nationally. Ford tried it with a car called the **Edsel**, the name that Henry Ford had chosen for his son. Many attributed the failure of that particular model to the nature of the name Edsel itself, and the fact that it was known to be a first name may have influenced the matter. It is difficult to say why, but first names do not convey the same impression of respectable solidarity as surnames used as trade names.

Other names become trade names, especially popular place names such as **Oxford** and **Cambridge**, but there appears to be a definite preference in modern trade-naming to form new names by various processes. One

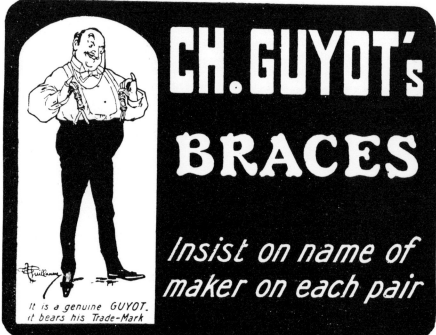

CH. GUYOT's BRACES

Insist on name of maker on each pair

It is a genuine GUYOT.
it bears his Trade-Mark

An advertisement in *The Graphic*, 1908.

problem with transferred names is that they are by their very nature shared with another entity. The trade name ideal lies in uniqueness. There are other ideals, of course. The name should catch the attention and be memorable. It should also work below the conscious level of the person who is exposed to it and appeal to the motives which really do cause him to buy a product, though he might be reluctant to admit it. As Vance Packard suggested by the title of his book some years ago, product names should be *Hidden Persuaders*.

Lipstick names

In 1968 Jill Skirrow looked at the names of some lipsticks that were then on sale to see what characteristics they revealed. The namers, she decided, had thought deeply about what was at the back of a woman's mind when she went into a shop to buy lipstick. She would be thinking about making herself look young, hence **Young Pink**. There would be thoughts of kissing, and **Snow Kissed Coral** could remind her of these thoughts while pretending to talk of something else. 'Snow' would also be suggesting coolness to her, with 'purity' lurking in the background, while 'coral' threw out hints of the South Seas. The combination of ideas in Snow Kissed Coral is illogical if one stops to think about it, but the namers knew that very few customers would try to analyse it. Even if they did it would not matter. As a slight obscurity will sometimes be used by a poet to make the reader or listener pay more attention, so an illogicality in a name may make customers notice it more.

The woman buying lipstick is presumably anxious to emphasise her femininity, the namers think, so they tempt her with **Moods of Red**, **Porcelain Pink**, **Tiger Rose**, **Quiet Flame**, **E. S. Pink**. Moods of Red, Jill Skirrow says, would appeal to the 'vampire instinct' in a woman, and I must accept her word for it. The 'porcelain' reference certainly suggests high quality and fragility, and E. S. Pink plays on 'extra sensory perception', flattering the feminine illusion about intuition. Tiger Rose and Quiet Flame show the male idea of a woman who wants to be docile yet passionate, and may even reflect the idea some women have of themselves.

The moistness of a lipstick is emphasised in **Dewy Peach**, the 'peach' probably linking with the idea of a 'peach of a girl'. **Pink Whisper** cleverly introduces a suggestion of intimate conversations and softness, while focusing the customer's attention on her mouth. **Gilt-Edged Pink** and **All Girl Gold** cater for the dreams of wealth that are lurking at the back of many a young feminine mind. Perhaps Miss Skirrow goes too far, however, in suggesting that 'gilt-edged' will also hint at excitement because of 'guilt'. The same is no doubt true when she says that names like **Bare Blush** and **Itsy Bitsy Pink** have partly been chosen because the lips are especially used to pronounce them. If she *is* right, then the namers have been too subtle, for when these names are most influencing the customer they are probably not being spoken aloud.

Lipstick names make a particularly interesting study because the namers are forced to be right up to date in the associations they build into a name. The customers will not be loyal to a particular lipstick for very long, and it is not really possible for the manufacturers to decide on a few names that they will then try to establish for all time. The namers are faced with a challenging situation in which customers will be running their eyes over a great many similar lipsticks, ready to indulge their whim of the moment in deciding which one to buy. While a customer is examining one colour rather than another, the lipstick names will be doing their work, planting suggestions in her mind. I suspect that they plant them in a man's mind too, for even I find myself going back to certain names again and again as I run my eye down the list. **Apricot Dazzle**, for example, attracts me very much as a name, though I can't begin to analyse why. I don't even like apricots.

Hotel names

At about the same time as Miss Skirrow was making her analysis of lipstick names, I was conducting an experiment into hotel names. I asked a large number of people to stop for a moment and look at several names. I then asked them to indicate which hotel of those mentioned they thought they would stay at if they had no other information but the name on which to base a judgment.

Names like **Grand Hotel** and **Queens Hotel** were rejected by many because they 'sounded expensive', but they were chosen by others because the names suggested luxury. The **Seaview Hotel** type of name did rather better than the **Sunshine Hotel** type, the former apparently being taken at its face value, the latter regarded with suspicion. Names which I planted experimentally to see whether they would make an appeal were ignored even more completely than I had expected. These were of the **Summer-joy Hotel**, **Magic Carpet Hotel** variety. Modern-looking names like **Hotel Two** failed to appeal to young or old, while **White Hermitage Hotel** made a quiet showing with older informants. By far the most popular name, particularly with women, was **Little Orchard Hotel**. I was conducting my survey in the centre of a city and presumably their choice revealed an emotional need for a rural retreat.

'Emotional need' is rather a key phrase in this context. Trade names of the kind we have been discussing are not meant to be prosaic descriptions, satisfying the mind with the facts they supply. If they are to be successful they must be like poetry, and the advertising men who suggest new names are commercial poets in their way. A typical poetical device, for instance, is the deliberate exploitation of polysemy—the different meanings that can be suggested simultaneously by the same word. This is constantly used in trade names. In *Trade Name Creation* Jean Praninskas quotes the example of a popular American detergent, **All**. This manages to suggest that it gets all the dirt out of clothes, that it can be used in all machines for all fabrics, does all cleaning jobs and does the work all by itself. For a simple word of three letters it is surely doing a great deal for the product it identifies. Its conversion to a trade name was a brilliant piece of inspiration.

Other poetical devices seen in trade names include rhyme, hyperbole, personification and metaphor. **Merry Cherry**, another lipstick name, shows the usual end rhyme, but one should include here the initial repetition of sound known as 'alliteration'. **Coca Cola** is an obvious example. Hyperbole is exaggeration that is not meant to be interpreted literally, so **Magi-Stik** does not really lay claim to occult powers. By personification a machine or device can be turned into a human servant, a **Handy Man** or **Brewmaster**. Metaphor simply compares the product being named with something having associated qualities, such as the speed and grace of a **Jaguar**.

Other trade name devices

But if one kind of trade name is a miniature poem, making intensive and subtle use of the language, another kind prefers to play games with the language. The various possibilities for playfulness are seen in names like **Helpee Selfee**, **Eat-A-Voo**, **Choc-A-Lot**, **Get Set** and **Ab-Scent**. Helpee Selfee manages to say to Americans that it is a laundry by implying that it has Chinese connections, although the same name elsewhere might suggest a self-service Chinese eating-place. These national associations are probably worthy of a special study in themselves. We have already noted the value of a Russianised name to a ballet-dancer and a French name to a hairdresser. There are presumably many other ways in which vague national associations can be exploited.

Eat-a-voo plays on the established 'rendezvous' element in many a restaurant name. Apart from making it clear that an eating-house is referred to the name also emphasises a down-to-earth attitude. 'Never mind the fancy foreign names,' it seems to say, 'we're more concerned with the real business of providing a good meal.' As with all jokey names, there is a suggestion that the namer means to entertain and establish a relaxed atmosphere.

Choc-a-lot identifies the product and adds a further enticement with its suggestion of quantity. Get Set takes a familiar phrase and deliberately re-interprets it. The reference is to a hair preparation and the joke obviously has point to it. What the name brilliantly implies is that having had one's hair set with this product the customer will then be ready to 'go' in the best sense. Ab-scent is a deodorant, and the name is etymologically satisfying as well as being a pleasant pun.

Trade name spellings

A problem created by trade names is referred to by my former colleague, Dr. Sven Jacobson, in *Unorthodox Spelling in American Trademarks*. As is well known, the lack of relationship between the sounds of English and English spelling already causes great difficulty to children who are learning to read. This difficulty is aggravated when children, and adults for that matter, are constantly exposed to spellings in trade names of the **Sox** and **Kwik** kind. Louise Pound commented on 'The Kraze for "K"' as long ago as 1925 in an article in *American Speech*. Other trade name crazes, as Sven Jacobson points out, include the use of hyphens in names like **Tys-Ezy** (plastic straps), **Sto-A-Way** (tables) and **Shat-R-Proof** (safety glass); the use of letter pronunciations in **E-Z-Chek** (brake

gauges) and **Trip-L-Bub-L** (chewing-gum); the use of 'x' for '-cks' in **Clix** (light switches) and **Hanx** (paper handkerchiefs); the use of 'z' for 's', as in **Stripzit** (paint-stripper) and **Kilzum** (insecticide).

Names like **Kehr-Fully Made**, used by Kehr Products Co., and the **Get It Dunn Safely** of Dunn Products are obviously not deliberately reformed spellings. They simply profit by a similarity of sounds that is suggested by existing names. It might be claimed that such names add to the orthographic confusion, but the language itself tolerates such an amazing variety of forms that a few more will probably do no harm. Consider how the same sound is represented, for example, in words like meet, meat, mien, me, seize and foetus.

Trade names are in any case virtually forced to resort to spelling variations as the search for new names becomes more difficult. At least 25,000 new consumer products and services come into being in the English-speaking world each year, and each of them needs a new name. They are not in the happy position of being able to borrow names from a small central stock, nor do they inherit names by family tradition. Their names must not resemble those already in existence for similar products, and there are many other restrictions placed on them.

The most notable restriction, however, is undoubtedly that of transfer within the system. What would be considered to be natural duplication elsewhere—when several namers independently arrive at the same name —is also banned. All names must be registered, and only one namer is allowed to be credited with a name in a distinctive business area. As far as possible, therefore, there is an insistence that a name should be truly individual.

This situation has already led, in the relatively short history of legally registered trade names, to there being more trade names on record than there are words in the English language. In 1961 Lippincott and Margulies, the American industrial design and marketing consultants, stated that a half-million trade names were already registered. At that time there were rather less entries in the mammoth *New English Dictionary*. Supplementary volumes of the dictionary have since been published, but it is inconceivable that the vocabulary of English increases at the rate of fifty or more words a day, which is the rate at which trade names multiply. Many of these names are then pounded into the minds of the public by the use of highly sophisticated techniques. Our medieval ancestors were educated by signs and pictures; we are forcibly given a literal education by way of trade names and advertising slogans.

Trademarks still supply a visual accompaniment to many names, but these are becoming design abstractions rather than meaningful symbols. Few companies today try to find a **Nipper** who will sit and listen to 'His Master's Voice' with an appealingly attentive ear, though such emotion-rousers add their own touch of aptness to any name. The tendency now is to favour initials and display them in an interesting way, but one suspects that the results often satisfy professional designers rather more than they satisfy the public. A display of graphical ingenuity is wasted if it is mere self-indulgence.

These initial names are unsatisfying in linguistic terms as well as visual, but as company names they are not obliged, perhaps, to create a public image. The companies concerned present themselves to the public by a wide variety of product and brand names, and a modern multi-national company, which has probably acquired many smaller businesses, is likely to own a very large number of names indeed. The latter represent a new phenomenon, a company nomenclature. This in turn must come to play an important part in the lives of employees, affecting their general use of language. The time will certainly come, if it has not done so already, when larger companies will be obliged to prepare dictionaries of these corporate languages for the benefit of employees.

Trade number names

With a few notable exceptions, trade-namers seem to have steered clear of number names. In an earlier chapter I discussed **4711**, to which one may add examples like **Seven Up** and **Vat 69**. Heinz showed a few years ago that '57' could be given an individual meaning, for that number always appeared in their advertising. Had it been converted to a number name at that point it would have been synonymous with **Heinz** itself. Number names are certain to come into their own before long, given the general situation of dwindling supplies of other names and ever-pressing needs. The first in the field will have a distinct advantage, being able to make use of numbers which carry a favourable meaning to many people. Late-comers might have to contend with **900424214** or something of the sort. If they choose that particular example I hope they will be gentle with it; it is already meaningful to me in that it is the International Standard Book Number of this book.

As it happens, it would not be as difficult to establish that number name as it might at first seem. Most of us these days successfully cope with several seven-digit number names, otherwise known as telephone numbers. We think of a certain person and the row of numbers comes into our minds. For anyone in a business where the customers need to telephone, the adoption of the telephone number as a trade name would seem to have several advantages. An advertising jingle could then be devised to fix the number name firmly in the mind.

A point that seems to have been missed where number names are concerned is that they have various verbal translations. The monstrous-looking nine-digit group quoted above could become 'nine hundred, four two, four two, one four' rather than 'nine hundred million, four hundred and twenty-four thousand, two hundred and fourteen'. The former breakdown enables a simple mnemonic to be constructed: 'Nine hundred four two, four two, plus one four you.' It would be possible to fit those words to a catchy little tune and have the entire number name nationally known in a few weeks by means of television advertisements.

The trade-namer is not yet in the position of having to accept arbitrary sets of numbers emerging from a computer as name suggestions, though he has for some years now been turning to a computer for new names. A computer can certainly supply combinations of letters that are 'names' of a kind, but the need is for names that will evoke an emotional response. These are needed, at least, in all those commercial areas where the buying of one product rather than another is likely to be a spur of the moment decision as far as the customer is concerned. Naturally there are many other instances where the price and quality of a product are what count, or where a particular product is uniquely associated with one name. When a customer is in what might be called a 'generic situation' the names come into their own. The customer is thinking: 'I need some soap, or a vacuum-cleaner, or whatever.' The trade name's job is to replace that generic, *without becoming a generic term itself*.

The latter point is reached if a person is able to speak of 'hoovering' the carpet and then use an **Electrolux** or other make of machine to do the job; if he thinks of 'cola' as a kind of drink which equally well describes both **Coca Cola** and **Pepsi Cola**. 'Launderette' may still be technically a trade name, but it has passed into the ordinary language and no longer suggests a particular company. Whoever formed the term forgot to leave a name-identifying element within it, a dash of strangeness that would have enabled it to stand outside the main vocabulary.

These generic replacement names are going to be the ones that are more and more difficult to find in the future. Praninskas concludes that industry 'will see to it that the names of their new products are created by literary artists', and there is much to be said for that argument. It is quite clear, for example, that Dickens would have made a superb creator of trade names. Many trade names discussed in this chapter also reveal, I would have thought, a high literary quality. Namers have already learned a great deal from the techniques of the imaginative writers.

What they need to study now, however, is not literature. Their way ahead lies in a study of other nomenclatures, where a million ordinary people have brought names into being. Transfer *within* the trade name system may not be possible, but transfer into it from other non-commercial systems—avoiding the over-worked first name, surname and place name nomenclatures—is not only possible but increasingly necessary.

There must be relatively few trade-namers, but we are all affected by their work. I have not made a full study of my children's speech, but in spite of restricted television viewing it is quite clear that they are familiar with a large number of commercial names. In the course of a few days I was personally able to write down 400 product names with which I was familiar, including those of many products—such as cigarettes—that I would never dream of using. However, these trade names are part of our lives and language.

Pleasures of trade names

For my own part I try to make the best of the situation and enjoy trade names. I am happy to read the yellow pages of the telephone directories to find **Thun-Thoots** and **Teeny Poons**, which are children's sun-suits and feeding-spoons. I like the **Mity Tidy** shelves and the **Kant Mis** fly-swatters, the **Bug-Shok** insecticide and the delightful **Slug-A-Bug**. I cannot wear **Enna Jettick** shoes, which are for ladies, or **Top Secret**, a hair-tint which presumably calls for a better supply of hair than I can boast, but their names are welcome.

I enjoy, too, the names of shops. The Greater Cincinnati telephone directory lists beauty salons called **Pamper Hut**, **Kut-N-Kurl**, **Magic Mirror Beauty Shop**. Some British equivalents are **Beyond the Fringe**, **The Pretty Interlude** and **The Cameo**. Antique shops are another pleasant group: **The Shop of the Yellow Frog**, **Granny's Attic**, **Passers Buy**, **The Tarrystone**, **Past Perfect**. A member of The Names Society, Sidney Allinson, reports on Canadian names such as **The Salvation Navy Store**, **Poise 'N' Ivy**, **The Bra-Bar**, **Juicy Lucy's**, **The Fig Leaf**, **Leg Liberation**, **The Wearhouse** and **Undieworld**, all of which sell clothes in Toronto. Meanwhile, the *boutique* game continues in London and elsewhere, with **Bootique**, **Beautique**, **Shoetique**, **Fruitique**, **Motique** (car accessories), **Junktique**, **Bespotique** (tailor's) and **Fishtique**.

Some of these names you may consider to be dreadful, but their collective message is clear. Trade name creators have not yet run out of ideas, and the English language is alive and well.

Chapter 17
No end of Names

I borrow my chapter title from Browning. It seems suitable for a chapter in which I want to emphasise that the names enthusiast draws his materials from a well that never runs dry. This book is obliged to be finite; the subject is not.

In ranging over a wide variety of name topics this chapter is likely to resemble a typical issue of *Viz.*, the newsletter of The Names Society. A discussion about names of all kinds has been going on in its pages since the first issue appeared in January 1969. Not that it was called **Viz.** at the time. That was naturally one of the subjects that came up for discussion— what to call a magazine devoted to names. Suggestions included **Onoma** and **Names**—which were already being used for similar publications— **The Nominist, Nomen, Name, The Onomatologist, The Nominist, Nomina, Namely, The Nomenclator, Philonoma, Nomenalia** and **Notamina**. The choice of *Viz.* led later to one conversation where I was mistakenly thought to be the editor of *Oz*, but apart from that the joke has usually been appreciated.

Other magazine names

Viz. is only one of countless small magazines that are non-commercial labours of love. Poetry magazines abound, for instance, and have names like **Poetmeat, Nightrain, Bean Train, Wild Dog, Long Hair, Software, Fish Sheets, Circle, Circuit, Nomad** and **Stand**. It would be easy to write a verse about them, for one finds a **Twice, Nice, Vice** and **Spice**, a **Choice** and **Voice, Ambit** and **Gambit**. An ever-increasing band of enthusiasts also collect science-fiction magazines, which usually have names that are suitably out of this world. Some examples are **Bweek, Zot, Erk!, Reverb Howl, Kangaroo Feathers, Egg, The Hog on Ice, Son of Fat Albert**. A few have names that could easily be absorbed into the English suburbs as house names, however. **Shangri-La** would certainly be at home there, as would **Soitgoze. Curse You** might cause a few mutterings among the neighbours, but **Powermad** might merely strike them as an honest statement.

'Alternative' publications in recent years have included **Wipe**, printed entirely on toilet paper, and **Arse**, published by the Architects' Revolu-

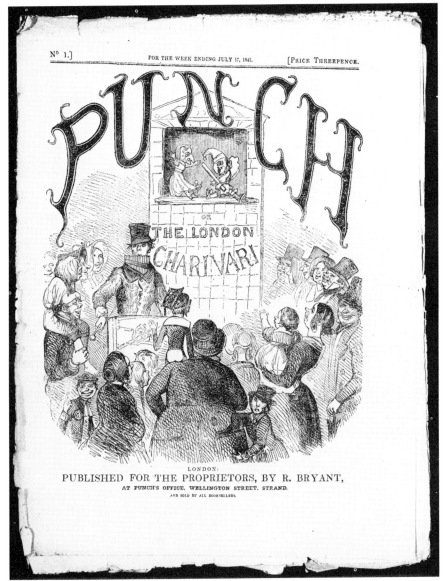

Nº 1.]   FOR THE WEEK ENDING JULY 17, 1841.   [PRICE THREEPENCE.

THE LONDON CHARIVARI

LONDON:
PUBLISHED FOR THE PROPRIETORS, BY R. BRYANT,
AT PUNCH'S OFFICE, WELLINGTON STREET, STRAND.
AND SOLD BY ALL BOOKSELLERS.

A clever use of a transferred name for a magazine, profiting from associations with popular entertainment but suggesting effective satire.

tionary Socialist Enclave. Others come and go, and *Viz.* quietly records their names with interest.

Names that share many of the magazine name characteristics are those of pop groups. In pre-pop days there were names like **The Andrews Sisters**, which followed the direct description tradition of the theatre. A dash of self-publicity led to **The Supremes**, **The Magnificent Men**, **The Spellbinders**. These are easy to understand as trade names of a type, making one think of professional wrestlers who try to boost themselves and frighten their opponents by means of fine-sounding names.

Another reminder of trade names comes with respelt names, used by famous groups such as **The Beatles** and **The Monkees**. A vaguely religious set of names was discernible in 1968 and has probably expanded considerably since then. At that time one heard of groups called **The Righteous Brothers**, **The Apostolic Intervention**, **The Angels** and **The Spiritual Five**. Names that with a slight change of form could easily have appeared on the covers of poetry magazines were also to be found, and some have endured well: **The Searchers**, **The Seekers**, **The Shadows**, **Saturday's Children**.

Names that showed an aggressive reaction to the Establishment were very similar to those of the alternative and 'underground' magazines. These were the groups called **The Enemies**, **The Animals**, **The Rejects**, **The Freak-Outs**, **The Barbarians** and the like. The science-fiction magazines translated into pop group names such as **The Grateful Dead**, **3½**, **The Mindbenders**, **U.F.O.**, **The Leathercoated Minds**, **The Happenings**, **The Mind Expanders**. All of these are meant to be attention-catchers, and some perform that function well. But names like **The Strawberry Alarm Clock** and **The Nitty Gritty Dirt Band**—the latter being rare in that it condescends to admit a connection with music—are like certain paintings. They are fine as exhibition pieces, but would be difficult to live with.

But we shall all, no doubt, get thoroughly used to such names as time passes. There is evidence on all sides of a new adventurousness in names which seems likely to affect a great many nomenclatures. Newly formed football clubs, for instance, are leaving aside traditional name elements such as 'Wanderers', 'Rovers', 'United' and 'Athletic'. There are already local teams called the **Alley Cats**, **Eskimoes**, **Stags** and **Juggernauts**. As it happens, many of the familiar club names have interesting anecdotes to account for them, such as the use of **Orient** by the crew from a ship of that name and **Wednesday** for a team that began by playing on that day.

Shop names, as we have seen, now reflect more modern trends, but by far the most important indication of the new onomastic atmosphere is seen in first name fashions. Yesterday's pop group fans are today's young parents, and their wide-ranging choice of names for their children shows the permanent effect their name environment has had on them. Historians of the future may, however, look back on the present naming era much as we look on the outbreak of Puritan names in the seventeenth century. There were excesses then, as now, but changes did come about that last to this day. The motivation then for the new names was religious fervour; today it is the fervour of a new generation which is determined to show that it thinks for itself. But before very long another generation will be wanting to show *its* individuality, and we must wait to see how that affects names.

Meanwhile, we can look back once again at some of the names given in the past. One area of great interest is the living world that surrounds man, the world of animals and plants. Another is that of man's various forms of transport—ships, locomotives, cars and the like, all man-made objects which are often felt to develop a personality of their own. There is enough material in those areas to fill another book of this size, so we must be brief.

Animal names

By animal names I mean the proper names of individual animals rather than the generic names of species used by a zoologist. We could all write down the names of several individual animals who are as well known to us as people. In many cases a pet is considered to be one of the family. Other animals are internationally famous. **Lassie** is far better known in Germany, for instance, than **Leslie**, as I often discovered.

A special group of animal names have become part of the English language. We can refer to a tom cat called **Percy** without it seeming strange, for 'tom' is no longer felt to be a form of **Thomas** in that context. Historians who are cat-owners will know that before Tom came on the scene, **Gib**—from **Gilbert**—was the usual name for a male cat. A 'tabby' looks suspiciously like a corruption of 'tib cat', which in some dialects remains the female equivalent of tom cat, but it has a different origin. Tabby is a striped taffeta and derives from the Arabic name of the place where it was made. A tabby cat was earlier described as 'tabby-coloured'. **Tib** was once the name of a low-class woman, the female equivalent of **Tom**, and was probably a diminutive of **Isabel**.

In medieval times cats and dogs were no doubt referred to by generic names and no others. These days individual names are bestowed on a wide range of pets and often display all the ingenuity we find in other nomenclatures. **Dora**, for instance, was owned by Annabel Bool and therefore known more fully as **Adorabool**. **Ocky** was **Octavius** on formal occasions and received that name because it was its owner's eighth cat. **Polly**, a corgi, was named from a resemblance to a television announcer of that name, and **Nelson** belonged to a **Hardy** family. Among my own favourite names are **Curlicue** for a curly tailed mongrel, **Edom** for a cat ('over Edom will I cast out my shoe'—Psalm 60), **Worthington** for a Basset hound and **Rover** for a budgerigar. The last example was intended to be an ice-breaker at parties.

Adrian Room's booklet on *Pet Names* (The Names Society) gives many more examples, some of which have already become minor classics. **Keith** and **Prowse** for a pair of cats are probably the best known, the agency of that name being famous for its advertising slogan: 'You want the best seats, we have them.' But children do a great deal of pet-naming and are not usually quite so subtle. They like incident names or descriptive names especially. My own children were probably typical when they named their white rabbit **Flash** because he was off 'like a flash' the first time they put him down.

Needless to say, these informal pet names are usually different from the registered titles of pedigree animals. I use the word 'title' deliberately, for they are often of the **Duchess of Bolcord, Lady of Arvon** type. A Kennel Club *Stud Book* I have by me shows that even formal names can be interesting, however. Among the bulldogs listed are **Abracadabra, Boom-De-Ay, Bully Boy, Derby Day, Queer Street, Rev. Dismal Doom, Bubbles, Cigarette, How Nice** and **Trifle**. There is even a bitch called **Buttercup**, though this would strike most of us as a typical name for a cow. Perhaps it was a humorous mis-naming, for many owners see no need to be too serious in the names they give. Chows with names like **Chin Chin** and **Yum Yum Victoria** are listed, and there is a Japanese spaniel called **Stoneo Brokeo**. **Spot XXVIII** is not without a certain humour, and has point in being basically the kind of shoutable name that is necessary for daily use.

The Buttercup example reminds us of non-domestic animal names, of which once again there are countless thousands. Some are worthy of special note, however. R. D. Blackmore mentions a cow called **Dewlips**, which has a definite charm, and the quinquemammalian cow called **Sanctity** discovered by a member of The Names Society who once looked into the subject would always belong in the Top Ten. Cows usually get suitably feminine names given to them, such as **Candy** and **Marigold**, but **Bullyface**, **Beefy**, **Droopy**, **Hoppy** and **Tango** are among other names that have been bestowed. One cow name that later became nationally known as a trade name was **Carnation**.

National attention was focused in Belgium a few years ago on the name of a donkey. A farmer who was protesting about agricultural policy arrived in Brussels with a donkey who bore the same name as the then minister of agriculture. This kind of satirical naming would probably not be allowed in Britain: it would be considered unfair to donkeys. I see from a show catalogue that British donkeys actually receive names like **Mrs. Donk**, which is a fascinating generic link name, **Jack the Ripper**, **Mockbeggar Gussie** and **The Vicar of Bray**.

Different kinds of horses receive names of different kinds, as one would expect. There was formerly a special point to the names of dray-horses, which always worked in pairs. Their partnership was often recognised in pairs of names like **Thunder** and **Lightning**, **Crown** and **Anchor**, **Might** and **Main**, **Time** and **Tide**, **Rhyme** and **Reason**, **Pomp** and **Circumstance**. No rules governed such names, such as those which have long been imposed by the Jockey Club on namers of racehorses. The restrictions do not prevent the creation of interesting names for the latter, however. Many are what could be called *notional blends*, a group we have not yet mentioned in connection with any other names.

Notional blends lead to names like **Mickey Mouse** by **Lightning Artist** out of **Cinema**, **Watchdog** by **Warden of the Marches** out of **Beagle**. A phonetic link may also be present, as in **Dial O** by **Diomedes** out of **No Reply**, and puns are possible: **Sea Pier** by **Duke of Buckingham** out of **Mollusca**. In the 1930s **Buchan** and **Short Story** had many bookish offspring, such as **Portfolio**, **Bookseller**, **Bibliograph** and **Birthday Book**.

Once the names come into being, by whatever means, they can exert a great influence on amateur punters. Horses are often backed because their names seem significant to a particular person at a particular time. The names are taken to be omens, in other words. We do not seem to be able to escape name magic wherever we look. One cannot help wondering, in passing, how much money has been lost to all but the bookmakers on poor horses that happen to have had brilliant names.

We must leave the animal world with a brief summary of what we have found, for there are wide areas still to cover. What is important in animal

Racehorse **Nimbus**, champion dairy shorthorn bull **Revelex Imperial Duke**, and giant panda **Chi Chi**.

names is not so much the predominance of one class of name rather than another, but the evidence one constantly finds of careful, affectionate naming. The names of pets, especially, have the friendly tone that one would expect and make a pleasant collection.

Flower names

If we turn now to flowers, our expectation might lie in the direction of lovely names rather than friendly ones. Oscar Wilde probably spoke for many people when he made Lord Henry, in *The Picture of Dorian Gray*, say:

> 'Yesterday I cut an orchid for my buttonhole. . . . In a thoughtless moment I asked one of the gardeners what it was called. He told me it was a fine specimen of **Robinsoniana**, or something dreadful of that kind. It is a sad truth, but we have lost the faculty of giving lovely names to things.'

We have not lost this faculty, as it happens, but one can see what Wilde meant. One has only to glance at a list of botanical names to understand also the remark of the nineteenth-century pamphleteer, Alphonse Karr, that 'botany is the art of insulting flowers in Latin and Greek'. The attractive names of flowers tend to be the folk names: **Sweet William**, **Jack-Go-To-Bed-At-Noon**, **Gill-Over-The-Ground**, **Good King Henry**, **Bitter Sweet**, **Morning Glory**, **Youth-And-Old-Age**, **Nancy Pretty** (or **None So Pretty**), **Old Man's Beard**, **Mourning Bride**, **Coral Bells**. The last named, to take one example, translates into the botanical name **Heuchera sanguinea**.

The botanists might argue, however, that scientific accuracy is of more importance to them than aesthetics. Historically speaking, it was logical for them to turn to classical languages that were internationally understood in order to create descriptive names. Those names may seem barbarous to the average person, but still more people would no doubt be offended if botanists made use of that other international language which begins '1, 2, 3'.

There are many signs that those who name cultivated varieties of flowers, such as the rose, make an attempt to find a name that suggests beauty. Rose varieties include **First Love**, **Maiden's Blush**, **Coral Dawn**, **Alpine Glow**, **Burning Love**, **Elegance**, **Golden Showers**, **Passion** and **Wildfire** as well as the famous **Peace**. Oddities occur, nevertheless. It is strange to find **Atombombe**, for instance, named in 1954 and presumably referring to a mushroom shape. One wonders also whether the reasons for choosing names like **Grumpy** and **Radar** really justified attaching them to roses. A number name that has been used for a rose, **Forty-Niner**, named in 1949, seems to fit in quite well with the names around it.

Scientists now say that there is some point in treating a plant as one would treat an animal, talking to it affectionately in order to make it grow better. We are therefore probably not far from the day when house plants will be named individually by their owners. Until that day comes, plant names remain at the generic level. It is probably just as well, for even at that level there are hundreds of thousands of names.

Apple names

The above statement about the vast quantity of names may be too general to impress itself upon the mind. Let us take a specific example. Whether we are gardeners or not, we all eat an apple from time to time. How many different kinds of apple are there? **Cox's**, **Granny Smith**, **Golden Delicious**—any more?

The *National Apple Register of the United Kingdom* lists 6,000 more, together with another 16,000 names that have been used as alternative descriptions for those same 6,000 cultivars. To be fair, many of these variant names are slight respellings of one another, abbreviations and so on. Translations of English names into other languages are also treated as variants. Nevertheless, the Golden Delicious, for instance, has also been known as the **Arany Delicious**, **Stark Golden Delicious** and

Yellow Delicious, and other apples have a long string of such genuine synonyms. **King of the Pippins** has such aliases as **George I**, **Hampshire Yellow**, **Pike's Pearmain**, **Princess Pippin**, **Seek No Further** and **Winter Gold Pearmain**. This is the kind of complexity that lies beneath not only 'apple' but most of the generic terms we use every day.

The apples that were popular in the seventeenth century were rather different from those in the shops today. One was the **Api**, or **Lady Apple**, carried by ladies in their pockets because it was very small and had no odour. It had been found growing wild in the Forest of Apis, in Brittany, and is known to have been in Louis XIII's garden by 1628. The **Catshead**, which 'tooke the name of the likenesse' according to a seventeenth-century writer, was later to be much used for apple dumplings. Particularly interesting were **Costards**, which at one time were sold for a shilling a hundred by costardmongers (the later costermongers). 'Costard' became a slang word for the head and occurred in the phrase 'cowardy costard', later corrupted to 'custard'. As an apple name it had originally referred to the apple's ribbed appearance (Latin *costa*, 'rib').

Another apple name well known in the seventeenth century was the **Nonpareil**, 'having no equal; peerless'. The word is unlikely to occur in a normal English conversation today, but it might well have done so in Shakespeare's day. He himself uses it in several of his plays—Miranda is said to be a nonpareil in her father's eyes, for instance. If there is ever a comprehensive *Dictionary of Names* which lists names that occur in several nomenclatures, 'Nonpareil' will be a typical entry. It names birds and moths, houses and a size of printing type among other things. In 1580 it became the name of a British warship, though this was renamed the **Nonsuch** in 1603.

Ship names

Since brevity is essential in this chapter, we must allow this mention of ship names (which has been carefully engineered) to lead us into the world of transport, which we mentioned earlier as another area of great naming interest. We move from the world of living things to one where inanimate objects are constantly being personified. Captain T. D. Manning and Commander C. F. Walker introduce the subject well in their *British Warship Names*:

> '... of all creations of men's hands, the ship—and especially the sailing ship—is surely the nearest approach to a living entity, possessing individual traits which distinguish her from her sisters, even of the same class. Small wonder, then, that the sailor, ever a sentimentalist at heart, has always endowed his vessel with an almost human personality and given her a name; or that, deprived as he is for long periods of the society of womankind, that personality should invariably be feminine— though by some illogical thought process he does not demand that the name should follow suit, and sees nothing incongruous in referring to an **Agamemnon** or a **Benbow** as "she".'

The Royal Navy has established over several centuries a stock of names that can be transferred from ship to ship. In this way names such as **Victory**, **Warspite**, **Orion**, **Ajax** and **Greyhound** have figured in great naval combats at widely differing periods. Because the ships were specifically built for these combats from the sixteenth century onwards, their names were often suitably war-like. **Warspite** probably represents 'war despite', showing contemptuous disregard for the dangers of battle. **Dreadnought** speaks for itself, as do **Triumph**, **Repulse**, **Revenge** and **Defiance**. **Swiftsure** is thought to be another contraction, this time of 'swift pursuer'.

In our discussion of place names in the New World we saw the influence of both Charles I and Charles II. The latter turned his attention also to his ships when he returned to England, immediately renaming the **Naseby**, which commemorated a Roundhead victory, the **Royal Charles**. Other ships became, for obvious reasons, **Royal Oak**, **Royal Escape** and **Happy Return**. The **Cleveland** was named after the Duchess of Cleveland, one of his mistresses. His highly subjective naming continued even with the **Loyal London**, which was paid for by the citizens of the city. The ship was sunk, but later raised and rebuilt. In spite of many hints thrown out by Charles, Londoners were less willing on this occasion to provide the funds. Charles struck out the 'Loyal' and allowed only 'London' to remain as the ship's name.

Unofficial renamings of ships by their crews are not unknown, and in at least one instance the Admiralty was forced to take action. They had named a sloop **Weston-Super-Mare** after the birthplace of the First Lord, A. V. Alexander. The name was quickly changed by the men to **Aggie-On-Horseback**, referring to Miss Agnes Weston, a well-known Navy benefactress. The ship's name was eventually altered to **Weston**.

Drake's **Golden Hind**, in which he sailed round the world, 1577–80.

British Warship Names contains an interesting essay which traces the historical development of the names. From a synchronic point of view, and going beyond British ship names to those of other English-speaking countries, we can safely say that all categories of names are represented on the high seas. There was even, at one time, a remarkable example of a physical blend name to add to the notional blends we found in racehorse names. The **Zulu** and **Nubian** were two destroyers that were both damaged in the First World War. A composite ship was assembled in 1917 using the forepart of *Zulu* and the after portion of *Nubian*. It was then named **Zubian**.

Some ship names, such as **Mayflower**, **Titanic**, **Mauretania** and **Cutty Sark** are world famous: at the other end of the scale completely are the names of yachts and smaller boats. Whereas modern ships like the great liners need dignified names, private vessels of all kinds allow whimsicality and humour to appear in their names. *Lloyd's Register of Yachts* for 1968, for instance, lists such examples as **Miss Conduct**, **Miss Demena**, **Bung Ho**, **C'est La Vie** (which I have seen elsewhere in the form **Sail La Vie**), **Annelory** and **Fairynuff**. The last named roughly translates a name I saw on a French chalet, **Sam Sufy** (*ça me suffit*).

Among other names I have collected from various sources are **Miss Mie**, **Miss Fitz**, **What Next**, **Bossy Boots**, **Koliwobbles**, **Q. Jumper**, **Tung Tide**, **Hare-Azing**, **Codswallop** and **Honey Don't**. I particularly like the names which link with the generic class name. 'Catamaran' is actually an adaptation of a Tamil word meaning a 'tied tree', but to many punsters who own one it is simply another kind of 'cat'. The names therefore emerge as **Nauticat**, **Kitti**, **Wild Cat**, **Cat Nap**, **Whiskers Two**, **Pussy Willow**, **Puss Face**, **Seamew**, **Sly Puss**, **Dupli-Cat**, **Show'er Puss** and **Pussy Galore**. 'Solo' class yachts receive names like **Solow**, **So-So**, **Soliloquy**, **Imalone**, **Solace**, **Slo Koche**, **Seule**, **Lone**, **So-Long**, **By Me Sen**, **Soloist**. In the 'Finn' class one finds names like **Huckleberry Finn**, **Tail Finn**, **Finale**, **Dolfinn**, **Finnigan**, **Finess** and **Finnisterre**. Even the National 'Flying Fifteen' class does not defeat the jokers. The two 'fs' in the title are picked up in names of the **Ffancy Ffree** type.

I have as yet seen no full-scale study of boat names, though the materials exist for it in various registers. All kinds of names occur, not just the jokey ones, and the standard generally is very high indeed. That is to say that if the namers decide to be witty they are usually very witty, often making learned or polyglot allusions. If they decide to be descriptive, convert words into names, link, transfer or invent names, they also seem to do these things well. There are not many nomenclatures where one finds names of the **Sailbad The Sinner** standard.

Train and locomotive names

The care with which boat-owners do their naming reflects the great enthusiasm the boats themselves arouse. An equal amount of enthusiasm is generated for some people by locomotives and trains, though this phenomenon appears to be almost exclusively British. Perhaps only an

A Selection of Yacht Names

A. Names that speak for themselves:

About Time II
Addynuff
Adorabelle
Allgo
Anuddha-Buddha
Any End Up
Anything
Appydaze
Aquadisiac
Avago
Azygos
Baise Mon Cul
Bald 'Ed
Bawdstif
Beezneez
B'Jabbers
Black Azelle
Blew Moon
Blow Mee
Blow-U-Jack
Blu Away
Bluebottle
Blue Over
Bluesology
Bosunover
Branestawm
Bright 'Un
Brillig
Buzz Off
Captain Cat
Cham-Pu
Chancalot
Clewless
Codswallop
Co Mo Shun
Coweslip
Craft E
Crusado
Cuffuffle
Daisy Dampwash
Dambreezy
Dammit
Dashtwet
Dinah Mite
Dinah Mo
Drip Dri
D Sea Bee
Dumbelle
Du-U-Mynd
Eb 'n' Flo
Elcat
Fair Kop
Fantabulous

Fast Lady
Fijit
First Luff
Flamin-Go
Flipincid
Fluffy Bottam
Flying Sorcerer
Foggy Dew
Forsail
Fred N Sign
Freelove II
Frivulus
Gaylee
Geewiz
Gercher
Get Weaving
Giggles
Gigolette
Gloo Pot
Golden B Hind
Gonpotee
Goonlight
Gozunda
Happikat
Hei Yu
Hell's Belles
Helluvathing
Herr Kut
Hot N Bothered
Hot Potato
Howdedo
Hows Trix
Icanopit
I.C.U.
Idunit
Infradip
Itsallgo
Jack's O.K.
Jest As Well
Jesterjob
Joka
Ketchup
K'Fuffle
Kippin
Koliwobbles
Konfewshun
Koolkat
Kriky
La-Goon
La Poussiquette
L For Leather
Loopey Llew
Luffabuoy

Luff Divine
Luffinapuff
Luft Behind
Maida Mistake
Maid Tumesshure
Mark 10:31
Maykway
Mea Tu
Merry Hell
Mighty Mo
Miss B Haven
Miss Carry
Miss Conduct
Miss Doings
Miss Fire
Miss Isle
Miss Myth
Mister Sea
Moanalot
Mrs. Frequently
My Goodness
Nap Kin
Nautitoo
Neveready
Nhit Wit
Nnay Llas
No Idea
Nowt
Nu Name
Nut Case
Nyctea
Odzanends
Oh-Ah
Ooops
Op-A-Bout
Owdonabit
Pen-Y-Less
Petard
Phlappjack
Phlash
Pink Djin
Plane Crazy Too
Potemkin
Puff-N-Blow
Red-E
Redrump
Reef Not
Rock-N-Roll
Rose Cheeks
Rosy Lee
Sa-Cas-Tic
Sail La Vie
Sally Forth

Scilly Whim
Scubeedoo
Seafari
Sheeza B
Shoestring
Sin King
Sir Fon
Sir Loin
Slo-Mo-Shun
Smart E
Soopurr
So Wet
Spraymate
Sudden Sally
Sue Perb
Sweet Fanny
Teas Maid
Tempers Fugit
Tern Up
The Pickle
Thou Swell
Tishoo
To Be True
Tomfoolery
Too Fax
Too-She
Tri-N-Ges
Tsmyne
Tuchango
Twilgo
Tyne E
Ucantu
U1-C
Up-N-Atom
Uskanopit
Utoo
Wacker Bilt
Waltzing Matilda
Water Lou
Weatherornot
We We
Windkist
Wotahope
Wotawetun
Wot-You-Fink
Wunnalot
Wych Syde
Y Dewin
Y Knot
Zom B
Z-Victor-One

B. Names that reflect special interests:

Arch Maid	Girl Friend	My Popsie	Shady Lady
Bright Eyes	Glamour Girl	My Spare Lady	She's Fast
Concubine	Heart Throb	Naughtilass	Slap N Tickle
Crumpet	Honeybunch	Nickers	Slick Chick
Cuddle	Honey Don't	Nifty Chick	Some Chicken
Curvaceous	Hot Tomato	Oui Oui	Ta Baby
Dabchick	Hunnibun	Painted Lady	Tangle Legs
Dancing Girl	Jezebel	Poppet	Taylor Maid
Dead Sexy	Jucy Lucy	Popsitoo	Tease
Easy Virtue	Katy Did	Provocative	Tempt Me
Enterprising Lady	Latin Lover	Saucy Puss	Temptress
Fast Lady	Lust	Sea Mistress	Testbed
Flirt	Meremaid	Sea Wife	Tiller Girl
Geisha	Mini The Minx	Sexy	Wayward Lady

Beer Bottle	Gin And Tonic	Pie Eyed	Sippers
Bottoms Up	Half Pint	Pink Gin	Soaked
Brandy Bottle	Hangover	Pinta	Souced
Brewer's Droop	Hot Toddy	Plastered	Sozzled
Bubbly	Lash Up	Quick One	Spree
Bung Ho	Mild And Bitter	Rum Baba	Still Sober
Cheers	Opening Time	Say When	Too Tipsy
Corkscrew	Pale Ale	Scotch Mist	Whisky
Foaming Ale	Pick Me Up	Shandy	Yo-Ho-Ho

C. Class names:

Flying Fifteen

Craffty	Ffickle	Fflame	Ffroff
Eleffant	Ffifi	Fflipinelle	Ffun
Family Fun	Ffillipp	Fflotsam	Fifty Fifty
Ffab	Fflagon	Ffluff	Flip Flop
Ffanfare	Ffirty Ffour	Ffolly	Nymff
Ffascination	Ffizzle	Ffortissimo	Sstutter
Ffelicity	Fflambuoyant	Ffreak	

Finn

Affinity	Coffinn	Finnatical	Muffin
Beefin	Enuffin	Finnomenon	Parafinalia
Boffin	Fickanfinn	Finny Hill	Skyfinn
Chafin	Finantonic	Laarfinn	Sumfinn
Chin Fin	Finbad	Micky Finn	Tiffin

Flying Dutchman

Dutch Uncle	Flying Fish	Ghost	Spectre
Fair Phantom	Flying Phantom	Jinx	The Dutchess
Flying Chum	Flying Scotsman	Sea Myth	Zeelust

Englishman (Cecil J. Allen) could write that many of the trains described in his book 'have become old friends to me', or that 'the route between Victoria and Dover is anything but easy *from the locomotive point of view*' (my italics). Both remarks occur in *Titled Trains of Great Britain*, a loving account of such trains as the **Broadsman**, **Flying Scotsman**, **Master Cutler**, **White Rose**, **Mancunian**, **Red Rose**, **Welsh Dragon**, **Capitals Limited**, **Granite City**, **Statesman** and **Red Dragon**. The *Statesman* was named because it connected with the sailings of the **United States**. The 'Limited' in *Capitals Limited* perhaps referred to the limited number of first-class seats available, and the other names all contain references to the places served.

Apart from named trains, most of the larger steam locomotives once had individual names. The practice was established in the early days of Stephenson's **Rocket** and pioneers such as **Novelty**, **Sanspareil**, **Invicta** and **Northumbrian**, but when **Locomotion** commenced work in 1825 it also bore the number name, **No. 1**. The many railway companies that sprang up had their own ideas about identifying locomotives, some considering number names quite sufficient, but the Great Western Railway consistently gave verbal names to its express passenger locomotives from the earliest days. When the railways were grouped into four companies in 1923 such names came back into general favour. Everything was set for the small boys (I was among them) who would later gaze upon the powerful giants with considerable awe and carefully underline those names in little books. Later still, 'enthusiasts' were to go much further, removing the nameplates from the driving wheel splashers completely if the opportunity presented itself.

Locomotive names were often grouped thematically as 'halls', 'castles', 'clans', 'granges', 'manors', 'counties', etc. The LNER named some Pacific locomotives after famous racehorses, though this led to the sight of **Sandwich**, **Spearmint** and **Pretty Polly** standing at the heads of trains and looking rather sheepish. As more and more locomotives were named, so the names were drawn from yet more sources. Many names were those which seem to be free-floating, likely to turn up in almost any nomenclature: **Atlas**, **Bonaventure**, **Pathfinder**, **Blue Peter**, **Vanguard**, **Meteor**, **Sunbeam**. Some names looked back to the immediate source of locomotive names, the stage coaches. These had borne names like **Vivid**, **Lightning**, **High Flyer**, **Nimrod**, **Royal Sovereign**, **Talisman**, **Vixen**, **Arrow**, **Dart**, **Comet**, **Red Rover**. A famous mailcoach bore the name **Quicksilver**.

We see once again how the world of names consists of countless overlapping nomenclatures. It is impossible to look through a book such as H. C. Casserley's *British Locomotive Names of the Twentieth Century* and not be reminded of ship names, place names, surnames, animal names and a dozen other kinds of name. One feels, too, that every name will have its day sooner or later. The stage coach **Red Rover** may have slipped into obscurity, but its name lives on as a pub name and as the name for a London Transport ticket. **Blue Peter** has earned a new kind of fame in Britain as the name of a television programme. Such names call for an individual approach which allows one to trace their path of transfer into different naming systems after their initial establishment as names. **Blue Peter**, for instance, possibly began as a French place name, **Beaupreau**, 'beautiful meadow'. A fabric made there, a kind of linen, was used to make flags. The fabric was called *beaupers* or *bewpers* in English. Professor Weekley suggested that the second part of this word may have been mistaken for **Piers**, which is another form of **Peter**. 'Beau' could then have been changed to 'blue' to suit the actual colour of the flag. Many well authenticated instances of similar word and name changes caused by folk etymology are recorded.

Stage-coach names often preceded locomotive names. Shown here is **The Telegraph**, which ran between Cambridge and London.

The railways as a whole were sources of very many names. Nicknames for the railway companies soon came into being, usually being based on the company initials. The London, Midland and Scottish was known by such names as **Ell of a Mess**, **Let Me Sleep** and **Lord's My Shepherd**. The Great Western became **Go When Ready** or **God's Wonderful Railway**, while the LNER was **Late and Never Early**. **The Bluebell Line** and **Cuckoo Line** were well known branches of the Southern Railway, and the Waterloo and City line of the Underground became **The Drain**. Much the same kind of process in the USA led to names like the **Apple Butter Route**, **Spud Drag**, **Original Ham and Egg Route**, **Bums' Own** and **Pennsy**.

Frank McKenna, in his *Glossary of Railwaymen's Talk*, mentions nicknames that were used by the railwaymen themselves. The footplatemen from Yeovil, for instance, were known as the **Apple Corps**; the **Master Cutler** was less reverently known as **The Knife and Fork**; an efficient fireman was **Terror of the Tongs**; the Leeds–Carlisle main line was the **Burma Road** because it was difficult to negotiate. One wonders whether many other occupations, other than military, have produced such collections of names. Mining language must include many examples. Geordie pitmen certainly used to name newly opened 'districts', according to one of my correspondents. **Spion Kop** was named after the battle for that hill had just taken place, and grim irony caused **White City** to be transferred below ground.

Lorry names in Malta

Philip Riley has written an interesting article about the names of lorries in Malta. He thinks that the custom of giving names began when hand-carts were the normal conveyors of goods. They had no registration plates but needed to be identified in some way. It became usual to display on them the nicknames of their owners.

The modern lorries which carry on the tradition of naming 'are almost exclusively privately owned', Mr. Riley says, which hints at ownership proclamation as the main reason for them. Most of the names are in English, the language used for educational purposes, but there is interference in the spelling of many names due to the influence of Maltese or Italian. A large group of names—which are apparently carefully painted in 'a spiked and ornate lettering, usually in bright red, yellow and green' —are the names of saints. These may be the patrons of villages where the drivers live or the patron saints of the drivers themselves. Other religious names refer to the Virgin Mary or may be statements of faith: **In God We Trust**.

Another large group of names draws its inspiration from the entertainment world. Song titles such as **Sonny Boy**, **High Noon**, **Congratulations**, **Thunderball** and **April Love** appear, and singers such as **Sandie Shaw** and **Cliff Richard** are honoured. Films have an influence, and **Peter Sellers**, **Steve McQueen**, **James Dean** are among those stars who drive round Maltese streets. **James Bond** (together with **007**) and **Goldfinger** are there with them.

A wide range of transferred names is called upon, and lorries called **Wilson** and **Kennedy** are seen beside **New York**, **Victoria**, **Melbourne**, **California** and **Germany**. A few lorry owners continue the former tradition of transferring their own nicknames, such as **Happy** or **Blue Boy**. One group Mr. Riley describes as 'prowess names, designed to enhance the owners' reputations'. He includes here such names as **Big Boy**, **Let Me Pass**, **Roadmaster**, **Hercules**, **King of the Road** and **Super Power**, which reflect drivers' attitudes with which we are all only too familiar. Some of the animal names, such as **Tiger** and **Lion**, might belong in this group, which are another form of personal trade names in a sense. A few names hint at prowess beyond the realm of driving, Mr. Riley suggests. He mentions names like **Lucky Lips** and **Kiss Me**, though these now have a curious innocence about them. They take us back to the 'sauciness' of seaside resorts just after the war.

Names take us everywhere, in fact. Not only into our social history, though they do that particularly well, but into every aspect of human activity. They take us everywhere English is spoken, showing the cultural differences that have evolved over centuries among peoples who often had a common origin.

This chapter, however, and those that have preceded it, are meant to have made that point. I have the consoling thought at the back of my mind that if the words I have written have failed to do it, the names will in any case have spoken for themselves.

Another form of transport which brought a set of names into being was the bicycle. The **Ordinary** (far left) was better known by its nickname, the **Penny-Farthing**. Also shown (this page) —the **Dandy** (or **Hobbyhorse**) and the **Boneshaker**.

Chapter 18
Name Games

As we have seen in previous chapters, names offer plenty of material for the serious student of history, language, psychology, sociology and the like who wants to make a scholarly investigation. But names also offer scope for a less serious approach. It is easy to play games with them in various ways, to treat them light-heartedly.

In the formal sense of playing an actual game, my children are fond of some simple name games that can be played on a car journey. One of these we refer to as *Animal Names*. They look at names of all kinds—street names, place names, shop names, pub names, etc.—and score a point for each animal they find. If they saw **Oxford** they would score one point, the **Fox and Goose** would give them two points, and so on. I would personally allow a point, and perhaps give a bonus, if the 'rat' in **Stratford** was pointed out, and if names are scarce one can also allow puns. I might give a point for 'eel' in **Ealing**, for instance (in addition to the 'ling' that is there), if the child claiming the point knew that he was making a pun. For the sake of my youngest child, who cannot yet read, I usually allow him to score a point for any advertisement, pub sign and the like that he sees that shows an animal. He also scores by seeing real dogs, cats, horses or whatever in streets or fields.

A simple street name game for a journey through a city makes use of the street name elements listed on pages 158 and 159. In my family we usually guess how many different words for 'street' we will see between the beginning and end of our journey, but there are many possible variations. One is to look for street names which have both parts beginning with the same letter, as in **Aragon Avenue**.

For longer journeys I once devised for the children's section of a national newspaper a place name game based on name elements. For common elements such as '-ton' or '-by', one point can be allowed. To these can be added three points for a tree, as in **Oakwell**, three for a river, as in **Burton-on-Trent**, and three for a first name, as in **Peterborough**. Five points can be given for colours, as in **Redhill**, fruits, as in **Appledore**, and the animals of **Molesey** and the like. Place names containing a number up to ten, such as **Seven Oaks**, score that number of points, but larger numbers score a maximum of ten points.

A more sophisticated game could easily be devised using the list of place name elements on pages 136 and 137, and there is no need to wait for a long journey. A map in a classroom or at home makes an effective substitute. It is not long before children start to ask questions as to why places have the names they do, and a good teacher will instantly respond to such a cue.

In a less formal sense, adults often play games with their own names, and it is surprising what one can do. Anagrams and name rebus have long been popular, and there are translations to be made, pronunciations to be changed, name files to compile, variant spellings to collect, and in certain cases, select clubs to join. From the point of view of name games, 'what's in a name?' turns out to have a host of new answers.

Games have names. **Blind Man's Buff** is universally popular. In Germany it is called **Blind Cow**, in Portugal **Blind Goat**.

Anagrams

A true anagram of a name was defined by William Camden in 1605. He explained it as a 'dissolution of name truly written into his letters as his elements, and a new connexion of it by artificial transposition, without addition, subtraction, or change of any letter into different words, making some perfect sense applyable to the person named'. The examples Camden gave were mostly in Greek and Latin, and he referred the first anagram to Lycophron, who is said to have turned the name of King **Ptolemaios** into '*apo melitos*', 'made of honey'. Anyone who has a few hours to spare and lots of patience might care to mix up the letters of his own name and see what he can make of them. He should take care, however. Camden gives the warning that 'some have been seen to bite their pen, scratch their heads, bend their brows, bite their lips, beat the board, tear their paper, when they were fair for somewhat, and caught nothing herein'. Those who have access to a computer can perhaps avoid the frustrations.

Darryl Francis has prepared a list of names that are mutually anagrammatical. Thus **Alice** becomes **Celia**, or vice versa, and **Arnold** becomes **Ronald** (or **Landor** or **Roland**). The following names are among those which are related in a similar way: **Christian—Christina**; **Mary—Myra**; **Ann—Nan**; **Theodora—Dorothea**; **Caroline—Cornelia**;

Dean—Edna; **Jane—Jean**; **Elmer—Merle**; **Amy—May**; **Marian—Marina**. The Mary example reminds one of George Herbert's little poem in the seventeenth century:

> How well her name an *army* doth present,
> In whom the Lord of Hosts did pitch his tent.

One should also note that **Myra** was invented by Fulke Greville, a seventeenth-century poet, and may have been a deliberate anagram of Mary.

George Herbert's poem shows the poet in light-hearted mood, and does not indicate a belief in onomancy, or name magic. Such beliefs were formerly widespread, and there are those even today who attach a great deal of importance to the words that can be formed by the letters of their names. Personally, I must include myself amongst Camden's head-scratchers, lip-biters and brow-benders, having 'caught nothing' in my own name.

Rebus

A name rebus can look like this: **Eur U** which example is meant to be decoded as 'Lo! "u" is past "eur"', or **Louis Pasteur**. Similarly, **Aristophanes**, **Lord Tennyson**, **King Solomon** and **George Washington** are to be found—by those who are ingenious enough—in the following:

Ar	Y	M	Gt
Hes	L/D Xn	K	Ge/Gew H

The construction and deciphering of such rebus, together with many other word and name puzzles, is the concern of the members of the National Puzzlers' League in the USA. My examples are taken from the January, 1973 issue of *Enigma*, the League's journal. Anyone unable to sleep because he is still trying to work out how they operate would be well advised to write to the Editor, Mary J. Youngqvist, 299 McCall Road, Rochester, N.Y. 14616. Similar intellectual name games, incidentally, are often to be found in the pages of *Word Ways*, the journal of recreational linguistics. This is edited by A. Ross Eckler at Spring Valley Road, Morristown, New Jersey 07960.

Two simple rebus that are among my own favourites have a satisfying visual appearance. It was J. Bryan who told me of the horse named **Potooooooooo**, and Mark Lower quotes **ABCDEFGHIJKMNOPQRSTUVWXYZ** in his nineteenth-century *Essays on English Surnames*. The number of 'o's' is important in the first, of course, as is the letter that is missing from the second.

Pictorial rebus have already been mentioned in connection with sign names, and it can be amusing to think of a way to illustrate one's own name. A suggestion for **Dunkling** was long ago given indirectly, I regret to say, by the boy who sat next to me at school. He delighted in calling out at quiet moments: 'Doesn't dung cling!' Other names may hint at a more pleasant illustration, particularly if it is the bearer of the name who is thinking about it. We tend to play unkind games with other people's names rather than our own. I am reminded of the entry in a parish register by the sexton who dug a grave for a Mr. **Button**. He wrote simply: 'To making one button hole: 4s 6d.'

Other name games

Some names translate well into other languages. My former colleague René **Quinault** becomes Mr. **Cinema** in Germany, where they pronounce his name as *Kino*. In a vaguely similar way, a Greek friend tells me that shifting the stress on his surname, **Melas**, changes him from Mr. **Black** to Mr. **Honey**. I can think of no English names that would change their meaning so drastically by an altered pronunciation, but some could perhaps be improved in sound. With some English surnames different families do in fact make use of different pronunciations.

There are those who are greatly offended by what they consider to be a mispronunciation of their name, and even more so by a misspelling. Several correspondents of mine have a more light-hearted approach. They keep a little notebook in which they collect variations of their own name. Their enthusiastic greeting of yet another form takes away all traces of irritation. One can go further and deliberately pun on one's own name. In the past many families did this when they adopted mottoes. The **Manns**, for example, adopted the phrase *Homo sum*, 'I am a man', and the *Festina lente*, 'hasten slowly', of the **Onslow** family is well known.

On the question of orthographic variations, my own name once appeared on a list near to that of Sheilah **Ward Ling**, and that naturally suggested a new train of thought. Would I instantly climb the social ladder a few rungs, I wondered, if I were to become Leslie **Dunk Ling**? I decided not in my own case, but once again there may be some surnames that would be much improved by conversion into double-barrelled form.

Another name game of a sort is to compile what might be called a 'name file'. The idea is to collect together all the information one can about one's own surname, including details of other people who have borne the name. Biographical dictionaries and encyclopedias can be consulted, but if no one famous has found his way into the reference books it may be necessary to write around to namesakes mentioned in telephone and other directories. There are those who claim to be the unique bearers of a particular surname, but this rarely turns out to be true when one looks into the matter. A name file, then, is a 'clan scrapbook' in a sense. It makes an interesting personal name project and may suggest something to educationists for classroom work.

There is a slight connection between the 'name file' idea and the Jim Smith Society, which we mentioned previously. Membership of that band is obviously open to all Jim Smiths, and for a fortunate few entry into another happy band may be possible. This is the 'My Name Is A Poem Club', open to those who have names like **Jane Cane**, **Newton Hooton** and **Nancy Clancy**. The president of the club, according to latest information, is **Hugh Blue**. Such names might be described as collectors' items, for there are many people around who do collect unusual names,

A Page From a Name Collector's Notebook

George F. Hubbard (210 East 68th Street, New York, N.Y. 10021) has a collection of nearly 10,000 unusual personal names. He collects only authentic names of real people, past and present. The following names are a small selection from his collection. To obtain their full flavour it helps to read them aloud.

Henrietta Addition	Mel Manny Immergut	Maid Marion Montgomery
Cyretha Adshade	Inez Innes	Malcolm Moos
Nancy Ancey	Melvin Intriligator	Seeley Wintersmith Mudd
Etta Apple	Chester Irony	Harriet Bigelow Neithercut
Oscar Asparagus	Frank Ix	Savage Nettles
Orville Awe	Lizzie Izabichie	Olney W. Nicewonger
Sterling Blazy	Hannah Isabell Jelly	Penny Nichols
Ilse Boos	Watermelon Johnson	Melvin Mackenzie Noseworth
Philip Brilliant	Amazing Grace Jones	Louise Noun
Duckworth Byrd	Boisfeuillet Jones	Belle Nuddle
George A. Canary	Halo Jones	Fluid Nunn
Dina Chill	Income Jones	June Moon Olives
Columbus Cohen	Pinkbloom Jones	Ichabod Onion
May Day	Love Joy	Memory Orange
Richard Dinners	Pleasant Kidd	Ada Garland Outhouse
Upson Downs	Maude Kissin	Freelove Outhouse
Mark Rile Dull	Rosella Kellyhouse Klink	Zoltan Ovary
Loveless Eary	Zeno Klinker	Victor Overcash
Luscious Easter	Royal Knights	Mollie Panter-Downes
Lilley Easy	Bent Korner	Sirjohn Papageorge
Ophelia Egypt	Joseph Wood Krutch	Hector Piazza
Ireland England	Rose Leaf	Human Piper
Alice Everyday	Michael Leftoff	Penelope Plum
Remington P. Fairlamb	Joan Longnecker	Omar Shakespeare Pound
Wanda Farr	Bernard Darling Love	George B. Proud
Thaddeus Figlock	Logwell Lurvey	Alto Quack
Charmaine Fretwell	Hunt A. Lusk	Florence A. Quaintance
Courter Shannon Fryrear	Sistine Madonna McClung	Nellie Quartermouth
Yetta Gang	Raven McDavid	Alberta Lachicotte Quattlebau
Bess Goodykoontz	Pictorial McEvoy	Pearline Queen
Henry Honeychurch Gorringe	Mussolini McGee	Flora Rose Quick
Gussie Greengrass	Spanish McGee	Freeze Quick
Tommy Gunn	Phoebe McKeeby	John B. Quick
Thomas Hailstones	Harry Maleman	Veasy Rainwater
Ima Hogg	Miriam Mates	Juanita Rape
Arabelle Hong	Marybelle Merryweather	Wanton Rideout
Louise Hospital	Lilla Mews	Pius Riffle
Rutgers I. Hurry	James Middlemiss	Murl Rigmaiden

Harry Rockmaker	Sory Smith	Sue Verb
Sarepta Rockstool	Burt Softness	Pleasant Vice
Dewey Rose	Minnie Starlight	Carrington Visor
Rose Rose	Sally Sunshine	Melvin Vowels
Violla Rubber	Daily Swindle	Dassah Washer
Little Green Russian	Rose Throne	Burson Wynkoop
Louis Shady	Yelberton Abraham Tittle	Thereon Yawn
Laurence Sickman	Milton Trueheart	Herbert Yells
Frederick Silence	Thomas Turned	Romeo Yench
Bess Sinks	Britus Twitty	Berma Yerkey
Ester Slobody	Nell Upole	Homer Yook
Adelina Sloog	Albertina Unsold	Ida Yu
G. E. Kidder Smith	Viola Unstrung	April Zipes

eagerly noting those that appear in newspaper reports and the like.

A great collector of the past was N. I. Bowditch, who published his *Suffolk Surnames* in 1858, and an edition seven times larger in 1861. The latter contains a very large number of unusual names that were to be found in America, especially Suffolk County, at the time. Bowditch rarely gives the origin of the names, but strings anecdotes together in a fast and furious way. One moment he is recounting how **Ottiwell Wood** spelt out his name ('*O* double *t*, *i* double *u*, *e* double *l*, double *u*, double *o*, *d*'), and immediately he remarks on the confusion of the sexes in Mr. **Maddam**, Mr. **Shee** and the like.

A collection need not concern itself with surnames. John Leaver and Gordon Wright are among those members of the 'Inn-sect' who fanatically collect pub names. Richard Luty, whose work is connected with the Ordnance Survey, is at least one collector of unusual place names known to me. In Fife, Eileen Ryan adds regularly to an already enormous collection of girls' first names. It is surprising that name collecting has not been organized in the same way as number name collecting, which is indulged in by so many small boys at railway stations and airports in Britain. It would be a relatively simple matter to provide children with materials for a names collection.

Name pieces

Of those adults who do collect names, many are tempted to make humorous use of them in literary pieces. These may take the form of short stories or poems, and a few examples will quickly make the point. A. A. Willis, for example, who used to write for *Punch* as 'A.A.', showed what a really clever writer could do with place names. In the middle of a longer article on the subject which appeared in *Punch* in October 1936, the following occurs:

'By way of light relief from cold classification, I have also compiled from village names a little modern romance. It is a love story of **Harold Wood** (Essex) and **Daisy Hill** (Lancashire), **Loversall** (Yorkshire) with **Pettings** (Kent). Follows naturally **Church** (Westmorland) with **Ring O' Bells** (Lancashire) for the **Bride** (Isle of Man). **Honeymoor** (Herefordshire) is obviously a honeymoon cut short—no doubt because the **New House** (Sussex) was **Fulready** (Warwickshire). Follows even more naturally **Nursling** (Hampshire) with **Cradle End** (Hertfordshire) and **Bapchild** (Kent). After a while Harold, being already very **Clubworthy** (Devon), takes to **Club Moor** (Lancashire), so he and Daisy begin to **Bicker** (Lincolnshire) and even **Wrangle** (also Lincolnshire), and are soon at **Loggerheads** (Staffordshire). She is thus left to her own **Devizes** (Wiltshire) with the result that there presently appears **Bill Brook** (Staffordshire), a **Lover** (Wiltshire) for her to **Skipwith** (Yorkshire). This should be the **Finish** (Ireland), but as I don't play with Irish names and anyway it's a modern romance, Harold treats this as a **Cause** (Shropshire) for Divorce (which unfortunately I **Havant** (Hampshire) been able to find anywhere), and all three end up in **Court** (Somerset).'

ALEXANDER ANN AUDREY CAROLINE CLARE

DAVID EDWARD FRANCIS JAMES JANE

LESLIE LOUISE MARY PAMELA SARA

Examples of 'blazonyms', which illustrate first names by designs based on heraldic principles.

Miss Muriel Smith has made use of her extensive knowledge of apple names to compose a similar story incorporating them. In the full version Miss Smith managed to build in no less than 365 different names. The story begins as follows:

'**Mrs Toogood**, whose daughter **Alice** was a **Little Beauty**, but rather a **Coquette**, despaired of ever seeing a **Golden/ Ring** on the **Lady's Finger**, although she had been **Queen** of the **May**, **Dainty** as a **Fairy**, with **Brown Eyes**, **Golden Cluster** of curls, **Pink Cheek**, **Sweet** expression (her **Family** called her **Smiler**) and had roused **Great Expectations** when she was a **Pretty Maid** of **Three Years Old**, a mere **Baby**, not out of the **Nursery**.'

In Miss Smith's epic, Alice eventually elopes with **Shannon**, an **Irish Giant**. Another rousing tale, based on the names of moths and assembled by Pauline Quemby, traces the adventures of **Grisette**, a **Small Quaker**, who is saved by a **Cosmopolitan** gentleman from the **False Mocha**. The highlight of this story occurs when a **Scarce Dagger** is plunged into Mocha's heart, causing his blood to flow out in a **Small Rivulet**. The landlord of the inn where this takes place then exclaims: 'Look what tha's done to ma **Ruddy Carpet**.'

Names in verse

From such compositions it is but a short step to writing verses about names. One must naturally distinguish here between true poems, such as the much quoted classic on American place names by Stephen Vincent Benét, and the consciously less serious attempts of other writers. Even great poets like Pope, for instance, could dash off a piece in a lighter moment about a name. In his case he chose to theorise about the name of the **Kit-Cat** Club:

> Whence deathless **Kit-Cat** took its name
> Few critics can unriddle;
> Some say from Pastry Cook it came,
> And some from **Cat and Fiddle** . . .

Pope goes on to give an explanation of the name that is more obscure than the name itself, which derives from Christopher (**Kit**) **Catling**, the keeper of the pie-house where the Club originally met.

In a similarly relaxed moment, Dryden played with his cousin's surname, **Creed**. After a discussion one evening about the origin of names he is said to have composed the following lines spontaneously:

> So much religion in your name doth dwell
> Your soul must needs with piety excel.
> Thus names, like well-wrought pictures drawn of old,
> Their owners' natures and their story told.
> Your name but half expresses, for in you
> Belief and practice do together go.
> My prayers shall be, while this short life endures,
> These may go hand in hand, with you and yours;
> Till faith hereafter is in vision drowned,
> And practice is with endless glory crowned.

By the nineteenth century James Smith was able to take up this theme of names and natures in his *Comic Miscellanies* and say that 'surnames seem given by the rule of contraries'. Sample verses from his long poem will illustrate his theme:

> Mr. **Child**, in a passion, knock'd down Mr. **Rock**,
> Mr. **Stone** like an aspen-leaf shivers;
> Miss **Poole** used to dance, but she stands like a stock,
> Ever since she became Mrs. **Rivers**.
> Mr. **Swift** hobbles onward, no mortal knows how,
> He moves as though cords had entwined him,
> Mr. **Metcalfe** ran off, upon meeting a cow,
> With pale Mr. **Turnbull** behind him.
> Mr. **Barker**'s as mute as a fish in the sea,
> Mr. **Miles** never moves on a journey,
> Mr. **Gotobed** sits up till half after three,
> Mr. **Makepiece** was bred an attorney.
> Mr. **Gardener** can't tell a flower from a root,
> Mr. **Wilde** with timidity draws back,
> Mr. **Ryder** performs all his journeys on foot,
> Mr. **Foote** all his journeys on horseback.

Smith turned his attention to a variety of name topics, not to mention allied subjects such as heraldry. He makes his contribution to the large body of poems about pub names, and is one of the very few writers I can think of who has tackled street names. Once again he was concerned with misnomers, this time of London streets:

> From Park Land to Wapping, by day and by night,
> I've many a year been a roamer,
> And find that no lawyer can London indict,
> Each street, ev'ry lane's a misnomer.
> I find **Broad Street**, St. Giles's, a poor narrow nook,
> **Battle Bridge** is unconscious of slaughter,
> **Duke's Place** cannot muster the ghost of a duke,
> And **Brook Street** is wanting in water.

Several more verses follow in a similar vein, and Smith does have the grace to admit that, even if he has proved 'That London's one mighty mis-nomer' it is in 'verse not quite equal to Homer'.

Name jokes

Jokes and minor anecdotes based on names have been circulating for a very long time, as William Camden once again makes clear. His *Remains Concerning Britain* contains a whole chapter on name puns, and in this we learn that the Romans, for instance, jokingly changed the name of **Tiberius Nero** because of his drinking habits. They made him **Biberius Mero**, or a 'mere imbiber' if one uses 'mere' in its early sense of undiluted wine. Camden also quotes the famous joke about the Angles ('not Angles but Angels'), which must be almost as well known as 'Thou art **Peter** [which means 'stone' or 'rock'] and upon this rock I will build my church.' Before this the Apostle had been called **Cephas**, the Aramaic equivalent of 'rock', though his real name was Simon.

Archie Armstrong wrote at roughly the same time as Camden, in the early seventeenth century, but he was far less learned in his *Banquet of Jests and Merry Tales*. His name jokes are not the kind to raise even a smile today, though he was popular at the time. A typical Armstrong joke is about the demand that was current in certain quarters to change Christmas to Christ-tide in order to avoid the Catholic reference to 'mass'. **Thomas**, Archie says, and one can almost feel him holding his sides, is worried in case he has to become **Thomside**. One anecdote in the book does provide additional evidence, if any were needed, about the badly painted name boards that were displayed in seventeenth-century streets. On a boar which had been taken to be a monster, Armstrong says that it is a sign that the painter was an ass.

By the nineteenth century the standard of name joke had improved somewhat. Bowditch writes of a doctor who, when he learnt that a Mr. **Vowell** had just died, instantly remarked that he 'was glad it wasn't *u* or *i*'. In modern times the best witticisms are perhaps to be found in the names themselves rather than in anecdotes about them. Those names which first aroused my own interest in the whole subject—suburban house names—hold their own well in this respect. They allow a retired teacher of mathematics to live in **After Math**, and an optimist who knows his Dickens to live in **Micawber** ('I am hourly expecting something to turn up'). In my view, that is the way the names game should be played, and while it is I shall continue to think it a privilege to be able to watch and record it.

Chapter *19*
Further Information and Bibliography

For those who seek further information about names, or would like to make contact with other names enthusiasts, here are some details of specialised societies.

The English Place Name Society

This Society was founded in 1923. Since that time it has been carrying out a survey of English place names, county by county, and has published an annual volume incorporating its findings. Each volume has become the authoritative work on the origins of the names of towns, villages, hamlets, farms, regions, rivers and forests in the region covered. The Society has always been fortunate in attracting scholars of very high quality, and the work they have done has earned the Society an international reputation.

Members of the English Place Name Society tend to be academics, particularly philologists, archaeologists and historians. While the area of interest of the Society is narrowly defined, it has much to offer students of other naming systems, particularly English surnames. The compiler of a local street name dictionary would also be able to look for help in the elucidation of medieval names in the appropriate county volume, and field name students would find similar help. Members of the Society receive the current volume free of charge and are able to purchase previous volumes at a preferential rate.

Enquiries about membership should be directed to:

> The Honorary Secretary,
> English Place Name Society,
> School of English Studies,
> University of Nottingham,
> Nottingham.

The American Name Society

On 29th December 1951, a group of American academics founded the American Name Society. They stated their aims to be 'the study of the etymology, origin, meaning and application of all categories of names—geographical, personal, scientific, commercial, popular—and the dissemination of the results of such study'.

The Society also saw itself acting as 'a clearing house for American nomenclature and an advisory agency for government offices, organisations and individuals concerned with the application, changing, spelling and pronunciation of names'.

The Society publishes a quarterly journal, *Names*, which contains articles and book reviews. These articles are usually highly specialised (e.g. 'Anglo-Saxon Onomastics in the Old English *Andreas*'), but from time to time articles of much wider interest appear. These deal, for example, with the psychology of first naming, or with the semantics of nicknames and diminutives. A serious researcher into names of any kind would be foolish not to consult the back numbers of *Names*, which over the years have dealt with a very wide range of subjects.

Members of the American Name Society also receive a newsletter which adopts a more light-hearted approach to names. The guest-editors pass on anecdotes about names and quote from popular newspaper articles. The Society therefore differs from the English Place Name Society both in admitting names of all kinds into the fold and in regularly permitting itself to smile. The fact that vital naming systems, such as trade names, receive relatively little attention in the Society's newsletter or journal presumably reflects a lack of interest in these areas among the present members. The constitution of the Society permits such names to be dealt with, and no doubt they will receive more and more attention in the future.

Enquiries about the Society should go to:

The Secretary-Treasurer,
American Name Society,
English Department,
State University College,
Potsdam,
New York 13676.

The Names Society

The Names Society was founded on 1st January 1969. Its members, who are scattered round the world, keep in touch by means of *Viz.*, the Society's newsletter. This contains a running discussion of the kind of name topics raised in this book, plus book reviews, anecdotes, queries and anything else to do with names.

The Society is building up a library of reference books and newspaper cuttings about names, and has several thousand letters giving information about house names, nicknames, etc., on file. The Society welcomes such letters at all times. Apart from collecting information about names, the Society attempts to answer questions about them from members and non-members. Many members of the Society have special interests and co-ordinate the work that is done in those areas. John Field, for example, is the focal point for field names; D. T. P. Mitchell is particularly interested in the educational applications of name projects.

The nature of the Society would best be shown by a sample copy of *Viz*. This is obtainable (20p post free), together with full details of membership, from:

> The Secretary,
> The Names Society,
> 7 Aragon Avenue,
> Thames Ditton,
> Surrey KT7 0PY.

(Canadian enquiries should be addressed to Miss Kathleen Sinclair, 128 Girton Boulevard, Winnipeg R3P OA5.
Australian enquiries should be addressed to Mrs. Cecily Dynes, 74 Wyong Road, Cremorne 2090, N.S.W.)

Books about names

There is an old joke about a person who picks up a telephone directory and starts to read it. After a time he remarks to a friend that there seem to be a lot of characters in the book but not much of a story.

For a student of names there are 'stories' in any list of names, as Charles Bardsley long ago tried to show in his *Romance of the London Directory*. Bardsley was a philologist, but directories have something for everyone. Those who think their own local directory, or telephone directory, is dull should try reading one from a completely different area, especially elsewhere in the English-speaking world. The surnames, trade names, street names and the like will quickly paint a portrait of the community concerned. This is also true of directories from the past, as the *Three Victorian Telephone Directories* reprinted by David and Charles in 1970 clearly demonstrated.

In America the Southern New England Telephone Company has gone a stage further in making its directories readable. Suggestions for name games that can be based on the directory are given inside the cover (they include the spotting of famous namesakes and collecting 'animal' surnames) and on nearly every page the list of names and numbers is interrupted to give the origins of surnames, or facts about historical figures who have borne the names. The directory is called *The Book of Names*, and the idea of adding interest to it in this way is one that other companies would do well to copy.

Directories and registers of every kind provide valuable source materials for name students, but books about names are obviously still more important. Several thousand discursive works and dictionaries of names have been published in various languages, especially about personal and place names. In the following pages is a list of books that I personally find most useful for general reference, together with others which I have consulted while writing this book.

Bibliography

1. Akrigg, G. P. V. and Helen B., *1001 British Columbia Place Names*, Discovery Press, 1973.
2. Alcock, Randal H., *Botanical Names For English Readers*, Reeve, 1876, reprinted Grand River Books, 1971.
3. Aldin, Cecil, *Old Inns*, Heinemann, 1930.
4. Allen, Cecil J., *Titled Trains of Great Britain*, Ian Allan Ltd., 1953.
5. Anderson, William, *Genealogy and Surnames*, Ritchie, 1865.
6. Armstrong, G. H., *The Origin and Meaning of Place Names in Canada*, Macmillan of Canada, 1972.
7. Aurousseau, M., *The Rendering of Geographical Names*, Hutchinson, 1957.
8. Baddeley, W., *Gloucestershire Place Names*, Bellows, 1913.
9. Barber, Henry, *British Family Names — Their Origin and Meaning*, Elliot Stock, 1902.
10. Bardsley, C. W., *Curiosities of Puritan Nomenclature*, Chatto and Windus, 1897, reprinted Gale, 1970.
11. Bardsley, C. W., *English Surnames, Their Sources and Significations*, Chatto and Windus, 1884, reprinted David and Charles, 1969.
12. Bardsley, C. W., *The Romance of the London Directory*, Hand & Heart Publishing Co., 1879.
13. Barfield, Owen, *History in English Words*, Faber, 1962.
14. Baring Gould, S., *Family Names and Their Story*, Seeley & Co., 1910.
15. Batchelor, Denzil, *The English Inn*, Batsford, 1964.
16. Bayley, Harold, *The Lost Language of London — a Tale of King Cole Founded on Folklore, Field Names, Prehistoric Hill Figures and Other Documents*, Cape, 1935.
17. Bebbington, Gillian, *London Street Names*, Batsford, 1972.
18. Belden, Albert D., *What Is Your Name?*, Epworth Press, 1936.
19. Benedictine Monks of St. Augustine's Abbey, Ramsgate, *The Book of Saints*, Black, 1921.
20. Bice, Christopher, *Names For The Cornish*, Lodenek Press, 1970.
21. Black, G. F. *The Surnames of Scotland*, New York Public Library, 1946.
22. Blair, Gardner, *Greenock Street Names*, Greenock Herald, 1907.
23. Bolitho, Hector and Peel, Derek, *Without the City Wall, An Adventure In London Street Names North of the River*, Murray, 1952.
24. *Book of Names, Bridgeport, Stratford*, Southern New England Telephone, 1972.
25. Bowditch, N. I., *Suffolk Surnames*, Trübner & Co., 1861.
26. Bowman, W. D., *The Story of Surnames*, Routledge, 1932.
27. Bowman, W. D., *What Is Your Surname?*, Faber & Faber, 1932.
28. Brookes, Reuben S. and Blanche, *A Guide to Jewish Names*, 1967.
29. Brown, Ivor, *A Charm of Names*, The Bodley Head, 1972.
30. Brown, Ivor, *A Word In Edgeways*, Cape, 1953.
31. Brown, Ivor, *Book of Words*, Cape, 1944.
32. Burke, Thomas, *The English Inn*, Longmans Green, 1931.
33. Burke, Thomas, *English Inns*, Collins, 1944.
34. Camden, William, *Remains Concerning Britain*, 1605, reprinted Russell Smith, 1870, reprinted EP Publications, 1974.
35. Cameron, Kenneth, *English Place Names*, Batsford, 1969.
36. Carter, G. A., *Warrington and the Mid-Mersey Valley*, Morten, 1971.

37. Casserley, H. C., *British Locomotive Names of the Twentieth Century*, Ian Allan, 1967.

38. Chaplin, Alethea, *The Romance of Language*, Sidgwick & Jackson, 1920.

39. Chicheley Plowden, C., *A Manual of Plant Names*, Allen & Unwin, 1972.

40. Clodd, Edward, *Magic in Names and Other Things*, Chapman & Hall, 1920.

41. *Collins Gem Dictionary of First Names*, Collins, 1968.

42. Copley, C. J., *English Place Names and Their Origins*, David & Charles, 1971.

43. Copley, C. J., *Names and Places*, Phoenix House, 1963.

44. Cottle, Basil, *The Penguin Dictionary of Surnames*, Penguin, 1967.

45. Crowley, Ellen T., and Thomas, Robert C., eds., *Acronyms and Initialisms Dictionary*, Gale, 1973.

46. Dauzat, Albert, *Dictionnaire des noms de famille et prénoms de France*, Larousse, 1951.

47. Dauzat, Albert, *Les noms de lieux*, Delagrave, 1951.

47a. Davey, L. S., *The Street Names of Lewes*, Lewes Borough Council, 1970.

48. Davidson, Gustav, *A Dictionary of Angels*, Free Press, 1968.

49. Davis, C. Stella and Levitt, John, *What's In A Name?*, Routledge & Kegan Paul, 1970.

50. Delderfield, Eric, *British Inn Signs and Their Stories*, David & Charles, 1972.

51. Delderfield, Eric, *Introduction to Inn Signs*, Pan, 1969.

52. Disraeli, Isaac, *Curiosities of Literature*, Moxom, 1849.

53. Dolan, J. R., *English Ancestral Names*, Potter, 1972.

54. Dracup, Roger, *House Names and Signs*, unpublished thesis.

55. Dunkling, Leslie, *English House Names*, The Names Society, 1971.

56. Dunkling, Leslie, *A Preliminary Survey of English Vocatives*, unpublished M.A. thesis, Stockholm University, 1967.

57. Edwards, Gillian, *Hogmanay and Tiffany*, Bles, 1970.

58. Edwards, Gillian, *Uncumber and Pantaloon, Some Words With Stories*, Bles, 1968.

59. Efvergren, Carl, *Names of Places in a Transferred Sense in English*, Ohllson, 1909, Gale 1969.

60. Ekwall, Eilert, *The Concise Oxford Dictionary of English Place Names*, O.U.P., 1966.

61. Ekwall, Eilert, *English River Names*, O.U.P., 1968.

62. Ekwall, Eilert, *Street Names of the City of London*, Clarendon Press, 1954.

63. Ellice, Edward C., *Place Names of Glengarry and Glenquoich and their Associations*, Routledge, 1931.

64. Endell, Fritz, *Old Tavern Signs*, Houghton Mifflin, 1916, Singing Tree Press, 1968.

65. Ewen, C. L., *History of British Surnames*, Kegan Paul, 1951.

66. Ferguson, Robert, *Surnames As A Science*, Routledge, 1884.

67. Field, John, *Discovering Place Names*, Shire, 1971.

68. Field, John, *English Field Names*, David & Charles, 1972.

69. Foxall, H. D. G., *A Gazetteer of Streets, Roads, and Place Names in Shropshire*, Salop County Council, 1967.

70. Franklyn, Julian, *A Dictionary of Nicknames*, British Book Centre, 1962.

71. Freeman, William, *Dictionary of Fictional Characters*, Dent, 1967.

72. Frey, Albert R., *Sobriquets and Nicknames*, Whittaker, 1887.

73. Gelling, M., Nicolaisen, W. F. H. and Richards, M., *The Names of Towns and Cities in Britain*, Batsford, 1970.

74. Guyot, Lucien and Gibassier, Pierre, *Les noms des plantes*, Presses Universitaires, 1967.
75. Guppy, Henry B., *Homes of Family Names in Great Britain*, Harrison, 1890.
76. Habben, F. H., *London Street Names*, Fisher Unwin, 1896.
77. Halliwell, Leslie, *The Filmgoer's Companion*, MacGibbon & Kee, 1967.
78. Harben, Henry, *A Dictionary of London*, Jenkins, 1918.
79. Harris, H. C. W., *The Origin of District and Street Names in Bristol*, typescript, 1973.
80. Hergemöller, B.-U., *Gebräuchliche Vornamen*, Regensburg-Münster, 1971.
81. Higgins, Vera, *The Naming of Plants*, Arnold, 1937.
82. Hindley, Charles, *Tavern Anecdotes and Sayings, including The Origin of Signs*, Tinsley Bros., 1875.
83. Hobbs, John L., *Shrewsbury Street Names*, Wilding, 1954.
84. Hughes, J. P., *Is Thy Name Wart?*, Dent, 1965.
85. *Index of Place Names*, England and Wales, Census, 1961. H.M.S.O.
86. *Inn-signia*, Whitbread & Co., 1948.
87. *Inn Signs*, The Review Press, 1969.
88. *Inns of Sport*, Whitbread & Co., 1949.
89. Jacobson, Sven, *Unorthodox Spelling in American Trademarks*, Almqvist & Wiksell, 1966.
90. Jacobs, N. J., *Naming Day in Eden*, Gollancz, 1958.
91. Johnson, Charles, and Sleigh, Linwood, *The Harrap Book of Boys' and Girls' Names*, Harrap, 1973.
92. Johnston, J. B., *Place Names of Scotland*, Murray, 1934, S.R. Publishers, 1972.
93. Josling, J. F., *Change of Name*, Oyez Publications, 1972.
94. Joyce, P. W., *The Origin and History of Irish Names of Places*, E.P. Publishing, 1972, reprint of 1875.
95. Joyce, P. W., *Irish Local Names Explained*, Gill, 1902.
96. Keverne, Richard, *Tales of Old Inns*, Collins, 1949.
97. Kirke Swann, H., *A Dictionary of English and Folk Names of British Birds*, Witherby, 1913, Gale, 1968.
98. Kneen, J. J., *The Personal Names of the Isle of Man*, O.U.P., 1937.
99. Lack, G. L., *Stevenage Street Names*, Stevenage Society for Archaeology, Arts and Natural History, 1972.
100. Lamb, Cadbury and Wright, Gordon, *Discovering Inn Signs*, Shire, 1968.
101. Larwood, Jacob and Hotten, John Camden, *History of Signboards*, Hotten, 1866.
102. Latham, Edward, *A Dictionary of Names, Nicknames and Surnames*, Routledge, 1904.
103. Linnartz, K., *Unsere Familiennamen*, Dummlers, 1958.
104. Long, George, *English Inns and Road Houses*, Werner Laurie, 1937.
105. Long, Harry Alfred, *Personal and Family Names*, Hamilton, Adams, 1883.
106. Lower, M. A., *English Surnames, an Essay on Family Nomenclature, Historical, Etymological and Humorous*, Russell Smith, 1875.
107. Luscombe, W. G., *A Book of Inns*, St. Catherine Press.
108. Mackenzie, W. C., *Scottish Place Names*, Kegan Paul, 1931.
109. MacLysaght, Edward, *The Surnames of Ireland*, Irish University Press, 1969.
110. Manning, T. D. and Walker C. F., *British Warship Names*, Putnam, 1959.

111. Marshall, Frederick, *Curiosities of Ceremonials, Titles, Decorations and Forms*, Nimmo and Bain, 1880.
112. Mathieson, J. M., *A Key to Highland Place Names*, An Comunn Gaidhealach, 1966.
113. Matthews, C. M., *English Surnames*, Weidenfeld & Nicolson, 1966.
114. Matthews, C. M., *Place Names of the English-Speaking World*, Weidenfeld & Nicolson, 1972.
115. McClure, Edmund, *British Place Names in their Historical Setting*, E.P. Publishing, 1972, reprint of 1910 edition.
116. McGivern, J. S., *Your Name and Coat of Arms*, Paper Jacks, 1971.
117. McGuire, Paul, *Inns of Australia*, Heinemann, 1952.
118. McKinley, R. A., *Norfolk Surnames in the Sixteenth Century*, Leicester University Press, 1969.
119. Milburn, R. L. P., *Saints and their Emblems in English Churches*, Blackwell, 1957.
120. Miles, Joyce C., *House Names Around the World*, David & Charles, 1972.
121. Miller, G. M., *B.B.C. Pronouncing Dictionary of British Names*, O.U.P., 1971.
122. Monson-Fitzjohn, C. J., *Quaint Signs of Olde Inns*, Jenkins, 1926.
123. Montague-Smith, Patrick, *Debrett's Correct Form*, Kelly's, 1971.
124. Moody, Sophy, *What Is Your Name?*, Bentley, 1863.
125. Moore, John, *You English Words*, Collins, 1964.
126. Muncey, R. W., *The Romance of Parish Registers*, Lincoln Williams, 1933.
127. *Münchens Strassennamen*, Baureferat der Landeshauptstadt München, 1965.
128. Munro, R. W., *Kinsmen and Clansmen*, Johnston & Bacon, 1971.
129. Opie, Iona and Peter, *Lore and Language of Schoolchildren*, O.U.P. 1959.
130. Packard, John, *Easton, Suffolk—The Fields and Field Names*, published by the author, 1972.
131. Park, B., *Roses—A Selected List of Varieties*, National Rose Society, 1958.
132. Partridge, Eric, *A Covey of Partridge*, Routledge, 1937.
133. Partridge, Eric, *Name Into Word*, Secker & Warburg, 1949.
134. Partridge, Eric, *Name This Child*, Hamilton, 1951.
135. Pawley White, G., *A Handbook of Cornish Surnames*, published by the author, 1972.
136. Payton, Geoffrey, *Payton's Proper Names*, Warne, 1969.
137. Philip, Alexander, *The Picts in Angus and their Place Names*, Routledge, 1925.
138. *Place Names of the Parish of Southend*, Kintyre Antiquarian Society, 1938.
139. Potter, Simeon, *Our Language*, Penguin, 1961.
140. Potter, Stephen and Sargent, Laurens, *Pedigree: Words From Nature*, Collins, 1973.
141. Praninskas, Jean, *Trade Name Creation*, Mouton, 1961.
142. Price, Roger and Stern, Leonard, *How Dare You Call Me That!*, Wolfe, 1966.
143. Rainbird, G. M., *Inns of Kent*, Whitbread & Co., 1949.
144. *The Ram Jam Inn*, a publicity handout explaining the name.
145. Rawlings, Gertrude B., *The Streets of London*, Bles, 1926.
146. Reaney, P. H., *A Dictionary of British Surnames*, Routledge & Kegan Paul, 1961.
147. Reaney, P. H., *The Origin of English Surnames*, Routledge & Kegan Paul, 1969.

148. Redmonds, George, *Yorkshire West Riding—English Surnames Series 1*, Phillimore, 1973.
149. *Personal Names In Scotland, 1958*, Registrar General's Office, 1962.
150. Richardson, A., *The Old Inns of England*, Batsford, 1934.
151. Room, Adrian, *Pet Names*, The Names Society, 1974.
152. Room, Adrian, *Place Names of the World*, David & Charles, 1974.
153. Rosenfeld, Hellmut, *Heimerans Vornamenbuch*, Heimeran, 1968.
154. Rosenthal, Eric, *South African Surnames*, Timmins, 1965.
155. Rostaing, Charles, *Les noms de lieux*, Presses Universitaires, 1965.
156. Rowland, R. N. G., *The Street Names of Acton, Middlesex*, published by the author, 1967.
157. Russen, Lilian and Ashmore, *Historic Streets of London*, Simpkin, Marshall, Hamilton, Kent & Co., 1923.
158. Salverté, Eusebius, *History of the Names of Men, Nations and Places* (translated by L. H. Mordacque), Russell Smith, 1862 and 1864.
159. Smith, Anna H., *Johannesburg Street Names*, Juta, 1971.
160. Smith, Al, *Dictionary of City of London Street Names*, David & Charles, 1970.
161. Smith, Elsdon C., *American Surnames*, Chilton, 1970.
162. Smith, Elsdon C., *New Dictionary of American Family Names*, Harper & Row, 1973.
163. Smith, Elsdon C., *Personal Names—A Bibliography*, New York Public Library, 1952, Gale, 1965.
164. Smith, Elsdon C., *Treasury of Name Lore*, Harper & Row, 1967.
165. Smith, Muriel W. G., *National Apple Register of the United Kingdom*, Ministry of Agriculture and Food, 1971.
166. Smythe Palmer, A., *The Folk and their Word Lore*, Routledge, 1904.
167. Spaull, Hebe, *New Place Names of the World*, Ward Lock, 1970.
168. Stapleton, Alan, *London Alleys Byways and Courts*, Bodley Head, 1925.
169. Stapleton, Alan, *London Lanes*, Bodley Head, 1930.
170. Stenhouse, T., *Lives Enshrined In Language*, Scott, 1922.
171. Stephens, Ruth, *Welsh Names For Children*, Y Lolfa, 1973.
172. Stern, G. B., *A Name To Conjure With*, Collins, 1953.
173. Stevenson, R. L., *The Philosophy of Nomenclature* (in *Virginibus Puerisque*), Heinemann, 1926.
174. Stewart, George R., *American Place Names*, O.U.P., 1970.
175. Stewart, George R., *Names On The Land*, Houghton Mifflin, 1967.
176. Stewart Fay, E., *Why Piccadilly?—The Story of the Names of London*, Methuen, 1935.
177. Stokes, H. G., *English Place Names*, Batsford, 1948.
178. Stone, Eugene, *Naming Baby*, Ward Lock, 1954.
179. Stow, John, *A Survey of London*, ed. Henry Morley, Routledge, undated.
180. Stuart, Marie W., *Old Edinburgh Taverns*, Hales, 1952.
181. Sturmfels, Wilhelm and Bischof, Heinz, *Unsere Ortsnamen*, Dümmlers. 1961.
182. Swan, Helena, *Girls' Christian Names—Their History, Meaning and Association*, Swan Sonnenschein, 1900.
183. Swan, Helena, *Who's Who In Fiction*, Routledge, undated.
184. Swift, C. R., *Inns and Inn Signs*, published by the author, 1935.
185. Sylvester Mawson, C. O., *International Book of Names*, Crowell, 1942.

186. Taylor, Isaac, *Names and their Histories*, Rivington, 1896.

187. Taylor, Isaac, *Words and Places*, Macmillan, 1893.

188. Thewes, Roma. *Name Your Daughter*, Corgi, 1969.

189. Thewes, Roma, *Name Your Son*, Corgi, 1969.

190. *Three Victorian Telephone Directories*, David & Charles, 1970.

191. Unbegaun, B. O., *Russian Surnames*, O.U.P., 1972.

192. Usherwood, Stephen, *Inns and Inn Signs* (History From Familiar Things), Ginn, 1972.

193. Usherwood, S. and H., *Place Names* (History From Familiar Things), Ginn, 1969.

194. Usherwood, S. and H., *Street Names* (History From Familiar Things), Ginn, 1969.

195. Vinel, André, *Le livre des prénoms*, Albin Michel, 1972.

196. Wagner, Leopold, *Names And Their Meanings*, Unwin, 1892.

197. Wagner, Leopold, *More About Names*, Unwin, 1893.

198. Wasserzieher, Ernst, *Hans Und Grete*, Dümmlers, 1967.

199. Watson, Godfrey, *Goodwife Hot and Others, Northumberland's Past as shown in its Place Names*, Oriel, 1970.

200. Watson, Rowland, *A Scrapbook of Inns*, Werner Laurie, 1958.

201. Weekley, Ernest, *Adjectives and Other Words*, Murray, 1930.

202. Weekley, Ernest, *Jack and Jill*, Murray, 1939.

203. Weekley, Ernest, *The Romance of Names*, Murray, 1928.

204. Weekley, Ernest, *Surnames*, Murray, 1916.

205. Weekley, Ernest, *Words and Names*, Murray, 1932.

206. Wheeler, W. A., *A Dictionary of the Noted Names of Fiction*, Bell, 1883.

207. Withycombe, E. G., *The Oxford Dictionary of Christian Names*, O.U.P., 1963.

208. Wright, Gordon, *At The Sign Of The Flagon*, Graham, 1970.

209. Yonge, Charlotte M., *History of Christian Names*, Macmillan, 1884, Gale, 1966.

210. Zettersten, Louis, *City Street Names*, Selwyn & Blount, 1926.

Surname researchers should remember that useful information about a surname is often to be obtained from a book on English place names. The best source of information is always the appropriate county volume of the English Place Name Society. The *Oxford English Dictionary* also provides valuable help with early meanings of words and words now obsolete.

A Select List

A small but comprehensive reference section on names of all kinds would probably include the books numbered in the Bibliography as follows:

First Names	207, 91	*Street Names (London)*	17
Surnames	146, 162, 44, 21, 109	*Pub Names*	101, 50, 100
Fictional Characters	71	*House Names*	55
Nicknames	70	*Ship Names*	110
Place Names	152, 60, 73, 174	*Plant Names*	39
Field Names	68	*Pet Names (Animals)*	151
River Names	61	*General*	136

Index (Italicised numbers refer to illustrations)